TZEENAH U-REENAH

A JEWISH COMMENTARY ON
THE BOOK OF EXODUS

Translation of the text on the title page of the Basel edition.

THE FIVE BOOKS OF THE TORAH, IN THE YIDDISH LANGUAGE

"Daughters of Zion Go Forth and Behold"

Behold the crown with which a man of great deeds has crowned you with the help of this wonderful compilation. He collected material in the valleys, and after the harvesters gleaned here and there in the Midrashim the Haggadoth, Rashi, Rabban, Bahya, Hazzekuni, Tzror-Hamor, Toldoth Yitschak, and other commentators who interpreted the Parashiyyoth of the Torah. All the comments which seemed closest to the Biblical text have been incorporated in this Yiddish book. Now the excellency, the might, and the strength of this work are destined to bring rest to the souls of men and women, through their understanding of the living word of God, written for them in an easy and pleasant language. Before this book was even published its nature became known all over the world, and the people of the town where it was published lauded it; because no book ever before included all the above named commentators. Come, therefore, and rally around the work of God published in the city of Lublin, and help to unravel the mysteries and the wisdom of God which have been brought to light by the present treatise.

The above book was later published, twice in the city[1] of Krakow, and no such work can be found in the whole of the Jewish diaspora in Germany, except perhaps one or two copies here and there.[2]

Still later we were, therefore, compelled to have this edition printed in the City of Basel.

Printed with great care and proof-read meticulously here in Basel.

------

1. The author calls it holy city.
2. The Hebrew idiom employed here for the words "here and there" is אחד בעיר ושנים במשפחה

TZEENAH U-REENAH

A

Jewish Commentary

on

The Book of Exodus

transl. by
NORMAN C. GORE

Author:

Jacob ben Isaac of Janow

(1550 - 1628)

VANTAGE PRESS
NEW YORK WASHINGTON HOLLYWOOD

31. OCT. 1967

CONTENTS

FOREWORD

by THE VERY REV. SHERMAN E. JOHNSON

Yiddish literature is an important part of the world's cultural heritage. A few Americans are acquainted with translations of Yiddish plays, poems, and short stories, but to the vast majority, the books are closed. Even in the Jewish community, English and Hebrew have largely replaced the charming and beloved old vernacular.

It is therefore, a reason for gratitude that Dr. Norman C. Gore has translated into English, that part of *Tzeenah U-Reenah* which deals with the Book of Exodus. The rich haggadic material embroidering the biblical account of deliverance from Egypt and the giving of the Law will give delight and wisdom to those who otherwise cannot read it. In addition, the reader will be initiated into the rabbinic tradition and a way of thinking that is foreign to the West and from which all of us have much to learn. Christians in particular will profit from a better understanding of the People of the Book who have preserved for us the Bible and the ancient traditions and who continue to enrich American life in countless ways.

The translator, a distinguished alumnus of the Church Divinity School of the Pacific, is to be congratulated on a translation that is clear and delightful.

VERY REV. SHERMAN E. JOHNSON
Dean, The Church Divinity
School of the Pacific

FOREWORD

by RABBI JACOB L. FRIEND

In the Middle Ages, when most people in Europe were steeped in darkness and in illiteracy, most Jews were literate. They knew Hebrew because their religion required it. In medieval Germany the Jews began to write German with Hebrew characters and gradually developed a distinctive language called "Yiddish". As time went on, Yiddish enriched its vocabulary with words borrowed from Slavonic languages and by the middle of the nineteenth century, Yiddish began to produce a first class literature. Many have read the works of J. L. Peretz, Sholom Asch, Sholom Aleichem (the Jewish Mark Twain), but few know that these literary giants wrote their books in the Yiddish language. To most people Yiddish literature is a closed field.

The *Tzeenah U-Reenah* was a most beloved and universally read book that occupied an honored place alongside the Hebrew Bible. The book recounts a multitude of rabbinic anecdotes, allegories, and pious observations. This unpretentious book proved itself to have been one of the supreme educators of the Jewish people because it enabled the Jewish woman to share in the religious and cultural life of her people. It taught her Jewish history and ethics. It was truly a household book for almost four centuries, guiding and training entire Jewish families in the religious traditions of their fathers. It is regrettable that this source of information has been inaccessible to many Jewish families in this country because of the language barrier. The appearance of this book in an English translation is, therefore, a welcome change. It will provide a source of popular religious knowledge, hitherto unaccessible to English readers. The translation is smooth and accurate. The many stories and legends from the *Talmud* strikingly bring the Biblical message close to home in a powerful manner. It provides an excellent source of religious and ethical material for our school children as well as for their parents. Our present world is in need of the ethical teaching of such a book. The translator, a scholar of great distinction, has spent many years of research in producing this volume and he deserves our appreciation for his labor of love. I wholeheartedly recommend this book to the Jewish public and express the hope that the remaining volumes covering the entire Torah will be made available in the English language.

RABBI JACOB L. FRIEND, F.R.A.S.

PREFACE

The translation is based on the Metz edition of 1768. There is indeed an older edition in existence, viz., the Basel edition of 1622, but it is not generally available.

The location of references to Rabbinical sources mentioned in the text of the "Tzeenah U-Reenah" is time consuming, for there is available no proper index to these works. An appendix has, therefore, been made of the passages in question.

The text of the "Tzeenah U-Reenah" is divided into פרשיות making up the portions for the weekly reading in the Synagogue and at home. The text knows neither chapter nor verse, and I have undertaken the task of dividing the text into chapters and verses, according to the order of the English Bible. This has involved transposing passages which were out of order, and placing them where they belonged in accordance with the Biblical text. There is no indirect form of speech in the text. The "Tzeenah U-Reenah" uses the direct form of speech, without quotation marks, like the Bible. Direct quotations from the Bible, when quoted at the beginning of a sentence, I have put in capital letters. Biblical quotations in the middle of the text I have placed in quotation marks, and in small letters.

I have sought to follow the text as closely as possible, without jeopardizing the translation itself. However, it should be borne in mind that the closer a translation is to the original text, the poorer is the translation, and this is especially true when the language of the original text is archaic.

Much forbearance has to be exercised in the transliteration of Hebrew letters, names or sounds, into the English language. For instance, the Hebrew title of our text, "Tzeenah U-Reenah," has been transliterated by various writers in half a dozen ways. The same is true regarding the transliteration of proper names. The abbreviation for the name God הקב״ה I have translated fully as "The Holy One, blessed be He," except once or twice where the name "God" was preferable. The title of the book has been transliterated in a variety of ways, such as "Tzehno-Urehno," "Tzeenah Ureenah" or "Tzeine Ureine." I chose "Tzeenah U-Reenah," which seems to me preferable.

The "Tzeenah U-Reenah" was the product of Polish Jewry. Therefore, this work is fitly dedicated to the millions of Jewish martyrs in Poland, victims of Hitler, to whom the "Tzeenah U-Reenah" is a memorial of piety and learning.

חבור זה הנני מקדיש לאלפי אלפי יהודי פולניה
שנהרגו על קדוש השם בימי היטלר הרשע.
"באי הרוח ופחי בהרוגים האלה ויחיו"
יחזקאל ל"ז'.

INTRODUCTION

THE RISE OF THE YIDDISH LANGUAGE AND LITERATURE:

Among the many languages and dialects spoken by Jews in various countries, Yiddish is nearest to the soul of the Jewish people. This vernacular expresses the characteristics of the Jewish minds and hearts with peculiar warmth and charm.

Some Yiddish scholars are of the opinion that a Swabian dialect, spoken by Jews in the "Siebenbürgen" district (Transylvania) as far back as the ninth century, A.D., was the ancestor of present day Yiddish. Scholars differ on that matter. Some maintain that up to the sixteenth century there was comparatively little difference between the German spoken by Jews of the Germanic countries and that spoken by their neighbors. Any differences which might have existed were slight and unimportant. Others argue, on the other hand, that there was a difference between the speech of the Jews and their non-Jewish neighbours and that the difference went back to the early beginnings of the Yiddish language. Now the fact that the Jews employed the Hebrew alphabet for the vernacular, and also the fact that the Jews of the Slavonic countries have exercised a strong influence upon the speech of the Jews in Germany would lend plausibility to the argument that there were considerable differences between Yiddish and German at the very beginning of the Yiddish language.

The language of our text, the "Tzeenah U-Reenah" is not mere German, written in Hebrew letters; for beside idiomatic phrases and expressions, peculiar to the Jewish mind, there are also a great many Hebrew words, and an occasional word which is neither of German nor of Hebrew origin, as, for instance, the words for steam[1] and for goats.[2] However, one cannot overlook the fact that the bulk of the vocabulary of the "Tzeenah U-Reenah" can be traced to the German language. Moreover, a study of the various editions revealed that the older the edition, the closer is its language to the German, and the later the edition the greater is the departure from that language.

Now with the rise of the Yiddish vernacular there arose a need for a literature in that language. It is assumed that this literature was born sometime between the years 1000 and 1200. Historians of Yiddish often quote a lost book by a Rabbi named Yehudah, a mystic, who died in the year 1217. The Rabbi, in his book "Sefer Hakhassidim," is cited to the effect that he warned his people against reading romances which were in circulation among Jews at that time. The inference is that there were books in Yiddish at that time. However, the earliest Yiddish written manuscripts available date back only to the fourteenth century. The fourteenth and fifteenth centuries witnessed the early start of the classical period of Yiddish. Eli Levita (or Elijah Bahur) who was born in Germany around 1469, and died in Italy in 1549, is often called the father of Yiddish literature. He was a philologist, lexicographer, poet, novelist and translator. For some time he served in Rome as Hebrew tutor to Cardinal Egidio da Viterbo. He was a prolific writer, and among others he wrote the popular book, the "Bovo Buch," which later

14

became known as the "Bobbe Masse." It is a verse epic of the adventures of Prince Bovo of Antona, published in 1541. Some Yiddish writers like to think of Elijah Bahur as the Jewish Chaucer.

Yiddish literature took its rise on the one hand, from the inner urge of the Jewish people to express its thoughts and feelings through its own writers, obscure and indigent as they were, and on the other hand, from the deep longing for religious knowledge. The two currents, the secular and the religious, often crossed and quarrelled with each other, but they stimulated Jewish life in the ghettos. There were intellectual currents whose impact from without had stirred up the stagnant pools of the ghettos, but also there were springs from within, which were the overflowing of an original national genius.

The large masses of the Jewish people, and especially the women who no longer understood the Hebrew language, wanted to be instructed in the Holy Writ; they longed for religious knowledge which would strengthen their spirits. The historical books of the Old Testament, the mighty deeds of the Jewish Kings, Judges, and Prophets, and the legends and love stories of the Jewish heroes, were like fountains of living water to thirsty souls.

Most Yiddish literature in the early periods consisted of translations, either from the Hebrew, the German or the Italian language. The Hebrew literature, with its rich Biblical and other religious sources, was the main fountain from which the translators drew. One must bear in mind that the early books in the Yiddish vernacular were written chiefly for women. They were written under feminine patronage and many of the books bear dedications to women. The author often called himself *"Der Schreiber fun alle Frume Weiber."*[3] This title, according to Max Erik,[4] would suggest that there had been professional writers or translators who earned their livelihood by providing reading material for women.

The expressions of early Yiddish literature have an emotional and peculiarly feminine character. The great figures of the Bible are no longer the patriarchs, but rather the heroines, and also the pious women of post-Biblical times. Thus, for instance, in the story of

15

Abba Hilkiah[5] greater piety and greater merit are ascribed to Abba Hilkiah's wife than to her husband. The style of the early Yiddish language is verbose and cumbersome, nevertheless it contains fascination and sweetness, making it appeal to a woman's heart. The women drew their inspiration, comfort, and joy from the numerous Biblical stories embellished with Haggadic fables and legends. The educated classes, however, looked down upon the Yiddish vernacular and its literary creation. They called Yiddish the language of the maidservants. The struggle of the Yiddish vernacular against the supremacy of the Hebrew language was not unlike the struggle of the German vernacular against the supremacy of the Latin language during the Reformation period. This was especially true with regard to religious literature, and since early Yiddish literature was mainly of a religious character, critics looked down upon it and considered it a most inferior production.

Bible translations formed the main source of early Yiddish literature, and the spread of that literature began in earnest, after the discovery of printing. From that period Bible translations of all sorts began to make their appearance.

Two printed translations of the Pentateuch in Yiddish, together with the Haphtaroth, appeared in 1544. One was the work of Michael Adam and issued at Constance. The other was made by Paulus Amelius and published in Augsburg. In the preface to the former, the translator says that his motive for making the translation was to promote knowledge of the Scriptures among the Jews and Jewesses who could not read Hebrew. The translator asserts that some Jews lived in villages, and could not find, nor afford, Hebrew teachers for their children. However, by using the translation in the vernacular, the parents themselves could teach their children the word of God. Later, in the year 1560, there appeared in Cremona a new translation of the Pentateuch, by Judah Leib ben Naphtali Bresh, a Polish Jew, who settled in Italy. Bresh's translation is mainly a reprint of Adam's version, but greatly improved, and this translation saw a second edition in 1583, and a third one

16

in 1603. Some translators developed a tendency to deviate more and more from the literal forms of translation, and introduced into the text Midrashic comments, stories and exegetical remarks. The most typical example of all such deviating paraphrases is our classic book, "The Tzeenah U-Reenah."

Two rival translations of the complete Old Testament were later made by Blitz and Witzenhausen and published in Amsterdam in 1676; and 1679, respectively. The one by Witzenhausen is preferable and saw a second edition. The translation was considered good enough to be included, along with the Dutch, Lutheran, Catholic, and Reformed versions in the "Biblia Pentapla." A most recent translation of the Old Testament into Yiddish, and a very beautiful one, was made by the Jewish poet, Yehoash. The Pentateuch was published in 1927; and the complete Old Testament was published in 1936, in New York.

THE TZEENAH U-REENAH:

The tendency to paraphrase and to introduce Midrashic and allegoric material into the text found its classical expression in the "Tzeenah U-Reenah," which soon became the standard Bible for Jewish women. More than that, it became their source of religious knowledge and fountain of piety. The book soon surpassed all other Yiddish books in quality and certainly in widespread distribution. The reason for this success was the love of the common people for homiletical explanation. Previous translators of the Pentateuch had not hitherto satisfied the popular readers because of their blind attachment to a verbal translation, which made reading obscure and dry. Jacob ben Isaac Ashkenazy, our author, however, introduced homilies which illustrated the text. He did not always give a faithful translation of the Hebrew text, but he retold the Biblical stories in his own words and in a popular and attractive manner. The heroes and characters of the Bible he thus popularized, and brought them nearer to the reader's own time. The influence exerted by that book can hardly be exaggerated. From it, generations of Jewish women drew their love and reverence for the past of their people.

The portrayals contained in the book, of the Jewish Saints and of righteous men and women, became models of conduct. The book inculcated in their hearts a desire for virtue and love of the Torah. It implanted in their souls a living hope for the redemption of Israel and for the deliverance from their sufferings.

The "Tzeenah U-Reenah" cannot be said to be a paraphrase of the Pentateuch, for the actual content of the Biblical text constitutes but a small part of the book. The greater part of the book consists of Haggadic passages, homilies and exegetic comments of all sorts, including cabbalistic elements. Its proper name should be a "Midrashic Commentary on the Pentateuch, in the Yiddish language." The author himself called it "The Five Books of the Torah." To this title he added a quotation from Canticles, Chapter III, verse 11, which reads צאינה וראינה בנות ציון "Tzeenah U-Reenah . . ." (Go forth, O ye daughters of Zion and behold). The quotation was intended only for the purpose of recommending the book to feminine readers, but the work soon became known as "Tzeenah U-Reenah." Saubert and Hersohn, however, call their translations "Rabbinical Commentary." [6] Oppenheimer's German translation is called "Frauenbibel."

Rabbi Jacob ben Isaac Ashkenazy, of Janow, drew upon the entire Jewish literature, the Talmud, Midrashim, books of legends and stories, and upon almost all leading Jewish commentaries, especially those of Rashi and Bahya ben Asher. At times he even cites oral comments or the *"bon mot"* from a contemporary scholar who is unknown to us. Rabbi Jacob displays great literary skill in weaving together the thousands of remarks, comments and homiletical explanations into one harmonious work. At times he gives the plain translation of the Hebrew verse first, and then continues to expound it by numerous quotations; at other times he marshals his moral teachings first and concludes with the verse. There are a large number of verse translations woven into the general narrative.

It is very unfortunate that so little personal history of this popular author has been handed down to us. All that is known can be said in a few words. Rabbi Jacob ben Isaac Ashkenazy, the author of the "Tzeenah U-Reenah," was born in Janow, Poland. The date of his birth is unknown, although Dr. I. Schipper [7] gives the date as 1550. Biographers also differ regarding the date of the author's death. According to Staerk and Leitzmann, this occurred in 1620; according to others he died in 1628. The 1620 date can be ruled out on the basis that the Basel edition, printed in 1622, does not lend itself to such an assumption. From the comments on the title page, one would be led to believe that the author was still alive at the time of that publication. A more accurate conclusion would be that Rabbi Jacob died in 1628, in Prague. The place of the Rabbi's birth is indeed given as Janow, but there were four towns by that name in Poland. Two of the four may claim the honour of having been the birthplace of Rabbi Jacob. The one is Janow, near Krakow, and the claim can be advanced on the basis of the fact that Rabbi Jacob's book, "Shoresh Yaakob," was published in Krakow. The second Janow is the one near Lublin, where the "Tzeenah U-Reenah" was first published. Of the two, the balance of probability seems to be in favour of the latter, although there is no conclusive proof.

Rabbi Jacob was a scholar of great erudition. He was a master of homilies, and he wove them into the text in a warm and pleasant way that made reading attractive. It is said that he was a descendant of Rashi and that he was a Rabbi. However, the term "Rabbi" does not necessarily imply that the author of the "Tzeenah U-Reenah" occupied a Rabbinical position in the Jewish community. It is more likely that he was a migrant preacher מגיד (Maggid) who supplemented his meagre earnings by selling books, most likely his own books. Besides the "Tzeenah U-Reenah," the author wrote "Shoresh Yaakob" (Krakow, 1585), "Sefer Hamaggid" (Prague,

1576), and the "Melitz Yosher" (Lublin, 1622). In the introductions to the "Sefer Hamaggid" and the "Melitz Yosher," the author explains the reasons why he wrote in the vernacular Yiddish. He states that the purpose of the writing in Yiddish was to enable the ordinary people to understand the Scriptures without interpreters or preachers. He goes on to say that people listen to sermons, but cannot always understand them because the preachers speak too fast. However, the people would be able to understand the Scriptures if they were to read them for themselves, in a language they understood, and read them slowly and meditated over them. The desire is interesting, that the people's book should take the place of the preacher and that the printed word should supplant the pulpit.

The old tradition of reading the Bible in the vernacular goes back as far as the time of Ezra, the Scribe, who interpreted the Torah to the people in their Aramaic dialect. Starting with explanation of the law, sermons on religion, and on conduct were added. Such sermons were preached in the vernacular in the synagogues on the Sabbath and on holidays, by preachers and teachers of the people. The famous heads of the Sanhedrin Shemayah and Abtalyon carried with them the title of "preachers," because they used to preach to the people, call them to repentance, comfort them, and strengthen their faith. Such sermons usually started with verses from the Bible, but the preacher did not dwell on the text. He often used the text only as an introduction to his sermon, in which he poured out his heart and not seldom showed off his oratorical gifts. These oral sermons later created a national literature.

The word "Midrash" is often used in Jewish writings, to describe a certain type of expository literature. The word "Midrash" comes from the Hebrew word "Darash," meaning to search out or to inquire, and it characterizes an attempt to interpret the spirit lying behind a Scriptural verse. The old "Midrashim" can broadly be divided into two classes: "Halaka" and "Haggadah." The former deals with legal and ritual matters arising out of the Scripture, while

20

the latter is an expository and homiletical interpretation of the Scripture. The Haggadah includes stories, legends, parables, allegories, customs, beliefs and all that might be called folklore. The "Midrashim" are sometimes described as a "Hammer which wakes to shining light, the sparks which slumber in the rock." This is a fitting description of the Midrashim. It was believed that the written word of the Bible had an infinite fullness and that every word of the Torah had seventy aspects. Philo of Alexandria held that there were no superfluous words in the Scripture, and, therefore, an exaggerated emphasis is often laid upon single words. For instance, commenting on the verse, "If thou wilt make me an altar of stone, thou shalt not build it of hewn stone; for if thou lift up thy tool upon it, thou hast polluted it" (Exodus 20:25). From the word "it," the Midrash Mekhilta infers that the prohibition of iron applies only to "it," meaning the altar and not the stones used in building the Temple. This "Halaka" is followed by a Haggadic explanation of the prohibition, viz., iron shortens life, while the altar prolongs life. Iron causes destruction, while the altar produces reconciliation between man and God; therefore, it should not be used in making the altar. Our "Tzeenah U-Reenah" follows in the footsteps of the Haggadah and quotes this passage from the Mekhilta almost verbatim.

The Haggadah assumed the mission of consoling, edifying, exhorting, and teaching a people threatened spiritually with stagnation of exile. From the time of the Babylonian exile, the practice grew among Jews to gather together for the purpose of hearing the Torah read and explained; and from this kind of assembly, the Beth ha-Midrash, that is to say, the house of the Midrash, came into being. Throughout the Talmudic period, and also in later ages, this was the school of the community, as well as a place of prayer. On the Sabbath afternoon the people would gather to listen to religious discourses which were intended to satisfy their needs—intellectual, moral, and spiritual. Homilies were discussed to instil hope and courage into a harassed community, and to preserve its will to live. The preacher or teacher was not satisfied with imparting to his listeners a dry interpretation of the text, but endeavoured to elucidate the Bible in a new light, and thus stimulate new thought.

The authors of the Haggadah were conscious of the fact that in order to hold the attention of the reader or listener the subject material must be interesting and entertaining. The very name "Midrash" suggests interpretation or explanation, but, for the purpose of illustrating the text, the teachers and preachers freely introduced Haggadic material not only from all over the Bible, but from far outside the Holy Writ. The Haggadah books were popular with most Rabbis, but there were some who did not care for them. For instance, Rabbi Joshua ben Levi[8] vehemently condemned these writings. The same Rabbi tells that the only time he ever looked into such a book he found in it some numerical correspondence between the Pentateuch and something else in the Bible, but the memory of this experience gave him a nightmare. Now, the "Tzeenah U-Reenah" made extensive use of the Haggadah and its homiletical material. No wonder that it incurred the wrath of some Rabbis. For, if some Rabbis of an earlier period disliked Haggadic material, even in its original language, the more reason for the later day Rabbis to dislike the "Tzeenah U-Reenah" in the vernacular Yiddish. The author of the "Tzeenah U-Reenah" not only widely used Haggadic material, but he follows a similar pattern. The Haggadic Homilies often begin a lesson with a verse from the Scripture and then the leader of the class will ask a question like this: "What does the verse teach us?" The "Tzeenah U-Reenah" often employed that form and says, "The verse teaches us that . . ." Now the value of the older homiletical Midrashim lies in the fact that they have preserved much of the religious and moral teaching of the second and third centuries in the name of the authors, who otherwise might have remained unknown to us.

The Midrashim, combined with the beautiful stories related by the preachers, have no known authorship. They came from the people and belonged to the people. The preacher made sermons out of the stories of different heroes and embellished them with verses from the Bible. The Midrashim, when they were written down, became the textbooks for the preachers of later generations who no longer preached in Aramaic, but in the vernacular languages spoken by Jews in the Dispersion. Thus, Rabbi Jacob ben Isaac Ashkenazy, from the little town in Poland, created the "Tzeenah U-Reenah" in the tradition of the Midrashic literature, and, although there is a difference in language between the Midrashim and the "Tzeenah U-Reenah," nevertheless the latter is a faithful continuation of the former. The two are linked together by the same creative genius of the people and they form a golden chain of an old culture. This ancient Yiddish literature was no mere "woman's" literature, but the literature of a people. The deep faith which permeates the "Tzeenah U-Reenah" gave it a special fascination, and that is the main reason why it became so popular. It was in every Jewish home and from that book, every Saturday, Jewish mothers read the stories to their children. The stories recorded the history of the Patriarchs, the heroes, the wise and righteous men and women of the past, written in the common language of everyday life, which the people could understand.

EVALUATION:

The originality of the author of the "Tzeenah U-Reenah" lies not so much in new ideas or new ways of interpreting the Scriptures, but in the use he makes of available material. On the title page the author states plainly that he collected material from various sources. He "gleaned here and there after the harvesters." However, the lessons he draws from the various sources are illuminating and helpful. For instance, commenting on Exodus Chapter XXI:28, regarding a man's responsibility for the damage caused by his ox, the author drives the lesson home, right into the woman's kitchen. He tells the women that they are equally responsible for throwing out garbage or pouring out unclean water in places where it causes people to stumble or slip and receive injuries.[9] An illustration of that kind, indeed, written in a language so plain, required no interpreter. In another instance, commenting on the story of the Creation, the author tells his readers that the sun and the moon[10] were at first created in equal strength, but that the moon, desiring to exalt herself over the sun, asked the Creator why there should be two luminaries of equal strength. The Lord, in wrath, answered and said that since the moon wished to exalt herself over the sun, let her light, therefore, be diminished. That is the reason the moon sheds less light than the sun. Naïve stories of that kind appealed to the uncritical readers, and in a way explained to them the universe. The author quotes many more interesting comments. He comments on the passage "Thou shalt not seethe a kid in its mother's milk" (XXIII: 19), in which the author quotes the Toldoth Itschak and explains the reason for the prohibition, namely, because it was a form of idol worship. This explanation is interesting and helpful. Of like interest is the explanation, why a thief pays a twofold indemnity while a robber does not have to do so. The reason being that a thief fears man more than God; therefore, the Holy Law places a larger fine on the thief. Comments of such nature awaken a human interest and make the Scripture interesting to ordinary people. Other comments carry with them more than mere human interest. Some bear theological significance, namely, the comment about "sinners suffering in hell only twelve months." This helps to abolish the notion of eternal damnation and eternal suffering.

As a popular production for meeting the need of Jewish women, the "Tzeenah U-Reenah" was supreme. The Jewish mother, who was the main strength of the Jewish household, passed on her faith, her piety, and her religious knowledge to her children. To the Jewish mother, the "Tzeenah U-Reenah" was a standard textbook in matters pertaining to faith and practice. When she nourished her child on her knee, or when she put him to bed, she told and retold to him the wonderful stories contained in the "Tzeenah U-Reenah." By doing so, she inculcated into her child's soul a deep love for the Bible. Before the child knew anything else, he knew the stories from the "Tzeenah U-Reenah." Thus, the book exerted a lasting influence in fashioning the mind and character of Jewish children at an impressionable age, and coloured their religious ideas and attitudes.

The language of the "Tzeenah U-Reenah," although archaic by modern standards, was nevertheless the best in its day. The style is lively and tinged with a poetic glow. In a warm and emotional tone it portrays pictures and scenes taken from daily life, adding local colour to the doctrinal terms of the Bible. By doing so, the author brought the message of the Bible closer to the people and made the Holy Writ more accessible and more meaningful to them. With some justification has Rabbi Jacob ben Isaac Ashkenazy been called the Luther of the Yiddish language.

The "Tzeenah U-Reenah" was the product of Polish Jewry, and its appearance on the scene marked the rise of a new Jewish cultural centre which illuminated Jewish intellectual horizons for about three centuries and a half, until crushed by the advent of the crooked cross.

DATE OF PUBLICATION:

The date of the first publication of the "Tzeenah U-Reenah" has not been definitely established. We know for certain that the oldest available copy is a fourth edition, published in Basel in 1622, as can be seen on the back of that publication. On the title page of the fourth edition, it is stated that there has been three previous editions; first in Lublin and two consecutive editions in Krakow. It seems that by the time the fourth edition was published, the influence of the "Tzeenah U-Reenah" was already felt. Scholars differ regarding the date of the first edition. Some put the date as far back as 1590; others 1600, and still others put it as late as 1618. By the year 1732, there were already over thirty editions, and the number grew steadily.

The success of the "Tzeenah U-Reenah" provoked the displeasure

25

of people who preferred to hold to the Hebrew text. These were joined in their criticism by authors and publishers who, for commercial reasons, wanted to see the downfall of the "Tzeenah U-Reenah." Alongside the German there also existed Spanish and Portuguese Jewish communities, among whom the study of Hebrew and the Bible was an important part of education. They looked down upon translations and paraphrases of the Holy Writ. Rival publishers joined in the crusade against the "Tzeenah U-Reenah" and secured from the Emperor, King Joseph II, an edict against the book. Moses Mendelssohn and his friends also took the field against the "Tzeenah U-Reenah," but they did not prevail. The "Tzeenah U-Reenah" maintained its popularity and spell over Jewish women for almost three hundred years. To this day there are several rival books bearing the name "Tzeenah U-Reenah" trying to take advantage of the popularity of Rabbi Jacob ben Isaac Ashkenazy's genuine work. Even Moses Mendelssohn tried to benefit by the popularity of the book against which he fought, and called his own translation of the Pentateuch "Tzeenah U-Reenah."

TRANSLATIONS:

The popularity of the "Tzeenah U-Reenah" encouraged translations into other languages. There are abridged translations and translations of parts of the book in Latin, French, German and English.

The Latin Translation was made by Johannes Saubert, in 1660, under the title *Commentaria Rabbinica.* The translation covers only the first five and a half chapters of Genesis, beginning with Chapter I, verse 1, and ending with Genesis, Chapter VI, verse 9 and constitutes the weekly reading in the synagogues. Saubert's translation can be found in Wolfe's *Bibliothecae Hebraeae,* Volume III.

French Translation—A French translation was made by Alexander ben Baruch Crehange, in Paris, in 1846. The Book of Genesis was published in 1846, and the rest of the Pentateuch in 1847. The French title of the book is *La Semaine Israelite,* with the

Hebrew subtitle צאינה וראינה ("Tzeenah U-Reenah"). The French title suggests that the translator recommended his translation to be read in weekly portions, which, of course, is correct. However, the French edition is hardly a translation, but rather a dramatization of the "Tzeenah U-Reenah," in which the translator did not feel bound to the original text. The translator introduced into his text a family by the name of Hadass, and the text is divided between various members of that family, the members of the family asking questions and the father answering them. The family consists of Josue Hadass, the father; Debora, his wife; Isaac, Jacob and Joseph, his sons; Rachel and Rebekah, his daughters; David and Solomon, his nephews, and Miriam and Naomi, his nieces. The French edition not only omits most of the original text, but also introduces material which was not in the original. The translation, as a whole, is so far removed from the original text of the "Tzeenah U-Reenah" that it becomes an original work of its own, independent of that of Rabbi Jacob ben Isaac Ashkenazy.

German Translations—Among the German translations, first place seems to belong to David Schweitzer's translation published in Fürth in 1861. The book is divided into chapters and covers the whole of the Pentateuch, but in an abridged form. The translation is good, except for the abridgments, which leave out much of the original text.

A second German translation was made by Goldschmidt and Marmorstein and published in series in the *Mitteilungen zur Jüdischen Volkskunde,* (Volume XIV. No. 1, 2, 3, Leipzig, 1911-1913). This translation covers only the Book of Genesis. The first thirty-seven chapters were made jointly by Goldschmidt and Marmorstein, but the rest was made by Goldschmidt alone. Like the other translations, this translation too omits many passages from the original text.

A more recent German translation was made by Bertha Oppenheimer, with an introduction by Dr. Goldring. The book was published in Frankfurt a. M. 1930. It is a luxurious publication, consisting, however, only of the Book of Genesis. The division of the text is left unchanged. However, like all translators, Miss Oppenheimer leaves out of the original text such passages as she considered spurious. For instance, in Chapter I, she leaves out the explanation why the letter ב has three sides closed and one open. She also leaves out a lengthy legend by Rabba bar bar Hanah, and other material. Miss Oppenheimer, in her introduction, makes no mention of previous German translations, and the reader could easily make the erroneous assumption that Miss Oppenheimer's translation is the first in the German language.

English Translation—The English translation of the "Tzeenah U-Reenah" covers only the Book of Genesis and was made by Paul I. Hershon, published in London in 1885, under the title *Rabbinical Commentary on Genesis*. The text is divided into chapters according to the Biblical order. However, Mr. Hershon left out certain passages from the original text. Moreover, in the introduction to the translation, Hershon quotes the year 1693 as the date of the first publication of the "Tzeenah U-Reenah," and he gives Frankfurt a. M. as the place of publication. This, of course, is wrong, as can be seen from the 1622 Basel edition.

The present work is a translation of the book of Exodus, and may claim to be not only the first translation of this book into English, but it may also claim to be a first attempt to a full and faithful translation from its original Yiddish.

The "Tzeenah U-Reenah" was a most popular book, and according to A. A. Roback[16] the book has gone through several hundred printed editions.

TRANSLATION OF THE

"TZEENAH U-REENAH" TEXT

BASED ON

T H E   M E T Z   E D I T I O N

1 7 6 8

CHAPTER I

1. *NOW THESE ARE THE NAMES*—King Solomon, may he
rest in peace, says in Proverbs, "As an earring of gold, and an
ornament of fine gold, so is a wise reprover upon an obedient ear." [1]
The verse teaches us that the best way of life is to accept the exhortations of wise men; therefore, King Solomon says here that as
jewels adorn the body, so the exhortations of a wise man adorn
the spirit, and this is especially true when such exhortations
are addressed to children, who at a tender age seek after vain
pleasures, for the יצר טוב (character) does not come to a boy before the age of 13,[2] therefore it is advisable to exhort him. For the
same reason, King Solomon says, "He that spareth his rod hateth
his son, but he that loveth him chasteneth him betimes." [3] King
David did not admonish his son Absalom, as a result of which Absalom grew wicked and lay with his father's wives at Jerusalem, and
David had to flee from that city because of him. Jacob, on the
other hand, did reprove his sons and trained them; therefore, they
all were pious and righteous, and this is implied in the text. Thus
the text says, "These are the names of the sons of Israel," i.e., they

29

were sons to a righteous father, who had brought them up to do what was good. Rashi asks why the Scripture has to count the names of the children of Jacob here when they are already counted in Genesis XLVI? The answer is that the Israelites are like the stars in heaven, which God brings out by number at eventide to lighten the darkness, and brings them in again by number at dawn. The Tzror Hamor and the Toldoth Yitschak say that the righteous are compared to the stars in heaven whom the Blessed One brings in and out by numbers, to teach us that as the stars shed more light at night than in the day, so the righteous have more honour and bliss in the world to come than in this world. Bahya, the Hazzekuni and the Imre No'am say that the verse teaches us that Jacob gave wives to all his sons and grandsons that they might contract no marriages with the Egyptians, and because of that the Egyptians had no pity on the Israelites.

EVERY MAN AND HIS HOUSEHOLD CAME—The Midrash, Bahya and the Tzror Hamor say that the verse shows us that God was also with Israel in exile in Egypt, for God is called "A Man of War" and He came with the sons of Jacob to Egypt in order to deliver them. Bahya asks why was the name of Joseph mentioned last in the text, and the names of Dan, Naphtali, Gad and Asher, the sons of the maidservants placed between Benjamin and Joseph, the sons of Rachel, the favourite wife of Jacob. The answer is that this was done in order to emphasize the fact that the sons of Rachel and of Leah should not lord it over the sons of the maidservants, but should honour them as equals. And Joseph was mentioned last to show that although he was a ruler, he, nevertheless, was humble, because the more honour the righteous have, the humbler they are in their own estimation.

5.⁴   *AND JOSEPH WAS IN EGYPT ALREADY*—Rashi comments that the text repeats the fact that Joseph was in Egypt to emphasize that although he was the ruler of Egypt, he nevertheless remained as pious as ever.

6. *AND JOSEPH DIED, AND ALL HIS BRETHREN*—Bahya comments that the verse intends to convey that although Joseph died, God in heaven remained alive, and therefore the verse is followed by one telling of the fecundity of Israel.

7. *AND THE CHILDREN OF ISRAEL WERE FRUITFUL, AND INCREASED ABUNDANTLY*—The Toldoth Yitschak says that every woman bore sextuplets and that there were no childless women, nor had they stillborn children, and the babes grew up rapidly as it is with animals and reptiles. The Tzror Hamor says that the Scriptures mentions again the sons of Israel [5] to show that, although they were only seventy souls originally, they soon became many tens of thousands. The same also points out that the Scriptural phrase, "came out of Jacob's loin" [6] using the singular (loin rather than loins) shows that the reason Jacob had only seventy souls was because the angel touched the hollow of his thigh[7] causing him to limp, and to have no more children.

AND THEY MULTIPLIED EXCEEDINGLY—Rabbi Abraham said he once saw a woman who gave birth to quadruplets. Now, if twins or quadruplets are weak, because the mother's strength has to be shared by two or four when it should go to one baby, the more so with sextuplets; therefore, the Scripture says, "they waxed exceedingly mighty," to emphasize that regardless of the number born at a time, they were exceedingly strong.

8. *NOW THERE AROSE A NEW KING*—The Hazzekuni states that whenever the Bible fails to say that "the old king died and a new king arose," it means that no new king arose, but that the same reigning king made many new evil decrees. Soon after Joseph's death, Pharaoh made new decrees, and forgot the good which Joseph had done for Egypt. Rashi says that in the Gemara,[8] Rab and Samuel disagree. One says it was a new king, while the other says it was the old king making the new decrees. The Tzror Hamor, commenting on the phrase, "a new king arose," says that when the Egyptians saw that the Israelites were growing numerous, they

counselled one another not to elect the heir of the old king, because the old dynasty looked favourably upon Joseph, and had made him ruler over Egypt; but they counselled to elect a new king, a wicked and unmerciful one.

9. *BEHOLD, THE PEOPLE OF THE CHILDREN OF ISRAEL ARE MORE AND MIGHTIER THAN WE*—The Egyptians thought that for three reasons they must destroy the children of Israel. First, because the children of Israel experienced miracles and wonders, and remembered how Jacob met his brother, Esau, when the latter came against him with four hundred men, but could not overcome him. Second, because they remembered how the two sons of Jacob completely destroyed the town of Shechem and did evil in selling their brother.[9] Third, because they were very many and strong. Therefore, the next verse says:

10. *COME, LET US DEAL WISELY WITH THEM.* We must in time outwit them. The king felt he was a stranger to the throne, and feared that the friends of the old dynasty might gather themselves together, and that should the children of Israel join with them they might overthrow the throne; therefore, said he, we must devise means whereby to destroy the children of Israel. Now, since their God has sworn that He will not bring again the flood upon the earth,[10] we will throw their children into the river, and as their God repays deed for deed, He will not punish us with water because of His oath. However, the Egyptians failed to see that God's oath not to bring the flood upon the earth[11] would not save them from drowning in the deep waters of the Red Sea, and thus make the punishment fit the crime. The Hazzekuni quotes the Talmud, tractate Sotah, to the effect that Balaam took part in the counsel how to afflict Israel and destroy them. But how could Balaam have lived for so long until the Israelites were in the wilderness, and have fought against the Midianites, and then be killed by Phineas, when the Talmud [12] itself says that Balaam lived only thirty-three years? The answer is that there were two Balaams, father and son, and the one who took part

in the counsel with Pharaoh was the father of the Balaam killed in the wilderness.[13]

[14] The Gemara in tractate Sotah[15] says that three men were associated with Pharaoh in the counsel to destroy the children of Israel. The first was Balaam, who counselled to destroy them all; therefore, he was killed by the Israelites in the wilderness. The second was Job, who sat silent; therefore, he was punished with tribulations. The third was Jethro, who ran away from such counsel; he merited, therefore, that his descendants should sit in the Sanhedrin.

THEY ALSO JOIN THEMSELVES UNTO OUR ENEMIES— The Toldoth Yitschak says that the Egyptians feared that in the event of an enemy invasion the children of Israel would surrender in order to save their lives, as it was customary to save the lives of those who surrendered, and the enemy might capture the city. 11. *THEREFORE THEY DID SET OVER THEM TASK-MASTERS*—Pharaoh appointed officers over the Israelites to tax them, because he did not wish to tax them himself, in order not to show how he hated them. The Rabbis say that Pharaoh wore a brick around his neck, and whenever a Hebrew complained that he could not work, then Pharaoh would point to the brick around his neck and say, why deemest thou thyself better than the king, who also maketh bricks? Thus Pharaoh deceived Israel. The Tanchumah says that Pharaoh gathered all Israel and asked them obligingly to work for him. The king himself took a shovel and dug with it, and then all the Israelites took shovels and dug in the clay. At the completion of the first day's work at eventide, Pharaoh ordered a count of the number of bricks made during the day and saw that there were many, for on the first day the people were strong and had made a great many bricks. Pharaoh then insisted that they make as many bricks every day, and for that purpose he appointed taskmasters to count the number of bricks made every day. And when the number was short, he ordered that the overseers be punished because they had failed to drive the workmen hard enough. But the overseers, who were Israelites, suffered stripes rather than betray the workmen who were short of the number assigned to them, lest these workers be punished: therefore, the overseers merited to be among the Sanhedrin that ruled Israel and be among the seventy elders in Egypt who, with Moses, saw all the miracles performed before Pharaoh. From this our sages infer that he who suffers for Israel's sake shall merit honour and high esteem.

14. *AND IN ALL MANNER OF SERVICE IN THE FIELD.* The Yalkut, commenting on the text, says that Pharaoh ordered the men to sleep in the fields and to live apart from their wives, to prevent the Israelites from begetting many children. However, the wives brought good food and drink to their husbands in the fields and comforted them, saying that God would deliver them from the bitter bondage. And when the husbands were comforted they united with their wives in the fields and begot children. The Lord, therefore, rewarded the Israelite women with much silver and gold, and made the Red Sea give up the dead pursuers, so that the Israelites might take from them their gold and silver. The Gemara, in the first chapter of the tractate Sotah,[16] says that the Israelites were delivered from the Egyptian bondage because of the merits of their pious views; for when a woman went to draw water, God caused half of her pitcher to be filled with water and the other half with fish. She boiled the fish in the water and brought to her husband in the field, the fish to eat and the liquid with which to wash and anoint his body, and again they united and the woman conceived. Now, when the time came for a woman to be delivered, she went into a field under an apple tree and was delivered of her infant, without the aid of any person. And God made the infant to be born clean, and the umbilical cord came off by itself as if a midwife had cut it off. And God prepared for every child two stones. Out of one flowed oil, and out of the other honey with which the infant was fed, as well as its mother. When Pharaoh learned about this, he sent

messengers to kill all the infants in the fields; but God performed a miracle, and the infants were hidden inside the ground so that Pharaoh could not find them. When Pharaoh learned of this, he ordered the ground to be ploughed up by oxen. Nevertheless, God delivered the children from Pharaoh's hand and made them come out of the earth like grass; and they came out in the tens of thousands. Later the same children recognized God at the Red Sea and exclaimed, "This is my God, and I will praise Him." (Chapter XV: 2.)

15. *AND THE KING OF EGYPT SPAKE TO THE HEBREW MIDWIVES*—Pharaoh told the Hebrew midwives secretly to destroy the Hebrew infants, if they were boys.

16. *AND SEE THEM UPON THE BIRTHSTOOL*—Pharaoh said: "You should take heed how the infant comes out of its mother's womb. If it is born with its face downwards to the ground it is a boy and you should kill him immediately, that the mother should not know it, and think the infant was born dead; but if the infant is born with its face upward, surely it is a girl and you should let her live." This comment is made by the Hazzekuni, and the Gemara in tractate Sotah[17] says the same. Rashi says that Pharaoh ordered the male children to be killed because the astrologers told him that the Messiah of Israel will be born in Egypt. The Hazzekuni adds another explanation, namely, that Pharaoh ordered all male children to be killed because they could become soldiers and go to war. Bahya says, on behalf of the Gemara tractate Sotah,[18] that the Birthstool upon which expectant mothers sat to be delivered was called אבנים "stones," because when a woman is about to be delivered, her feet and her limbs become as cold as stone. Thus Pharaoh gave the midwives the sign saying: "When you see a woman whose limbs grow cold, know ye that she is going to be delivered." The name of one midwife was Shiphrah, who was Jochebed, but because she washed the newborn babies and made them look handsome, she

was called Shiphrah. The name of the second was Puah, who was Miriam, the daughter of Jochebed, mother of Moses and Aaron. She was called Puah because she comforted the babies when they cried. The Ba'al Hatturim adds that Jochebed was called Shiphrah because when a woman gave birth to a stillborn, as happened occasionally, she would make a duct from a feather and blow breath into the child to revive it. Jochebed was therefore called Shiphrah, meaning "duct" through which one blows. And the two midwives let the children live and looked after them. The Hazzekuni, the Toldoth Yitschak, and the Imre No'am, say that the two midwives must have been in charge of many others, for it is impossible that two midwives could have been sufficient to serve the whole of Israel. The Ba'al Hatturim, commenting on the Gemara tractate Sotah,[19] says that Pharaoh lusted to consort with the two midwives, but they would have nothing to do with him, though he was a king, because they were exceedingly pious and would not commit adultery. The Imre No'am tractate Sotah further says that a large bribe was offered to the midwives that they should kill the infants, but they refused because they feared the Lord.

18.   *AND THE KING OF EGYPT CALLED FOR THE MID-WIVES AND SAID UNTO THEM, WHY HAVE YE DONE THIS THING, AND HAVE SAVED THE MALE CHILDREN ALIVE?*

19.   *AND THE MIDWIVES SAID*—They excused themselves before Pharaoh, saying that the Hebrew women are like the beasts of the field that are delivered without the help of midwives; they are their own midwives, and do not need us.

21.   *THAT HE MADE THEM HOUSES*—Rashi, quoting from the Gemara tractate Sotah,[20] says that God rewarded the midwives; that out of Jochebed came priests and Levites, and out of Miriam came kings. Bahya says that the phrase, "he made them houses" means that Pharaoh placed one Egyptian between two Hebrew houses to make certain that when an infant boy was born, he should

be thrown into the river. The Hazzekuni says, Pharaoh built houses in which he confined the expectant mothers and guarded them in order that their male offspring should be thrown into the river. Regarding the midwives, Bahya explains that the text uses the word להם which is masculine, and not להן which is feminine, to indicate that God rewarded the midwives with as much reward as if they were men, who fulfilled the Law faithfully.

22. *AND HE CHARGED ALL HIS PEOPLE.* Rashi and the Tanchuma, and also the Gemara in the tractate Sotah, say that the astrologers told Pharaoh what day the Messiah of Israel would be born, but could not foretell whether he would be an Israelite or an Egyptian. However, they predicted that he would meet his end through water. Pharaoh then ordered that even the Egyptian children should be thrown into the river, on that particular day. The astrologers, however, were mistaken. Moses was only punished through water, but not destroyed. When the Lord ordered Moses to speak to the rock in the wilderness that it bring forth water, Moses struck the rock. For that reason God punished him by forbidding him to enter the Promised Land.

CHAPTER II

1. *AND HE TOOK THE DAUGHTER OF LEVI*—Rashi, the Hazzekuni, and Bahya, quoting from the Gemara tractate Sotah,[1] say that Amram, the husband of Jochebed, was the greatest man of his generation; and when Pharaoh ordered all children to be thrown into the river, he separated himself from his wife and gave her a divorce, and that many righteous men of the Hebrews did the same. But, Miriam, Amram's daughter, came and said to her father that his decree was worse than that of Pharaoh, for Pharaoh ordered only the male children to be destroyed, but her father caused the loss of both male and female. Amram thereupon took back his wife and so did all the others; therefore, the text says, "and he took the

daughter of Levi," for he remarried her; and Aaron and Miriam danced before them as one does before a bridegroom and his bride and sang, "our father remarried our mother." The Rabban asked how could Aaron, who was but three years old, have had the intelligence to sing, dance, and make merry. The answer is that the Holy One, blessed be His Name, gave him the intelligence to make merry, and Miriam taught Aaron and led him in the dance. Jochebed was at that time one hundred and thirty years old, yet the verse calls her "daughter," meaning a young maiden, to show that she became as young as a maiden, and became beauteous and her face was without wrinkles; and she conceived and bore children without pain. From the example of Jochebed we learn that pious women bear children without pain.

The Pirque de-Rabbi Eliezer says that all the children who were thrown into the river survived, for the water threw them out into the wilderness, where the Holy One provided every child with two stones; out of one stone came oil, and out of the other came honey.

2. *AND THE WOMAN CONCEIVED*—And Jochebed gave birth to a son, and he was Moses.

AND SHE SAW HIM THAT HE WAS A GOODLY CHILD [2] —She saw that he was goodly because he filled the house with light, and also because he was born circumcised, and she had no need to circumcise him. Therefore, she longed to save him, and she hid him for three months.

3. *AND WHEN SHE COULD NO LONGER HIDE HIM, SHE TOOK FOR HIM AN ARK OF BULRUSHES AND DAUBED IT WITH SLIME AND WITH PITCH AND SHE PUT THE CHILD THEREIN AND LAID IT IN THE FLAGS BY THE RIVER'S BRINK.* The Egyptians counted the time when Amram remarried his wife, and expected the coming of a baby after the usual nine months. Moses, however, was born after six months and one day. Therefore, his mother could hide him at home for three months; and after that period of time, when the Egyptians came

and asked for the babe, she told them that it was thrown into the river. And Moses was born on the seventh day of Adar[3] and was kept hidden until the sixth day of Sivan;[4] and because he was destined to receive the Torah on the sixth day of Sivan, he was saved from the water on that day. That is the opinion of Bahya and the Hazzekuni.

4. *AND THE SISTER STOOD AFAR OFF* [5]—Now Miriam was the babe's sister, and had prophesied that her mother would bear a son who would deliver Israel from the hands of the Egyptians, and therefore she stood by the river afar off to see whether her prophecy would be fulfilled.

5. *AND THE DAUGHTER OF PHARAOH CAME DOWN TO BATHE AT THE RIVER*—And when she saw the ark, she ordered her maids to fetch it out of the water; but they tried to dissuade her, so God intervened and the maids perished instantly. And the Lord performed a miracle, and the arm of Pharaoh's daughter was lengthened so that she could reach the ark.

6. *AND SHE OPENED IT* and saw the Shekinah abiding upon the babe, and the babe crying loudly with the voice of a grown-up boy because the angel Gabriel came and struck the child, and made him cry loudly so that the daughter of Pharaoh might take pity on him. And the daughter of Pharaoh said, this is one of the Hebrew children whose mother was afraid that the Egyptians would drown him in the river, and she therefore hid him in an ark upon the water. The Rabban says that she saw that he was born circumcised and therefore she said, "This is one of the Hebrew children." And the daughter of Pharaoh asked several Egyptian women to give suck to the baby but he refused to suckle, for the mouth that was to speak with God could not take suck from idolaters.

7. THEN SAID MIRIAM TO PHARAOH'S DAUGHTER, SHALL I GO AND CALL THEE A NURSE OF THE HEBREW WOMEN THAT SHE MAY NURSE THE CHILD?

8. AND SHE SAID, GO AND CALL ONE. AND MIRIAM

WENT AND CALLED THE CHILD'S MOTHER.

9. AND PHARAOH'S DAUGHTER SAID TO THE MOTHER, TAKE THY CHILD UNTO THEE—Prophecy came into the mouth of Pharaoh's daughter, and she said: "Take what is thine," that is to say, it is thy babe. "And I will give thee thy wages," and take no other infant to feed. From this statement we learn that when a woman undertakes to give suck to a babe, she has no right to take a second babe. Bahya says that God shows great favour to the righteous, for not only did Jochebed receive her babe back, but she also received a reward for feeding him.

10. AND WHEN THE CHILD WAS WEANED, SHE BROUGHT HIM TO PHARAOH'S DAUGHTER, AND THE LATTER LOOKED UPON HIM AS HER OWN SON, and embraced and kissed him. Pharaoh too embraced him and kissed him and played with him, as with a child. And Moses seized the crown from Pharaoh's head and threw it on the ground, which was as it were an indication that through Moses God would put an end to Pharaoh's reign.[6]

AND PHARAOH'S DAUGHTER CALLED HIS NAME MOSES, BECAUSE SHE DREW HIM OUT OF THE WATER —And God, blessed be His Name, put into her mind to give him that name and the name remained with him.

11. AND WHEN MOSES WAS GROWN UP, he went into the field and saw how hard the Hebrews worked, and it grieved him greatly, and he also saw an Egyptian smiting a Hebrew. This Egyptian was wicked, for he awoke the Hebrew at midnight, at the crowing of the cock, and when the Hebrew left his house the rascal went in and lay with the man's wife. The woman thought him to be her husband, and she conceived and bore a wicked son, who later was stoned because he cursed the name of God. And when the Hebrew came home and found out what had happened, and when the Egyptian also learned that he had been discovered, he cruelly persecuted the Hebrew at work. Moses knew all that transpired, and

perceived that no child would come from the Egyptian who might become an Hebrew proselyte; Moses therefore laid his hands on the Egyptian and slew him with the Tetragrammaton, and hid his body in the sand so that no man could find it.

13. AND ON THE SECOND DAY Moses went out and saw Dathan and Abiram striving one with the other. And he said to him who was in the wrong, "O sinner, why attemptest thou to smite thy fellow?" From this, we infer that when a Jew lifts up his hand to smite his fellow, he is a sinner; for here they were not yet at blows, but one lifted up his hand against the other in readiness to strike a blow, and for that alone Moses called the one a sinner.

14. WHO MADE THEE A PRINCE OR A JUDGE OVER US? —Dathan and Abiram said to Moses: "Who made thee a prince or a judge over us? Thou art too young to be a judge" (for Moses was only twelve years old at that time); "wilt thou kill us as thou hast killed the Egyptian yesterday, and buried him in the sand?" And Moses was afraid and said: "Now I well know why Israel is in bondage in Egypt, because they are informers, accusing their own before strangers."

15. *NOW WHEN PHARAOH HEARD THIS THING*—Pharaoh heard of this thing through Dathan and Abiram, who reported it.

HE SOUGHT TO SLAY MOSES, but with the help of the Tetragrammaton, Moses made himself invisible and escaped from the hand of Pharaoh. The Midrash says that Moses was handed over to an executioner for decapitation, but the sword could not touch his neck. And Moses fled into the land of Midian, and sat down by a well. Now Jethro was a lord over Midian, and because he had abandoned idolatry the people ostracized him, and no one wanted to look after his flocks, and as he had no sons, his daughters had to do it.

16. AND THEY CAME TO WATER THEIR FLOCKS, but the shepherds came and drove them off and took their water away.

17. AND MOSES CAME AND HELPED THEM against the

shepherds and watered their flocks, and they returned to Jethro, their father.

18. AND HE ASKED THEM, HOW IS IT THAT YE ARE COME SO SOON TODAY?

19. AND THEY SAID UNTO HIM, AN EGYPTIAN DELIVERED US OUT OF THE HANDS OF THE SHEPHERDS— The Torah calls Moses an Egyptian because the slaying of an Egyptian brought him to Midian. And the daughters reported that when he was about to draw the water, the water of the well arose to meet him.

20. AND JETHRO SAID, "WHY HAVE YE LET HIM GO?— He might marry one of you;" for Jethro knew if the water of the well arose to meet him, he must have come from the seed of Jacob.

21. *AND MOSES WAS CONTENT*—Bahya asks why Moses married a daughter of Jethro, and the same answers that it was because he feared that Pharaoh might search after him and find him. But the king had no power over the priests, and if a man, though guilty of death, took refuge with the priests, the king could not touch him. Therefore, Moses wanted to marry a daughter of a priest, provided she would turn to the Hebrew faith, and in the hope that she would not betray him to Pharaoh's agents. And Moses went to Jethro because he had many daughters; as the verse says, he had seven daughters, and Moses thought that he surely would not be against his marrying one. And Moses swore to Jethro that he would not leave the country without his permission, and then Jethro gave him his daughter Zipporah for a wife. She was called "Zipporah," which means bird, and she ran after Moses as fast as a bird; a second reason why she was called Zipporah is because she shone like the morning star, and she was most beautiful.

22. AND SHE CONCEIVED AND BORE A SON AND HE CALLED HIS NAME GERSHOM—Moses called him Gershom because he said that he was a stranger in a strange land.

23. AND THE KING OF EGYPT DIED—The king of Egypt

was smitten with leprosy, and he daily killed a hundred Jewish children to bathe himself in their blood; therefore, the Israelites mourned.

24. AND GOD HEARD THEIR CRY, and remembered Abraham, Isaac and Jacob, who were exceedingly pious.

CHAPTER III

1. *NOW MOSES WAS KEEPING THE FLOCK OF JETHRO, HIS FATHER-IN-LAW.* It was a custom among righteous men in ancient days to occupy themselves with tending sheep in the wilderness, in order to remain in solitude; for they held that many evils, such as gossip, jealousy, evil talk and trespassing upon the rights of others, result from association with others.

THE BACK OF THE WILDERNESS. Moses kept the flock far out in the desert, in order to prevent it from grazing on other people's property. The sages say that Moses dwelt forty years in Egypt, forty years in Midian, and forty years in the wilderness; likewise did Rabbi Akiba, who was in business for forty years, studied for forty years, and taught for forty years.

AND MOSES CAME TO MOUNT HOREB, WHERE THE TORAH WAS GIVEN.

2. AND GOD APPEARED IN A FLAME OF FIRE OUT OF A BUSH, AND THE BUSH WAS NOT CONSUMED. The Hazzekuni and Bahya say that God appeared in fire, in order that Moses might grow accustomed to fire, in preparation for the receiving of the Torah, which was given to him in the midst of fire upon Sinai. And the Lord appeared in a burning bush to symbolize His suffering with the Hebrews in their bondage, because whosoever touches thorns must feel the prick of them.

3. AND MOSES SAID I WILL GO AND SEE WHY THE BUSH IS NOT BURNED.

4. AND GOD CALLED UNTO HIM AND SAID, MOSES,

43

MOSES, AND HE ANSWERED, HERE AM I.

5. AND GOD SAID UNTO HIM, TAKE OFF THY SHOES FROM OFF THY FEET, FOR THE GROUND WHERE THOU STANDEST IS HOLY. And he heard the call "Moses" twice because the voice from Heaven is very powerful and sounds like two voices. A second explanation for the repetition of the call is that, since at the first hearing of a voice from Heaven, mortal man becomes frightened and cannot answer, it is therefore necessary that the Heavenly voice should repeat itself.

6. I AM THE GOD OF THY FATHER AMRAM.[1] In mentioning Moses' father by name, God revealed to Moses that his father was dead, for God does not reveal Himself in the name of a living person. And God revealed to Moses the death of his father, because He knew that Moses would not accept a position of leadership as long as his father was alive.[2]

AND MOSES HID HIS FACE, AND WAS AFRAID TO SPEAK WITH GOD.

7. AND THE LORD SAID, I HAVE SURELY SEEN THE AFFLICTION OF MY PEOPLE.

8. AND I AM COME DOWN OUT TO DELIVER THEM AND TO BRING THEM UNTO A GOOD LAND FLOWING WITH MILK AND HONEY.

10. COME NOW THEREFORE, MOSES, AND GO TO PHARAOH AND BRING FORTH THE ISRAELITES OUT OF EGYPT.

11. BUT MOSES ANSWERED AND SAID, "WHO AM I THAT I SHOULD GO UNTO PHARAOH, and what merit have the children of Israel that they should be delivered?" Thus Moses contended and said, "I am a person of low estate to speak with a king, he might even strike me down. Who am I to bring out a people so worthy and so wise? And even when they be delivered from the cruel bondage, they may not wish to go to Canaan, because of fear of the mighty heathen nations."

12.   AND GOD ANSWERED MOSES TWO QUERIES AND
SAID—"Regarding thy fear to speak with Pharaoh, know thou
that I will be with thee at all times and thou needest not be afraid;
and second, as to why Israel should be delivered, I tell thee that
they will receive the Torah on Mount Sinai, and on that merit they
will be delivered out of the bondage of Egypt. The fire which
thou seest shall be a sign unto thee that thou shalt not fear
Pharaoh, and that the Israelites shall not fear the strong nations
in Canaan, whom I will consume with fire."

13.   AND MOSES SAID, WHEN THE ISRAELITES ASK ME
WHAT IS THE NAME OF THE GOD WHO WILLS TO DE-
LIVER US, WHAT SHALL I SAY UNTO THEM?

14.   AND GOD SAID, TELL THEM THAT MY NAME IS, I
AM THAT I AM, that is to say I am always with you in the present
bondage and in any other future bondage.

16.   GO AND GATHER THE ELDERS OF ISRAEL TO-
GETHER AND SAY UNTO THEM, THE GOD OF YOUR
FATHERS HAS SENT ME TO DELIVER YOU AND SAY
THE WORDS, "I HAVE SURELY VISITED YOU." For Jacob
used the words "surely will visit" and so did Joseph.[3] They will
therefore believe, if thou usest the same words.

18.   GO UNTO PHARAOH AND SAY, THE GOD OF THE
HEBREWS HATH MET WITH US, and hath commanded us to
go to the wilderness and sacrifice to Him.

19.   AND I KNOW WELL THAT PHARAOH WILL NOT
LET YOU GO, but I shall first have to show him My mighty hand
and try him with plagues, and after that he will let you go.

21.   AND I WILL GIVE YOU FAVOUR IN THE SIGHT OF
THE EGYPTIANS, and they will lend you gold and silver and ye
shall spoil the land of Egypt. Bahya asks: "How cometh it that
the Lord encouraged Israel to borrow and to steal?" The same
explains the query, and says that the Israelites did not borrow those
things, but asked that they be given to them as gifts, because the

45

Lord gave the children of Israel favour in the sight of the Egyptians.

CHAPTER IV

1. AND MOSES SAID UNTO GOD, perhaps they will not believe me, that thou hast sent me.

2. AND THE LORD SAID, WHAT IS THAT IN THINE HAND? AND MOSES ANSWERED, A ROD.

3. AND THE LORD SAID, CAST IT ON THE GROUND, AND MOSES CAST IT ON THE GROUND AND IT BECAME A SERPENT, AND MOSES FLED FROM BEFORE IT.

4. AND THE LORD SAID, TAKE IT BY THE TAIL, AND MOSES TOOK IT, AND IT BECAME A ROD AGAIN. Rashi says, God turned the rod into a serpent, to show Moses that he was speaking against Israel in saying that they would not believe him, just as the serpent spoke evil against God.

6. THE LORD SAID FURTHER UNTO MOSES, PUT THINE HAND INTO THY BOSOM, AND HE PUT HIS HAND INTO HIS BOSOM, AND IT BECAME LEPROUS. By that sign God showed Moses that he who speaks evil is stricken with leprosy, and that Moses also spoke evil against Israel, saying they would not believe in God.

7. THEN THE LORD SAID, PUT THINE HAND INTO THY BOSOM AGAIN, AND HE PUT HIS HAND INTO HIS BOSOM AGAIN, AND IT TURNED CLEAN AS IT WAS BEFORE.

8. AND THE LORD SAID UNTO MOSES, THOU SHALT SHOW THESE THINGS UNTO ISRAEL, AND IF THEY WILL NOT BELIEVE IN THE FIRST SIGN, THEY WILL NOT BELIEVE IN THE SECOND: Thou wert smitten with leprosy because thou spokest evil against them and they know of old that he who wrongs Israel is smitten with leprosy, as was Pharaoh, who took Sarah to lie with him, and also as Abimelech was smitten for the same reason.

9. AND IF THEY WILL NOT BELIEVE THESE TWO SIGNS,

THOU SHALL TAKE OF THE WATER OF THE RIVER AND
POUR IT UPON THE GROUND AND IT SHALL TURN INTO
BLOOD.

10. AND MOSES SAID, I PRAY THEE, LORD, I AM NOT
ELOQUENT. For when Moses took off the crown from Pharaoh's
head [1] and cast it upon the ground, the king wanted to have him
slain, for the astrologers said: "We warned thee some time ago
that a son was to be born, who will save Israel from their bondage,
and surely this is he." And Pharaoh appointed three men, Jethro,
Job, and Balaam, to judge the matter. One said: "He is guilty of
death," but the other said: "He is still a child and has no understanding." A dish laden with gold and another dish laden with fire
were placed before Moses, to see which he would choose. If he
chose the one laden with gold and not the one with fire, it would
prove that he possessed discernment, and that he should be put to
death. Moses preferred the dish with the gold, but an angel pushed
him toward the one with the fire. And Moses took a coal of fire and
placed it in his mouth and burned his tongue; therefore, he was not
an eloquent speaker. Thus said Moses: "In my youth I could not
speak well, and the more so now in my old age." Bahya says that
God did not heal Moses' infirmity because he did not pray to be
healed, and the reason why he did not pray was that he might have
an excuse before God for being unable to speak; that the Holy One,
blessed be He, might not send him on the errand to Pharaoh.

11. *WHO HAS MADE MAN'S MOUTH*—And God said:
"Thou refusest to go because thou art not eloquent, but who made
thee speak before Pharaoh when he was seeking thy life for having
smitten the Egyptian? Or who maketh man dumb? Who made
Pharaoh dumb, that he did not order thee to be executed? Or who
made deaf the ears of Pharaoh's servants, that they did not hear
when they were told to seek thy life? Or who blinded them, that
they did not see thee escape? He who did all these, can also
make thee speak before Pharaoh."

13. AND MOSES SAID, "SEND AARON, for he is preferable to me; and also in view of the fact that I am not to lead Israel into the Promised Land, since I am to die in the wilderness; send unto Pharaoh those same messengers who will come into the Promised Land."

14. *AND THE ANGER OF THE LORD WAS KINDLED AGAINST MOSES, AND HE SAID*, "Because thou speakest thus, the priesthood shall not be given unto thee, but unto thy brother Aaron, and thou shalt be a Levite and he shall be thy spokesman unto Pharaoh. And Aaron shall come forth to meet thee and will be glad in his heart for the privilege which is thine and he shall not be envious." Therefore, Aaron was counted worthy to bear upon his heart the breastplate which contained precious stones, because his heart was free from envy.

15. GO, THEREFORE, AND TELL AARON ALL THE WORDS THAT I HAVE SPOKEN UNTO THEE, AND THOU SHALT BE LORD UNTO HIM AND HE SHALL BE THY SPOKESMAN UNTO PHARAOH.

17. *AND THOU SHALT TAKE IN THINE HAND THIS ROD, WHEREWITH THOU SHALT DO THE SIGNS.*

18. *AND MOSES WENT AND RETURNED TO JETHRO, HIS FATHER-IN-LAW.* Moses went and took leave from his father-in-law to go to Egypt, and said, "I will go and see how my brethren fare." And Jethro said, "Go in peace."

19. AND GOD SAID UNTO MOSES, "GO INTO EGYPT, for Dathan and Abiram, who have spoken to Pharaoh against thee, are dead." He called them dead although they were still alive, because they were impoverished, and poverty is like death. They were no longer able to slander Moses, because no one heeded their words after they were impoverished.

20. *AND MOSES TOOK HIS WIFE AND HIS SONS AND SAT THEM UPON AN ASS.* The ass belonged to Abraham; which

he rode when he led Isaac to be sacrificed on Mount Moriah. On the same ass will the Messiah ride when He cometh.

21. AND GOD SAID UNTO MOSES: "With the rod which thou holdest in thine hand shalt thou perform all the miracles before Pharaoh, and I will harden his heart that he should not let the people go, in order that I may multiply my wonders through him."

22. *AND THOU SHALT SAY UNTO PHARAOH*: "The God of Israel has sent me to say unto them, ISRAEL IS MY SON, MY FIRST BORN."

23. "Israel is my esteemed people, thou shalt therefore let them go to serve me and, if thou refusest to let them go, I WILL SLAY THE FIRST BORN." Although the slaying of the first born was the last of the plagues, it is mentioned first, because the Lord, blessed be His Name, wished to impress Pharaoh with the strongest of the plagues.

24. AND IT CAME TO PASS ON THE WAY AT THE LODG-ING PLACE THAT AN ANGEL OF THE LORD SOUGHT TO KILL HIM, BECAUSE HE FAILED TO CIRCUMCISE HIS SON, ELIEZER. Rabbi Yossi says that it was not the intention of Moses to neglect the commandment of circumcision, but that Moses was faced with the dilemma of either circumcising his son and risking to carry a sick child with him on the journey, or else waiting three days until the wound was healed, and risking thereby a delay in executing the commandment to go to Egypt. As long as Moses and his family travelled, the angel did no harm, but when the party reached a lodging place and Moses began to busy himself with his own affairs and not with the commandment of circumcision, the angel sought to kill him. Bahya says that an angel came and swallowed up Moses from his head down to his penis, and that explained to Zipporah the reason for the divine intervention.

25-26. AND ZIPPORAH UNDERSTOOD THAT THE IN-TERVENTION OF THE ANGEL WAS ON ACCOUNT OF THE

CIRCUMCISION, AND SHE TOOK A SHARP FLINT AND
CUT OFF THE FORESKIN OF HER SON, AND THE ANGEL
DEPARTED. Bahya quotes Rabbi Hananel, saying that Moses
himself did not circumcise his son, because he was not present
when the incident took place, and that the angel did not attempt to
swallow up Moses but the child. Rashi, however, maintains that
Moses was present and that the angel did attempt to swallow up
Moses. But Moses was sick and could not circumcise his son,
therefore Zipporah, his wife, performed the circumcision. Bahya
also says that it is not written "the angel went away from him,"
but "the angel let him go," because the angel did not go away.
Zipporah had only cut off the foreskin, but did not perform the
act of "Periah," [2] therefore the angel did not go away until she did
so. Zipporah then said "a bridegroom of blood art thou because of
the circumcision"; and she used the plural term   למולת   implying
two actions, one for the cutting off of the foreskin, and second for
performing the act of "Periah." The Midrash says the child was
circumcised with a sharp flint, and not with a knife, because it was
customary in those days to use flint. Later, when King David threw
his stone to kill Goliath, who wore an iron helmet on his head, the
angel in charge of stone said to the angel in charge of iron: "Let
the iron give way to the stone that it may enter into the head of the
Philistine, and I will reward thee in this manner, that, as until now,
people use flint for circumcision, they shall from now onward use
knives, which are made of iron." Therefore, since those days circumcision has been performed with a knife, because the iron on
the Philistine's head gave way to the flint.

27. AND THE LORD SAID UNTO AARON, GO TO MEET
MOSES, AND HE WENT AND MET HIM.

28. AND MOSES TOLD AARON ALL THE SIGNS GOD
HAD SHOWN HIM.

29. AND MOSES AND AARON GATHERED TOGETHER
THE ELDERS OF THE CHILDREN OF ISRAEL.

30. AND DID THE SIGN WITH THE ROD IN THE SIGHT OF THE PEOPLE.

31. AND THE ISRAELITES BELIEVED, THAT THE LORD SENT MOSES TO DELIVER THEM OUT OF BONDAGE, AND THEY BOWED THEIR HEADS IN WORSHIP, GIVING THANKS TO GOD FOR THE GOOD NEWS.

CHAPTER V

1. AND AFTERWARDS MOSES AND AARON WENT UNTO PHARAOH, but the elders departed from Moses and Aaron because they feared to go to Pharaoh, and therefore they did not merit to be with Moses on Mount Sinai.

AND MOSES AND AARON SAID UNTO PHARAOH, the God of Israel has appeared unto us, and commanded thee to let Israel go, that they may hold a feast unto Him in the wilderness.

2. AND PHARAOH SAID, I KNOW NOT THE LORD. The Midrash says that Pharaoh had a book in which the names of all strange gods were recorded, but he could not find in it the name of the God of Israel. Bahya says that Pharaoh was very clever and knew the name of every reigning king; he therefore said, "I know not the Lord" because he knew of no country on earth over which the Lord reigned. However, Pharaoh did not know that God reigned over all the kings who rule over the earth. Our sages have compared Pharaoh's folly with that of a foolish man who was servant to a priest. One day the priest was out and the servant inquired after him at the cemetery. People laughed at him and called out, "Oh, you fool, why do you look for a priest at a cemetery,[1] when priests are not supposed to visit cemeteries." Likewise, Moses asked Pharaoh why he was looking for the name of the Lord among idols, which are dead, and have no dominion, when the God of Israel is alive and is King over all the kings on earth. Then Pharaoh asked what the God of Israel could do. And Moses said that He

had created heaven and earth, that He giveth rain and maketh all things grow; and that He appointeth kings upon the earth, and removeth kings from the earth. But Pharaoh said: "I am the lord of the universe. I have created myself, and I alone made the river Nile; who then is your God?" The Lord then said unto Moses: "Because Pharaoh boasted about the Nile, thou shalt turn the water of the Nile into blood." Moreover, Pharaoh said: "I have no need to listen to your God, for He did not appear unto me when I took Sarah, but only to Abimelech when he had her. Your God appeared to him at night, but not to me. I therefore know Him not. Nor do I want to heed His word."

3. AND MOSES AND AARON SAID TO PHARAOH: "Let us go, and if not, God will smite thee with pestilence and with the sword."[2]

4. AND PHARAOH SAID UNTO THEM: "LOOSE NOT THE PEOPLE FROM THEIR WORKS, for all Israel hearkens to your words and does not work. Get you unto your burdens. Get you home, you Moses and Aaron, attend to your work and do not interrupt the people in their work." Pharaoh, however, did not order Moses and Aaron to slave for him, for the Levitic tribe was free from labour, since Pharaoh let the Levites study the Torah so that they might teach Israel the laws and the precepts. The Hazzekuni says that the Levites were not pressed into work, because Pharaoh himself first worked together with the people in the hope that they would continue later on their own, but the tribe of Levi from the very beginning refused to work. Moreover, since Jacob forbade the children of Levi to carry his bier, because they were destined to bear the Ark of the Lord with the holy vessels of the Tabernacle, and not biers with dead bodies, the Levites were all the more determined in their refusal to carry burdens for Pharaoh, and so they remained free. For, from the very beginning Pharaoh did not press the tribe of Levi to do forced labour, as the rest were, until they were set free.

6-7. AND THE SAME DAY PHARAOH COMMANDED THE TASKMASTERS SAYING, THAT NO STRAW BE GIVEN FOR THE MIXING OF THE CLAY BUT LET THEM GO AND GATHER STRAW FOR THEMSELVES. Pharaoh told Moses and Aaron that they interrupted the people in their work, therefore, he ordered that no straw be given for the mixing of the clay, but that the people should gather their own straw.

8. AND THEY SHALL MAKE THE SAME NUMBER OF BRICKS DAILY, AS MADE HERETOFORE WHEN STRAW WAS GIVEN TO THEM, THAT THEIR BURDEN BE MADE HEAVIER AND THEY CEASE FROM SAYING LET US GO INTO THE WILDERNESS AND SACRIFICE TO OUR LORD.

12. AND THE PEOPLE SCATTERED TO GATHER STRAW.

13-14. AND THE TASKMASTERS BEAT THE JEWISH OFFICERS WHO SUPERVISED THE WORK THAT THEY FORCE THE PEOPLE TO WORK AND MAKE THE SAME NUMBER OF BRICKS AS IN THE DAYS BEFORE WHEN STRAW WAS GIVEN. The Hebrew officers merited to be numbered among the seventy elders in the Sanhedrin that ruled Israel, because they suffered stripes on behalf of their brethren, and did not punish those who were short on the number of bricks expected of them.

19. *AND THE OFFICERS OF THE CHILDREN OF ISRAEL DID SEE THAT* THEY WERE IN EVIL CASE. The officers saw how hard the Israelites had to work, especially so when they were not given any straw, and had to supply the required number of bricks daily.

20. AND THEY MET MOSES AND AARON AS THEY CAME FORTH FROM PHARAOH.

21. AND THEY SAID UNTO THEM, THE LORD LOOK UPON YOU AND JUDGE, BECAUSE YOU MADE THE WORK OF THE ISRAELITES HARDER.

22. AND MOSES SAID UNTO THE LORD: "Wherefore hast

Thou done evil to Israel that they blame me, since I am God's messenger, and now Pharaoh has made their work harder? The fault is mine, because I was the cause of it; moreover, Pharaoh is still unwilling to let Israel go out of Egypt."

CHAPTER VI

1. *AND THE LORD SAID UNTO MOSES*, "Thou art not like Abraham to whom I first promised that in Isaac shall his seed be, and later when I asked him to sacrifice his son, when he was thirty-seven years old, he made no complaints against me and was immediately ready to sacrifice him; but thou, Moses, complainest much against my deeds. *NOW, THEREFORE, THOU SHALT SEE* what I will do in Egypt, but thou shalt not see the portents which I will do to the thirty-one kings in Canaan. For thou shalt not lead Israel into the Promised Land, but Joshua will lead them, and thou wilt not be present to see these portents. Bahya says Moses asked why the Israelites fared badly and suffered, while Pharaoh and his people, who were wicked, fared well; for as a rule people suffer either as a result of sin committed, or they suffer in this world in order that they might fare well in the world to come. Now, therefore, for which of the two was Israel supposed to suffer? And the Lord answered and said: "Thou shalt soon see the downfall of Egypt, together with Pharaoh, and their rejoicings shall soon come to an end. I have made the work of Israel heavy that I may double their reward, provided they bear their afflictions gladly; and Pharaoh will I punish for his sins." And as it was at the redemption from Egypt, so will it be at the redemption from the present exile, even if it be prolonged, and grow worse daily. In our present situation, too, God will multiply our reward if only we accept our lot gladly. And God will punish the heathens even more for their sins, which they committed against us in the long exile.

3. *AND I APPEARED UNTO ABRAHAM*, UNTO ISAAC, AND UNTO JACOB AND TOLD THEM THAT MY NAME WAS GOD ALMIGHTY, BUT MY NAME YAHWEH I DID NOT REVEAL UNTO THEM—Moreover, if, under the name of God Almighty, I gave them what I promised, the more shall I do the things I promised under the name of Yahweh.[1]

6-7. WHEREFORE, GO AND SAY UNTO THE CHILDREN OF ISRAEL, I WILL KEEP MY OATH WHICH I SWORE TO THEIR FOREFATHERS AND I WILL BRING THEM OUT OF EGYPT—Bahya says that the Scripture uses four terms of redemption; "I will bring you out," "I will rid you out," "I will redeem you," and "I will take you," to show that God promised four things to Israel: (1) He will free them from their masters. (2) He will separate them from their masters. (3) He will divide the waters of the Red Sea. (4) He will give them the Torah.

Firstly, He promised they will be free from their masters, for He said, "I will bring you out from under the burdens of the Egyptians." That means that they will cease from their labours six months before the redemption. As our sages have said, they ceased from their labours on Rosh Hashanah [2] and were redeemed on the fifteenth of Nisan.[3] Secondly, God promised to rid them of the Egyptian dominion, for He said, "I will rid you out of your bondage; I will free you entirely from your forced labours and you will escape their dominion in the month of Nisan." Thirdly, He promised to divide the Red Sea, for He said, "I will redeem you." As long as the master is alive, an escaped slave fears that his master may take hold of him again, but when the Red Sea was divided, the Israelites saw that their masters were drowned, for the sea had cast them out. Then every Israelite saw that their masters were drowned, for the sea had cast them out. Then every Israelite knew he was redeemed, since he recognized his dead master and rejoiced. Fourthly, God promised them the Torah, for He said, "I will take you to me for a people."

By receiving the Torah they became the people of God to serve Him and no other God.

8. AND I WILL GIVE IT YOU FOR AN HERITAGE. The Lord said: "I have lifted up my hand and have sworn to give you the Land of Israel for an inheritance." Bahya says that the Scripture uses the term מורשה and not ירושה, to show that the Israelites who came out of Egypt will not inherit the land, but will die in the wilderness and that their children will inherit the Promised Land.

9. *BUT THEY HEARKENED NOT UNTO MOSES.* Moses came to the Israelites and said: "I have come to deliver you from your bondage"; but they hearkened not unto him, because of the anguish of spirit which they suffered, on account of the heavy work they were made to perform.

10-11. AND THE LORD SPAKE UNTO MOSES, GO, SPEAK UNTO PHARAOH AND TELL HIM TO LET ISRAEL GO OUT OF EGYPT.

12. AND MOSES SAID, BEHOLD, THE ISRAELITES, TO WHOM IT IS GOOD NEWS, HAVE NOT HEARKENED UNTO ME, HOW THEN SHALL PHARAOH HEARKEN UNTO ME?

13. AND THE LORD SPAKE AGAIN UNTO MOSES, and commanded him to go to Pharaoh and pay homage to him, in spite of the fact that he was wicked, because he was a king, even though a king of heathens. The Lord also commanded Moses not to be angry with the children of Israel.

14. *THESE ARE THE HEADS OF THEIR FATHERS' HOUSES*—These are the heads of the families at the time of Israel's redemption.

The Scriptures record Israel's genealogy in order to praise the Israelites above the Egyptians, who had no ancestry worth mentioning. The genealogical account of Moses and Aaron is given to show that they came from worthy parents. The account begins with Reuben and continues to Levi. The Scriptures record that Levi lived one hundred and thirty-seven years, to tell us that the children of Israel were not enslaved as long as a single son of Jacob was still alive. Levi lived longer than any of the sons of Jacob, and the Egyptian bondage began after his death. The verse, therefore, gives us Levi's age to indicate the time when the Hebrews' slavery in Egypt began.

23.   *THE SISTER OF NAHSHON*—Aaron took unto him a wife, Elisheba, the daughter of Amminadab, the sister of Nahshon. The verse tells us who Elisheba's brother was to teach us that when a man wants to marry a wife he should see what kind of brothers the woman has, for the children take after the mother's brothers.

26.   *THESE ARE THAT AARON AND MOSES*—The Scripture places sometimes Aaron before Moses, to show that he was equal in dignity with Moses. He was older than Moses, but Moses excelled his brother in prophecy.

30.   *BEHOLD, I AM OF UNCIRCUMCISED LIPS*—God said to Moses: "Go to Pharaoh," but Moses answered and said: "I cannot speak, because I am of uncircumcised lips." Bahya says that, at the time when the Lord spake unto Moses and unto Aaron, and gave them charge unto the children of Israel, and unto Pharaoh, King of Egypt, Moses did not say, "I cannot speak," because at that time the commandment was also given to Aaron, and Moses thought that his elder brother would do the speaking; but now when God commanded only Moses to go to Pharaoh, he replied that he was of uncircumcised lips. The Hazzekuni says that in order to restrain the two brothers, God ordained Moses and Aaron should come from Amram, who married his aunt, a thing the Torah later prohibited. Had they become proud, one could have told them that they were of a wedlock prohibited by the Torah. Here the question arises: "Wherefore does a woman need to marry her uncle, while a man may not marry his aunt?" The reason is that man rules over his wife. Therefore, when a man takes his aunt, and he strikes her

as a man may, it is considered a grave sin to strike one's aunt; but a woman is allowed to marry her uncle, for if he strikes her occasionally, when she deserves it, then it is no sin.

CHAPTER VII

8. AND THE LORD SPAKE UNTO MOSES SAYING.

9. WHEN PHARAOH SHALL ASK FOR A SIGN, THOU SHALT TAKE THY ROD AND CAST IT DOWN BEFORE PHARAOH AND IT SHALL BECOME A SERPENT. Bahya says that the rod became a serpent and not anything else, because Pharaoh was like the serpent that spoke evil against God and made Adam sin; Pharaoh spoke in the same vein when he said: "Who is the Lord that I should hearken unto his voice?" Pharaoh, therefore, was to reap the same reward as the serpent. Moreover, as a serpent twists his body here and there, so Pharaoh twisted his words; when the plague was sore he said he would let Israel go, but when relieved he soon after hardened his heart.

10. *AARON CAST DOWN HIS ROD BEFORE PHARAOH AND BEFORE HIS SERVANTS, AND IT BECAME A SERPENT.*

11-12. AND PHARAOH CALLED FOR HIS WISE MEN AND THE SORCERERS AND THEY WITH THEIR ENCHANTMENT ALSO TURNED THEIR RODS INTO SERPENTS: BUT AARON'S ROD SWALLOWED UP THEIR RODS. This was an indication that on account of Israel the Egyptians will finally be swallowed up by the Red Sea. Bahya says it is written of the rods of the sorcerers, "and they became serpents." The rods of the sorcerers, through enchantment, appeared as though they became serpents, but as a matter of fact, they never did; the sorcerers bewitched the people and made them believe the rods became serpents.

13-14. AND PHARAOH'S HEART WAS HARDENED AND HE REFUSED TO LET ISRAEL GO.

15-16. *GET THEE UNTO PHARAOH.* Go early in the morning and thou shalt surely find him by the river; for Pharaoh thought himself to be a god and claimed that he ate and drank and had no need to relieve himself; but he went privately to the river in the early morning, to relieve himself, where no man would see him. The Lord therefore said unto Moses: "Go and meet him by the river and tell him to let Israel go. But I know that he will not let them go until I will smite all the first born in the land of Egypt."

17. THOU SHALT SAY UNTO HIM, BEHOLD, I WILL SMITE WITH THE ROD THAT IS IN MINE HAND UPON THE WATERS WHICH ARE IN THE RIVER, AND THEY SHALL BE TURNED INTO BLOOD.

18. AND THE FISH THAT IS IN THE RIVER SHALL DIE, AND THE RIVER SHALL STINK THAT THE PEOPLE SHALL NOT BE ABLE TO DRINK THEREOF.

19. AND THE LORD SAID UNTO MOSES, GO UNTO AARON AND TELL HIM TO TAKE THE ROD AND STRETCH IT OVER THE WATERS OF EGYPT, OVER ALL THE RIVERS AND OVER ALL THE PONDS THAT THEY MAY BECOME BLOOD. AND THERE SHALL BE BLOOD IN ALL THE VESSELS OF WOOD AND IN ALL THE VESSELS OF STONE.

Aaron, not Moses, smote the river because the river had been kind to Moses when, as a child, he was thrown into it: he was therefore not to smite it. The same is true with regard to the frogs which came out of the water; it was Aaron and not Moses who brought that plague. Likewise, the plague of lice was brought not by Moses, but by Aaron, because the plague was wrought by smiting the dust of the earth which saved Moses when he smote the Egyptian and hid him in the sand.

22.*   AND THE MAGICIANS DID IN LIKE MANNER, and turned water into blood. Bahya says the magicians dug new wells and the water they found they turned into blood; for all the existing waters had been previously turned into blood by Aaron. The explanation is that they dug water out of the earth, and turned it into blood, because the plague of Moses and Aaron was only upon the water which was available, but the water which was still below the surface of the earth was not turned to blood. It was from such sources that the magicians drew water and turned it into blood. The Hazzekuni also maintains the same view.

21-24.   AND THE FISH THAT WAS IN THE RIVER DIED: AND THE RIVER STANK, AND THE EGYPTIANS DIGGED ROUND ABOUT THE RIVER FOR WATER TO DRINK, FOR THEY COULD NOT DRINK THE WATER OF THE RIVER.

25.   *AND SEVEN DAYS WERE FULFILLED.* Seven days passed after the plague came, but Pharaoh refused to let Israel go. Every plague lasted seven days, which is likened to the menstruation period of a woman, when she is considered unclean for seven days.[1] For the remaining twenty-one days of the month, between one plague and the other, Pharaoh had peace. At the coming of a new plague, the same day Moses exhorted Pharaoh and warned him of what was to come.

CHAPTER VIII

1.   WHEN THE LORD SPAKE UNTO MOSES, GO UNTO PHARAOH AND SAY UNTO HIM,

2.   IF THOU STILL REFUSE TO LET ISRAEL GO, I WILL SMITE ALL THY BORDERS WITH FROGS.

3.   AND THEY SHALL COME INTO THINE HOUSE AND

---

*Verse 22 comes in our text before 21, but could not be reversed because 21 runs as part of verse 24.

INTO THY BEDCHAMBER. AND UPON THY BED, AND INTO THE HOUSE OF THY GOVERNORS AND THY SERVANTS, IN THINE OVENS AND IN THY KNEADING-TROUGHS, of which thou bakest thy bread, and there shall be frogs everywhere. Bahya said that the king of Egypt had previously quarrelled with the king of Ethiopia. The king of Egypt accused the king of Ethiopia of having taken some of his land; and the king of Ethiopia made a similar charge against the king of Egypt. However, when the frogs descended, it was shown for certain where the Egyptian border ended, for the frogs were only in the land of Egypt reaching to the Ethiopian border, but did not cross it; and as a result of that sign, the quarrel between the two kings was ended.

4. *UPON THEE, AND UPON THY PEOPLE.* The frogs shall enter into the bellies of the people, and make croaking noises within.

6. AND AARON STRETCHED OUT HIS HAND OVER THE WATERS OF EGYPT AND THE FROGS CAME UP. There was one gigantic frog in the water, and when Aaron smote it, multitudes of smaller frogs came out of it, and they filled the land.

7. *AND THE MAGICIANS DID IN LIKE MANNER WITH THEIR ENCHANTMENTS, AND BROUGHT UP FROGS.*

8. AND PHARAOH SAID UNTO MOSES AND AARON, ENTREAT YE THE LORD TODAY THAT HE TAKE AWAY THE FROGS FROM ME TOMORROW. Then shall I send out Israel. And Moses asked: "When do you want me to entreat, and for what time do you want relief from the frogs? However, they must remain in the river." And Pharaoh said: "Entreat the Lord today that He take away the frogs from me tomorrow." Bahya, Nahmanides and the Hazzekuni say that Pharaoh, therefore, said "that he take away the frogs from me tomorrow," because Pharaoh reasoned in his heart that the frogs might disappear today of their own accord, and had he asked that they be taken away today, Moses and Aaron might say that they went because of their intercession.

He therefore asked that they be taken away tomorrow, so that if they went today of their own accord and not because of Moses' intercession, the latter would have been shown to be a liar. From thenceforth Pharaoh always said "tomorrow," and Moses also said the same. The Hazzekuni and the Ba'al Hatturim say that when Moses made intercession, all the frogs died, except those which on the commandment of God entered into the ovens and into the fire, and the same later returned alive into the waters. From this we learn that whoever sanctifies God's name attains eternal life. The Imre No'am asks why it should be written in one case, "and the frogs shall depart," and in another case, "and the frogs died?" The answer is that the frogs which were within the people's bellies came out and departed alive; also those which were in the house of Pharaoh departed, out of respect to the king, but that the rest died.

12.   *AND MOSES CRIED UNTO THE LORD.* The Imre No'am says that Moses had to cry for the removal of that plague, because he had spoken proudly when he had said to Pharaoh, "Glory over me;" therefore God did not hearken to his prayer immediately, and Moses had to cry. From this we deduce that one need not cry out aloud in prayer. Rabbi Isserles says that the plague of blood affected the vessels made of wood and the vessels made of stone, but not the vessels made of iron. From that we infer that when the seasons of the year come,[2] a piece of iron should be thrown into the water that the season may not suffer. As it was the case in Egypt, where there was no blood in the iron vessels.

16.   AND THE LORD SAID UNTO MOSES, BECAUSE PHARAOH REFUSES TO LET ISRAEL GO, SAY THERE-FORE UNTO AARON TO STRETCH OUT THY ROD AND SMITE THE DUST OF THE EARTH AND IT WILL BECOME LICE.

17.   AND AARON DID SO,[3] but not Moses, because the earth had covered the Egyptian whom Moses had smitten and hidden beneath the earth, and thereby the earth protected Moses from death

62

by the hand of Pharaoh.

18. AND ALSO THE MAGICIANS TRIED TO BRING FORTH LICE, BUT THEY COULD NOT. Demons have no power over objects smaller than a grain of barley. Bahya says the magicians could turn water into blood because this was not a creation. Water was available and they could change it into blood. The same is true with respect to the frogs; they were available in the waters, and it was only necessary to make them come out. That the magicians could do. But to make lice out of dust involved an act of creation, and this the magicians could not do; therefore, they recognized in that plague the finger of God, and said that they could not do it, and henceforth they were held in low esteem by the Egyptians, and Pharaoh no longer called them in at the coming of the rest of the plagues. "And there were lice upon man and upon beast," and all over Egypt.

20-22. THE LORD SAID UNTO MOSES, BECAUSE PHARAOH'S HEART IS HARDENED AND HE REFUSES TO LET ISRAEL GO, BEHOLD I WILL SEND EVIL BEASTS INTO ALL THE HOUSES OF THE LAND OF EGYPT, BUT IN THE LAND OF GOSHEN WHERE THE CHILDREN OF ISRAEL DWELL, THERE WILL BE NO EVIL BEASTS. Bahya says that it is customary for a king who plans evil against his enemy to keep his plans secret that the enemy be not on his guard, but the Lord warned Pharaoh before every plague, because no one can hide before the Lord.

23. AND I WILL PUT A DIVISION BETWEEN MY PEOPLE AND THY PEOPLE. The Lord says that the evil beasts will cause harm to man and beast, but not to the Israelites, who will be able to go about Mitzraim freely.

25. AND PHARAOH SAID UNTO MOSES AND UNTO AARON, "GO YE, SACRIFICE TO YOUR GOD HERE, and do not go into the wilderness."

26. AND MOSES AND AARON SAID, IT IS NOT MEET

FOR US SO TO DO. SHALL WE SACRIFICE THE GODS OF THE EGYPTIANS AND WILL NOT THE PEOPLE STONE US? Therefore we must go far into the wilderness, so that the Egyptians may not see us sacrificing their gods.

28. AND PHARAOH SAID, I WILL LET YOU GO: ONLY YE SHALL NOT GO VERY FAR AWAY: ENTREAT FOR ME.

29. AND MOSES SAID, BEHOLD I GO OUT FROM THEE AND I WILL ENTREAT THE LORD THAT THE EVIL BEASTS MAY DEPART FROM THEE TOMORROW, THAT THOU THINK NOT THAT THEY DEPARTED OF THEIR OWN ACCORD; ONLY REPENT NOT FROM LETTING ISRAEL GO.

31. AND HE REMOVED THE SWARMS OF FLIES. Moses prayed and God removed the evil beasts. Bahya says: "Why did God allow the evil beasts to escape? Why did He not kill them, as He killed the frogs?" The reason is that the frogs stank and defiled the whole country and made life miserable for the Egyptians, but had God left the "evil beasts" to die, the Egyptians would have benefitted from their excellent hides, since foxes, wolves, and more costly varieties were amongst them. And the Lord let them escape into the wilderness, so that the Egyptians might not benefit from them.

The Hazzekuni says that the magicians could not imitate the plague of the lice, because the earth was covered with lice, and man had to stand on them without being able to touch the ground, but a magician could not perform his magic tricks unless his feet touched the ground.

32. AND PHARAOH HARDENED HIS HEART THIS TIME ALSO, AND HE DID NOT LET THE PEOPLE GO. Bahya says that at this plague, the verse adds the words "this time also" Pharaoh hardened his heart, because at the previous three plagues the magicians hardened Pharaoh's heart. But with the plague of the

"evil beasts" the magicians did not come to counsel Pharaoh, since they saw in the case of the plague of lice that they could not reproduce it, and thereby they acknowledged it to have been the work of God. Therefore, the text implies that the magicians did not harden Pharaoh's heart, but rather softened it, nevertheless Pharaoh hardened it himself.

CHAPTER IX

1. THEN THE LORD SAID UNTO MOSES, GO IN UNTO PHARAOH AND SAY UNTO HIM.

2. IF THOU REFUSEST TO LET ISRAEL GO.

3-6. BEHOLD, THE HAND OF THE LORD IS UPON THY CATTLE, WHICH IS IN THE FIELD. Bahya says that the warning was given regarding the cattle in the field, because most cattle were in the fields; but the cattle which were indoors were not spared either. Nahmanides maintains that it is therefore written "in the field" because the Egyptians worshipped animals, and therefore kept them far away from people in the towns, keeping the cattle in the fields near Goshen, where the Hebrews dwelt. However, the cattle belonging to the children of Israel were not far from the cattle belonging to the Egyptians, yet the Scripture says, "all the cattle of Egypt died; but of the cattle of the children of Israel died not one."

7. AND PHARAOH SENT, AND, BEHOLD, THERE WAS NOT SO MUCH AS ONE OF THE CATTLE OF THE ISRAELITES DEAD. BUT THE HEART OF PHARAOH WAS STUBBORN AND HE DID NOT LET ISRAEL GO.

8. AND THE LORD SAID UNTO MOSES AND UNTO AARON, TAKE INTO YOUR HANDS ASHES OF THE FURNACE AND SPRINKLE IT TOWARD THE HEAVEN, IN THE SIGHT OF PHARAOH.

9. AND IT SHALL BRING FORTH BOILS UPON MAN AND

UPON BEAST. By a miracle Moses was able to hold in one fist the ashes which had filled both his hands and also that which was in Aaron's hands, and then threw it high towards the skies. Now, the throwing of the ashes was also miraculous, because ashes cannot be thrown high, for they scatter easily.

12.   AND THE LORD HARDENED THE HEART OF PHARAOH, AND HE REFUSED TO LET ISRAEL GO OUT OF EGYPT. Bahya asks: "Why does it say here 'And God hardened the heart of Pharaoh' and at the former plagues it says 'and Pharaoh hardened his heart?' " The reason is that at the first plagues the magicians came and hardened Pharaoh's heart, but here, at the plague of boils, the magicians were ashamed to come to Pharaoh's home, since they themselves were covered with boils. Therefore, the text says that "God hardened his heart" because God, Himself, hardened Pharaoh's heart.

Rashi asks how the verse can say that boils came upon the cattle, when all the cattle of Egypt were supposed to have died in the previous plague? The answer is that a few Egyptians feared God and sheltered their cattle indoors, and these were spared. However, these same were smitten with boils.

13-18.   AND THE LORD SAID UNTO MOSES, GO AND SAY UNTO PHARAOH, IF THOU WILT NOT LET ISRAEL GO, I WILL CAUSE TO RAIN A VERY GRIEVOUS HAIL THAT WILL BREAK EVERY TREE AND SMITE THE CROPS IN THE FIELDS.

19.   NOW, THEREFORE, SEND AND GATHER IN THY CATTLE AND ALSO THE PEOPLE FROM THE FIELD, THAT THE HAIL KILL THEM NOT.

Bahya says that all the cattle perished by the pestilence in the previous plague, but the Egyptians later purchased new cattle from the neighbouring peoples; these were the cattle which God commanded to be gathered in. Also, there were cattle that belonged to both Israelites and Egyptians by virtue of common ownership, and these did not perish in the Pestilence; and God ordered that these cattle be gathered in, that the hail destroy them not. One could ask why, if the cattle that belonged to Jewish and Egyptian common ownership did not perish in the Pestilence, should they be in danger of being killed by the hail? The answer is because here in this case God warned the people to gather in the cattle. Bahya also says that the hail, which broke the trees, contained fire and water. The hail broke the trees and the fire burned up the roots on the ground, and yet the water did not quench the fire. This situation can be illustrated by a story about a king who had two governors who hated each other. Once the king had to go to war, and was in need of the service of both his governors, so he made peace between them. The Holy One, blessed be His name, likewise made peace between His angels in Heaven, where Michael is in charge over water and Gabriel is in charge over fire, yet both angels serve God, who makes peace between them.

24.[1] AND THE LORD SENT THUNDER AND HAIL. God first sent thunder to smite the people and afterwards hail.

25. *AND THE HAIL SMOTE EVERY HERB OF THE FIELD*, including the flax and the barley, man and beast, all were smitten.

26. *ONLY IN THE LAND OF GOSHEN WHERE THE CHILDREN OF ISRAEL WERE, THERE WAS NO HAIL.*

27. AND PHARAOH SENT, AND CALLED FOR MOSES AND AARON AND SAID, THE LORD IS RIGHTEOUS AND I AND MY PEOPLE ARE WICKED, because we let not Israel go.

28. ENTREAT THE LORD THAT THERE BE NO MORE MIGHTY THUNDERINGS, FIRE AND HAIL, AND I WILL LET YOU GO.

29. AND MOSES SAID, AS SOON AS I AM GONE OUT OF THE CITY, I WILL ENTREAT FOR THEE THAT THE HAIL AND FIRE CEASE, THAT THOU MAYEST KNOW THAT THE GOD IN HEAVEN IS ABOVE ALL GODS.

33. *AND MOSES WENT OUT OF THE CITY* to pray, because the city was full of idolatry. The Hazzekuni says that Moses asked that the cattle be gathered in before the hail, a thing he did not do before the plague of Pestilence, because the hail smote both man and beast; therefore God exhorted the Egyptians to gather in people and cattle. However, in the case of the Pestilence, there was no risk to human lives, for only the cattle died, but not men; therefore, God did not warn the people to gather in their flocks from the fields. The Hazzekuni also says that Moses went out of the city to pray in order to show that he feared not the mighty hail nor the fire in the field. Bahya says that Moses lifted up his hands in prayer to God in this case more than in the previous plagues, because the hail smote man and beast and there was a great cry among the people.

AND THE RAIN WAS NOT POURED UPON THE EARTH.[2] Bahya says the hail remained suspended between heaven and earth for forty-one years, until Joshua came and fought against the thirty-one kings, whom the hail smote together with their peoples. And the thunder was suspended until the coming of Elisha, in whose days the king of Assyria came with many people against the City of Samaria. Then the Lord caused the thunder to come down upon the invaders and made them fear greatly, and they left their tents with all that was within them and the Israelites captured their booty.

34. AND HE SINNED YET MORE. The wicked, as long as the affliction is upon him, is submissive and fears God, but as soon as the affliction leaves him, he becomes wicked again. The righteous, however, are always humble; therefore they are honoured, as it is written "but he that is of a lowly spirit shall obtain honour."[3]

CHAPTER X

1. GO IN UNTO PHARAOH. King Solomon, may he rest in peace, says, "Happy is the man that feareth alway," [1] that no evil

come out of his deeds. The verse used the term[2] אדם to show that although man was created from the dust of the earth, he nevertheless can use his understanding to think of doing all that is good; and when he wants to eat or drink, let not his aim be carnal pleasures, but let it be for the purpose of strengthening his body in the service of God. And the Scripture also says, "But he who hardens his heart against God will fall into evil," like Pharaoh, who hardened his heart against God and, therefore brought much evil upon himself; and since he hardened his heart first by his own volition, God later hardened it for him, in order to punish him severely for his misdeeds. For God leads man on the path of his own choice; if he chooses the good way, God leads him in it, but if he chooses the evil way, God likewise leads him in it, that He may punish him. The Lord therefore said to Moses, "go in unto Pharaoh," and warn him and say unto him: "How long wilt thou refuse to let my people go and how long will thou ignore the signs I performed, and refuse to humble thyself before me?"

4. BEHOLD I WILL BRING LOCUSTS.

5. AND THEY SHALL COVER THE FACE OF THE EARTH AND THEY SHALL EAT UP ALL THE TREES AND ALL THE HERBS OF THE FIELD.

6. AND THY HOUSES SHALL BE FILLED WITH THEM THAT NEITHER THY FATHERS NOR THY FOREFATHERS HAVE SEEN THE LIKE. Bahya says that the Holy One, blessed be His name, warned Pharaoh at two places, by the river, because he boasted of having created it, and in the house, because he boasted of his luxurious dwelling. God therefore warned him at both places, and humiliated him. Likewise, Nebuchadnezzar, when he boasted of being a god, the Lord humbled him and turned him into a beast and made him eat grass like a beast, and caused him to dwell in a forest for seven years. Bahya also says that the plagues came in the following order. First, on the fifteenth day of Nisan, God

69

appeared unto Moses in the midst of a burning bush and commanded him to go unto Pharaoh. On the twenty-first day of Nisan, Moses took leave from Jethro, his father-in-law, to go into the land of Egypt, since Moses had sworn not to leave Midian without Jethro's permission. He now wanted to be free from his oath, in order to go unto the land of Egypt and warn Pharaoh to let Israel go. It took Moses eight days to reach Egypt and to deliver the message, and by then the month of Nisan was complete. Then for the following three months, Iyar, Sivan and Tamuz, Moses was in hiding from Pharaoh and was away from Israel; and the plague of blood began in the month of Ab. A plague lasted for seven days and then followed three weeks of relief for Pharaoh, between one plague and the other. The plagues repeated themselves in that way until the beginning of Nisan. Now, the locusts came at the beginning of the month of Nisan and lasted seven days; then, soon after, came the plague of darkness and it too lasted seven days, until the fourteenth of Nisan. On the fifteenth of Nisan came the plague against the first born, so that all the plagues came within twelve months, i.e., one full year. In the month of Nisan of the previous year, Moses forewarned Pharaoh about the final plague, which came after twelve months. Like the wicked who suffer in hell for twelve months; so Pharaoh and his people suffered plagues and tribulations for twelve months.

AND HE TURNED, AND WENT OUT FROM PHARAOH. Moses went out from Pharaoh in great anger, he warned him about the locusts, that Pharaoh might consult with his counsellors and let Israel go before it was too late, since the locusts were a great calamity in the eyes of Pharaoh, because they would eat up all the crops in the field.

7. AND AS SOON AS MOSES WENT OUT, PHARAOH'S SERVANT SAID, HOW LONG SHALL THE ISRAELITES BE A SNARE UNTO US? LET THEM GO THAT THEY MAY

SERVE THE LORD THEIR GOD, KNOWEST THOU NOT THAT EGYPT IS DESTROYED BECAUSE OF THE PLAGUES?

8. AND MOSES AND AARON WERE BROUGHT AGAIN UNTO PHARAOH: AND HE SAID UNTO THEM, GO SERVE THE LORD YOUR GOD, BUT TELL ME WHO ARE THEY THAT SHALL GO?

9. AND MOSES SAID WE MUST ALL GO: WOMEN AND CHILDREN TOO, FOR WE MUST HOLD A FEAST UNTO THE LORD. By the feast Moses meant the Feast of Pentecost, for on that day Israel received the Torah.

10. AND PHARAOH SAID, "WHY SHOULD THE CHILDREN GO? GO YE THAT ARE MEN. For ye desire to sacrifice to God, but women and children do not sacrifice. I can see you plan to run away in the wilderness, but look out, *FOR EVIL IS BEFORE YOU*. I see an evil star appearing against you in the wilderness signifying blood, which means ye will perish in the wilderness."

The name of that star was Ra'ah (evil), for it causes evil to people. In truth Pharaoh was right. The star did foretell of blood, for when Israel made the Golden Calf, God wanted to destroy them, but owing to Moses' intercession, God changed their blood for the blood of circumcision, which Israel underwent in the wilderness under the direction of Joshua, before they entered the Promised Land. Therefore, Moses in his intercession said, "Wherefore should the Egyptians speak, saying for evil did he bring them forth." [3] If thou destroyest Israel, the Egyptians will say, have we not foretold it that their God brought them out by the star Ra'ah, in order to destroy them in the wilderness? And now, all the signs and wonders which Thou has wrought in Egypt will be forgotten and become meaningless.

11. AND PHARAOH DROVE MOSES OUT OF HIS HOUSE.

12. *AND THE LORD SAID UNTO MOSES, STRETCH OUT*

THINE HAND OVER THE LAND OF EGYPT FOR THE LOCUSTS THAT THEY MAY COME.

13. AND MOSES STRETCHED FORTH HIS HAND, AND THE LORD BROUGHT A MIGHTY EAST WIND ALL THAT DAY AND ALL THAT NIGHT, AND THE WIND BROUGHT THE LOCUSTS.

15. AND THEY COVERED THE FACE OF THE WHOLE EARTH, SO THAT THE LAND WAS DARKENED, AND THEY DID EAT EVERY HERB OF THE LAND AND ALL THE CROPS OF THE FIELD. The word "locusts" occurs seven times in the Parashah,[4] because there were seven kinds of locusts, small, large, red, black, white, green, and brown.

16. AND PHARAOH SAID UNTO MOSES AND UNTO AARON, I HAVE SINNED AGAINST THE LORD, YOUR GOD, AND AGAINST YOU, FOR I CALLED FOR YOU AND AFTERWARDS DROVE YOU AWAY.

17. NOW I PRAY YOU ENTREAT THE LORD YOUR GOD THAT HE MAY TAKE AWAY FROM ME THIS BITTER PEST OF LOCUSTS. Bahya says that the locusts stung the Egyptians in their eyes and caused them to die, therefore Pharaoh said, "that He may take away from me this death only."

18. AND MOSES ENTREATED THE LORD.

19. AND THE LORD TURNED A WEST WIND, WHICH TOOK UP THE LOCUSTS AND DROVE THEM INTO THE SEA. The Imre No'am says that God drove the locusts into the Red Sea, and that when the Egyptians pursued the children of Israel into the Red Sea the locusts took vengeance on the soldiers of Pharaoh, for all the plagues which the Lord brought upon Egypt were repeated at the crossing of the Red Sea.

THERE REMAINED NOT ONE LOCUST. Even the locusts which the Egyptians conserved for food revived and flew away to the sea that the people might not benefit from them. Bahya says that Moses' prayer brought everlasting help to Egypt, for since Moses prayed that the locusts be taken away from Egypt, the country no longer suffers from that pest; and although the land of Israel does occasionally suffer from the locusts, Egypt does not, and even if the locusts do sometimes pass through Egypt, they cause little damage. Now regarding the frogs of which Moses said, "they shall remain in the river," only one large monster-frog remained alive in the water, and from time to time comes out on the dry land and devours three people at a time. A bow and arrow cannot touch it, for the frog has a powerful poison that even if one pierced its belly and killed it, anyone touching the dead frog would die.

21. AND THE LORD SAID UNTO MOSES, STRETCH OUT THINE HAND TOWARDS HEAVEN THAT THERE MAY BE DARKNESS, EVEN DARKNESS WHICH MAY BE FELT. The Holy One, blessed be His name, said that when the darkness of the night disappears and it will begin at dawn, then let darkness come again that it be known to all that it is a plague coming from God. The Hazzekuni and the Imre No'am ask: "Why did not Moses warn Pharaoh with the words, 'if thou wilt not let Israel go, I will bring darkness upon thee'?" The reason is that had anyone warned the Egyptians, they would have hidden all their gold and silver, and Israel would not have been able to borrow anything from them. Therefore, when the darkness descended upon Egypt the Israelites came and asked the Egyptians, "Lend me your silver goblet or jug, or your gold chain." Thereupon, if the Egyptian answered: "I have not any. Why do you ask?" Then the Israelites would say: "I see all the vessels standing there, all that I desire." The Egyptian then said: "Since you see in the dark and I do not see in the dark, I will lend them to you." Rashi says that darkness came upon Egypt because there were many sinners among Israel who refused to leave Egypt, and the Holy One, blessed be His name, caused them to die while darkness lasted, that the Egyptians might

not see them and say: "The Israelites are smitten like we are smitten." Therefore, the Lord brought darkness that the wicked might die and be buried in the darkness.

22-23. AND THE DARKNESS WAS SO THICK THAT HE WHO SAT COULD NOT RISE FROM HIS PLACE. The thick darkness lasted only six[5] days, although all other plagues lasted seven days, but in this case the seventh day was reserved for the time when the Egyptians pursued the Israelites to the Red Sea, where darkness struck them again.

BUT THE CHILDREN OF ISRAEL HAD LIGHT IN THEIR DWELLINGS. The Hazzekuni asks why is it not said that there was light in Goshen, where Israel dwelled, as in the case with the other plagues, where it was pointed out that Israel was not afflicted? The same answers, that it is written there was light where Israel dwelt, meaning to say, when an Israelite entered the house of an Egyptian, the Egyptian was in darkness, but the Israelite could see. For that reason the Torah does not say that there was light only in Goshen, because an Israelite could see in all places wherever he went.

24. AND PHARAOH SAID UNTO MOSES AND UNTO AARON, GO YE ALL OF YOU INTO THE WILDERNESS AND SERVE THE LORD: ONLY LET YOUR FLOCKS AND YOUR HERDS STAY BEHIND AS A BOND.

25. AND MOSES SAID, THOU MUST ALSO GIVE INTO OUR HANDS EVEN OF THINE OWN FLOCKS, FOR WE KNOW NOT HOW MANY OFFERINGS THE LORD OUR GOD WILL ASK OF US.

28. AND PHARAOH SAID UNTO MOSES, GET THEE FROM ME, TAKE HEED TO THYSELF, SEE MY FACE NO MORE.

29. AND MOSES SAID, THOU HAST SPOKEN WELL AND IN THE PROPER TIME, THOU SHALT SEE ME NO MORE, FOREVER.

CHAPTER XI

1. AND THE LORD SAID UNTO MOSES, YET ONE PLAGUE MORE WILL I BRING UPON PHARAOH, AND AFTERWARDS HE WILL LET YOU GO HENCE.

2. SPEAK NOW, THEREFORE, IN THE EARS OF ISRAEL AND LET EVERY MAN ASK OF HIS NEIGHBOUR SILVER AND GOLD. And let him take it with him out of Egypt, for I promised to Abraham that "they shall come out with great substance." Moreover, because the Egyptians made the children of Israel slave for them, let them lend their silver and gold to the Israelites.

4-5. AND MOSES SAID UNTO PHARAOH: THUS SAID THE HOLY ONE, BLESSED BE HIS NAME, ABOUT MIDNIGHT I WILL SMITE ALL THE FIRST BORN IN THE LAND OF EGYPT, THE FIRST BORN OF HIS FATHER OR OF HIS MOTHER, PRINCE OR KING; ALSO THE FIRST BORN OF THE CATTLE; for the Egyptians worshipped animals.

6. AND IN THE NIGHT THERE SHALL BE A GREAT CRY IN EGYPT FOR THERE SHALL NOT BE A HOUSE WITHOUT ONE DEAD. But Pharaoh himself was not touched that he might see the wonders at the Red Sea, and tell of them to other people.

7. BUT AGAINST ANY OF THE CHILDREN OF ISRAEL SHALL NOT A DOG MOVE HIS TONGUE.[1] The Imre No'am says: The dogs did not bark against the children of Israel, because there were no corpses among them. But among the Egyptians there were many corpses, due to the first born who had been smitten; therefore, the dogs barked at them. The Gemara, therefore, says that when dogs play in the streets, it is a sign that Elijah is in the town, for when Elijah killed the four hundred false prophets he threw the corpses to the dogs. Therefore when they see him coming, they are pleased and think he will give them meat again.

8. AND MOSES SAID UNTO PHARAOH, THY SERVANTS SHALL COME DOWN UNTO ME AT NIGHT AND BOW DOWN, SAYING, GET THEE OUT, AND ALL THE PEOPLE THAT FOLLOW THEE: THEN I WILL GO OUT. AND HE WENT OUT FROM PHARAOH IN HOT ANGER.

CHAPTER XII

1. AND THE LORD SPAKE UNTO MOSES AND UNTO AARON IN THE LAND OF EGYPT OUTSIDE THE CAPITAL CITY.[1] The city was full of idols; therefore, the Lord declined to give His precepts in that city. And the Holy One, blessed be His name, said unto them: "Go out of this city, and I will give you a commandment that you observe the New Moon festival every month." Our sages say, that if Israel were to have no other merit than that of observing the New Moon festivals regularly, it would be enough for them. For in welcoming the New Moon one bids peace to one's Lord, lovingly. The people must stand and bless the appearance of the New Moon, because the moon testifies of Him who created the universe, as He directs the reappearance of the full moon every month.

3.* AND THE LORD SAID, THOU SHALT TAKE A LAMB FOR AN HOUSEHOLD. On the tenth of Nisan a lamb was set aside and kept secure for four days, until the fourteenth of Nisan, the eve of the Passover. And all Israel sacrificed a Passover lamb.

4. AND THE LORD SAID, IF THE HOUSEHOLD BE TOO LITTLE FOR A LAMB, LET THE HOUSEHOLD SHARE IT WITH ITS NEIGHBOUR. The Torah teaches us not to be wasteful, and not to spend more than has to be spent. Bahya says, that

---

*For missing passage, see Chapter XI: 7, which was transposed according to Biblical order. `

God ordered a lamb to be killed because, according to the accounts of the astrologers, the planet Aries טלה מזל rules in heaven in the month of Nisan. Therefore, a lamb was killed that the children of Israel might not think that the planet helped them, but the Holy One, blessed be His name, He alone delivered them from Egypt. Another reason God commanded that a lamb be killed was that the animal was sacred to the Egyptians, and they worshipped it. And the lamb was not to be boiled, but it was to be roasted, that the Egyptians might recognize it was a lamb, an animal sacred to them. And the whole lamb was held on a spear and roasted with fire, that everybody could see what it was.

5.* A LAMB WITHOUT BLEMISH. Ye shall take a lamb without blemish, that the Egyptians say not that the lamb has defects and is disqualified from being sacred, and that therefore there was no cause for alarm. It is also written that the lamb must be a male, one year old, fit for worshipping purposes, that the Egyptians be speechless against Israel. The lamb was held in confinement four days, that the Egyptians might hear their idol bleating, and yet be powerless to do anything.

6. THE WHOLE ASSEMBLY OF THE CONGREGATION OF ISRAEL. Together they must slaughter the lamb, that no Israelite might excuse himself before an Egyptian by saying: "I did not slay your idol." The Passover lamb shall be slaughtered in the evening, between day and night, when the Egyptians return home from work, so that they might see their sacred animals being slaughtered.

7. AND YE SHALL SPRINKLE OF THE BLOOD UPON THE LINTEL AND UPON THE TWO SIDE POSTS, as a public witness to the whole world. And the blood was sprinkled upon the

---

*Verses 5, 6, 7, 8, which follow verse 35 in our text, have been transposed here in accordance with the Biblical order.

lintel and upon the two side posts, which formed the shape of the letter ה for חיים meaning life for Israel.

8. AND THE LAMB SHALL BE ROASTED, that by its smell the Egyptians should know what was taking place, and be rendered speechless.

AND WITH BITTER HERBS THEY SHALL EAT IT, in order to disgust the Egyptians.

FOR THERE WAS NOT A HOUSE WHERE THERE WAS NOT ONE DEAD.[2] The first born of some houses may have been dead for a long time, but it was an Egyptian custom to paint on the walls the face of a first born, if he died, as an everlasting memorial to him. Therefore in the night when the first born were slain God caused the paintings to be effaced, and made it seem as if the subjects of the paintings of the deceased had just died. Another explanation is that the Egyptians were accustomed to burying the dead first born in their homes. But on the night in which God smote the first born, dogs came and dug out the corpses of the first born that had been dead for some time, and dragged them around, so it looked as if they had died that night; therefore, there was no house where there was no dead.

AND THE PEOPLE CARRIED THEIR DOUGH UPON THEIR SHOULDERS [3] because the asses were already laden with gold and silver.

11.* AND YE SHALL EAT THE PASSOVER LAMB IN EGYPT, WITH YOUR LOINS GIRDED, YOUR SHOES ON YOUR FEET, AND YOUR STAFF IN YOUR HAND, READY FOR THE JOURNEY.

12. AND AGAINST ALL THE GODS OF EGYPT, I WILL EXECUTE JUDGMENTS. The Holy One, blessed be His name, said: "The first born will I smite and their heathen worship will I destroy, a wooden idol shall rot away, and iron or golden idols

---

*Missing passage transposed according to Biblical order.

shall be melted down and disintegrated." The Torah places the destruction of the idols near to the destruction of the first born, to teach us that had the Lord destroyed the idols alone, the Egyptians would not have known this immediately, as they did not go at once to their places of worship: therefore, God did strike down the first born that very night; and then the Egyptians had to go and bury their first born, and, since they used to bury their dead in their places of worship, they could not help soon to see what had happened to their idols.[4]

15. AND THE LORD COMMANDED TO CLEAN THE HOUSES OF LEAVEN AND EAT UNLEAVENED BREAD FOR SEVEN DAYS, AND WHOSOEVER SHALL EAT LEAVENED BREAD SHALL BE CUT OFF FROM THE WORLD AND DIE.

22. AND THE HOLY ONE, BLESSED BE HIS NAME, SAID, YE SHALL DIP IT IN THE BLOOD OF THE LAMB AND SPRINKLE THE LINTEL AND THE TWO SIDE POSTS WITH THE BLOOD: AND THAT NO ISRAELITE SHALL GO OUT OF THE DOOR OF HIS HOUSE DURING THE NIGHT WHEN THE FIRST BORN IN EGYPT ARE SMITTEN.

23. *AND WHEN HE SEETH THE BLOOD UPON THE LINTEL*, THE LORD WILL PASS OVER THE HOUSE THAT NO ONE WITHIN IT BE SMITTEN. Bahya says that the blood itself did not save Israel, but the public witness which Israel bore by sprinkling the doors of their houses, showing thereby that they feared not to sacrifice the sacred animals of Pharaoh. By their utter confidence in the God of Israel, they merited that night that their lives be spared.

30. *FOR THERE WAS NOT A HOUSE WHERE THERE WAS NOT ONE DEAD*. In the houses where there was no first born, the eldest of the family was smitten: it is therefore customary for the eldest of the families to fast on the eve of the Passover.

31-32. *AND HE CALLED FOR MOSES AND AARON BY*

NIGHT. Pharaoh searched for them from house to house during the night and said: "Get you all, man, woman and child, out of Egypt, and take your flocks with you and serve the Lord as you have desired."

BUT AGAINST THE CHILDREN OF ISRAEL SHALL NOT A DOG MOVE HIS TONGUE.[5]

The Hazzekuni says that it is customary for dogs to bark at night when people pass by carrying staves. However, when the Israelites went out of Egypt at night, with staves in their hands, the dogs did not bark. The Lord, therefore, rewarded them and decreed that animals which die a natural death, or have been torn in the field by wild beast, should not be used as human food but be given to the dogs.

Bahya says that God brought ten plagues upon Egypt in retaliation for the ten evils the Egyptians did to the Israelites. Firstly, the Egyptians made the Israelites draw water for their flocks and fields and vineyards, therefore the Lord turned the water into blood, and their flocks could not drink of it. Secondly, the Egyptians made the Israelites arise from their beds early in the morning to afflict them with hard labour, which made them groan in their hearts, therefore the Lord brought upon the Egyptians frogs which entered their beds, and did not let them sleep. Thirdly, they prevented the Israelites from bathing and caused them to become infested with lice, therefore the Lord sent lice upon Egypt. Fourthly, they made the Israelites guard their flocks in the fields, therefore the Lord sent the pestilence upon their flocks, and they died in the fields. Sixthly, the Egyptians made the Israelites to warm for them water to bathe in it, therefore the Lord sent upon them boils. Seventhly, the Egyptians cast stones upon the Israelites, whenever they saw them, therefore the Lord sent upon them the hailstones from Heaven. Eighthly, the Israelites were forced to spread manure on the fields, therefore the Lord sent the locusts which ate up everything in the fields. Ninthly, they imprisoned the Israelites in dark cells, therefore the Lord sent upon them darkness. Tenthly, they wanted to destroy Israel, whom God calls "my first born," therefore; the Lord smote the first born of Egypt.

The Midrash says the Holy One, blessed be His name, plagued Egypt in the order in which a king invades a country. Firstly, he cuts off the cities' water supplies, thereby forcing the inhabitants to surrender: so God turned the water into blood, that the Egyptians could not drink it. Secondly, the king causes his troops to make a mighty noise with his men and his horses, to intimidate the inhabitants: so God brought the frogs, which made a great noise and frightened the Egyptians. Thirdly, he orders his troops to shoot with arrows: so God plagued Egypt with lice, whose bite stung like the prick of an arrow. Fourthly, he sends formations of troops of many tribes and nationalities to storm a city: so God sent all kinds of wild beasts upon Egypt. Fifthly, he sends wild horses which trample upon the flocks: so God sent the pestilence which killed all the flocks in Egypt. Sixthly, he captures some of the people and tortures them with fire, to get information from them about the plan of a city and how it could be captured: so God plagued the Egyptians with boils which burned their bodies like fire. Seventhly, he orders his troops to throw heavy objects and destroy the city walls: so God sent upon Egypt a hail of large stones, which killed men and beasts. Eighthly, he sends troops to possess the city: so God sent locusts to occupy Egypt. Ninthly, when he conquers the city, he throws people into dark prisons: so God plagued Egypt with darkness. Tenthly, the victor smites the notables of the city: so God smote the first born of Egypt. And all the plagues which came upon Egypt God will bring again upon the heathens in the days of the coming of the Messiah.

33. *AND THE EGYPTIANS WERE URGENT UPON THE PEOPLE.* The Egyptians urged the Israelites to leave the land of Egypt, because of the ten plagues.

Pharaoh first asked Moses: "Who is your God? All other gods

have written to me, except your God; therefore, I do not know him." Pharaoh called his wise men and said unto them: "We have heard that the God of Israel is a son of the wise." The Holy One, blessed be His name, thereupon said, "Ye call Me only a son of the wise, but for yourselves you claim to be the wise men; behold, wisdom shall soon be taken from you and perish away. And thou, Pharaoh, who claimest to know not the Lord, behold thou shalt soon say 'the Lord is righteous'; and instead of thy refusal to let Israel go, thou wilt rather beg them to go." The same can be compared to a parable about a prince who sent his servant to buy fresh fish, but the servant bought a dead fish, which stank. The prince was wroth and said to the servant: "Choose for thyself one of these three punishments, you either eat the fish yourself, receive a hundred strokes, or pay a fine of one hundred gulden." The servant chose first to eat the fish, but he could not eat it all, so he changed for the one hundred strokes. But he could not bear them, and after he had suffered a few strokes, he begged to be permitted to pay the one hundred gulden, for he feared that he might die. Thus, he suffered all three punishments. He ate stinking fish, and he was beaten, and he paid the fine. Likewise, Pharaoh suffered the ten plagues, lost his gold and silver to the Israelites, and finally had to let them go out of Egypt. All these calamities came upon him because of the hardness of his heart.

34. AND THE PEOPLE TOOK THEIR DOUGH, BOUND IT UP IN THEIR CLOTHES AND PLACED IT UPON THEIR SHOULDERS. Although they had many beasts of burden to bear the dough, the Israelites carried it upon their own shoulders, because they were extremely eager to fulfill the divine commandment and preferred to carry the dough upon their own shoulders.

35. AND THE CHILDREN OF ISRAEL ASKED OF THE EGYPTIANS JEWELS OF SILVER AND OF GOLD AND COSTLY RAIMENT. Bahya says that the raiments were more valuable than the silver and gold, and therefore they are men-

tioned last, because the more valuable things are listed last. Silver is mentioned first because it is less valuable than gold, therefore the raiments which are mentioned last must have been more valuable than the gold.

The Hazzekuni says that the Israelites took a lamb on the tenth of Nisan, which was a Sabbath Day, and tied the lamb with a loose knot to the bed, for it was not permitted to make a tight knot on the Sabbath; yet the lamb did not untie itself. This was a miracle. A second miracle was that the Egyptians could say nothing to prevent their sacred animal from being tied to a humble place at the bedside, and later slaughtered. The Sabbath preceding the Passover is therefore called the Great Sabbath, because of the great miracle which occurred on that day, and that the Egyptians were speechless.

39. *NEITHER HAD THEY PREPARED FOR THEMSELVES ANY VICTUAL.*[6] The Israelites took no food with them on the journey, because they trusted in the Lord, blessed be His name, that He would sustain them even in the wilderness, where nothing grew.

46. *NEITHER SHALL YE BREAK A BONE THEREOF*[7] because the Passover lamb was intended to provide the Israelitish households with a sufficiency of meat: thus not requiring them to break the bones for further sustenance, and to avoid making one appear a glutton.

CHAPTER XIII

2. *SANCTIFY UNTO ME ALL THE FIRST BORN* of their mothers. Bahya says that the Holy One, Blessed be He, commanded Moses to sanctify the first born of the mothers and not the first born of the fathers, as, for instance, in the case of Egypt, where God smote the first born of the fathers. The reason is that it is more certain who is the first born of a mother than of a father, since the

father might have begotten children out of wedlock and in secret, whereas with a woman it is a certainty. The Holy One, blessed be He, said unto the children of Israel: "If ye keep my commandments, I will bring you into the Land of Israel." Bahya further says that, although the land of Israel was inhabited by seven nations, it was, nevertheless, called "The Land of Canaan" and not after another nation, because Canaan was cursed to become a servant of Shem,[1] and whatever a slave possessed belonged to his master. The Holy One, blessed be He, therefore, called the land of Israel, "the Land of Canaan" to show that the land inhabited by the Canaanites was not theirs, but that of Israel, their master. The Hazzekuni says the children of Heth honoured Abraham, and when they heard that the Holy One, blessed be He, was going to give it to Israel, the Canaanites left it on their own accord; therefore, the Holy One, blessed be He, said, because you have left the land on your own accord, I will give you another land—Africa—and I will call forever the Land of Israel in your name—The Land of Canaan.

13. *AND EVERY FIRSTLING OF AN ASS THOU SHALT REDEEM WITH A LAMB.* The firstling of an ass was redeemed and not that of a horse or that of any other unclean animal, because the ass had helped to carry the gold and silver out of Egypt; for every Israelite had ninety asses upon which were borne the spoils of Egypt into the wilderness.

16. *FOR A SIGN UPON THINE HAND.* The phylacteries thou shalt place on thy left hand, because a man generally works with the right hand and that hand is more likely to be soiled. Rabbi Simon ben Lakish said that he who prays with his phylacteries on daily merits to live long.

17. AND IT CAME TO PASS, WHEN PHARAOH HAD LET THE PEOPLE GO, THAT GOD LED THEM NOT BY THE WAY OF THE LAND OF THE PHILISTINES, ALTHOUGH IT WAS THE SHORTER WAY TO THE PROMISED LAND,

because the Holy One, blessed be He, wanted to try them, whether they would follow Him, with their wives and with their children, through a wilderness in which there were very large serpents, thick as logs.

Another reason why the Lord led the Israelites through the wilderness was to prevent them from returning to Egypt, in case of war. He therefore led them by the way of the wilderness beyond the Red Sea. And although Amalek came against Israel in the wilderness, he did not cause a war great enough to make Israel wish to return to Egypt on account of it. Rabbi Hananel says that The Holy One, blessed be He, is always ready to work miracles for the righteous. He also wished to work miracles for Israel in the wilderness by giving them Manna and good birds, called quail, for meat, and water out of a rock, and for that reason He led them through the wilderness. A similar interpretation may be made in the case of Hananiah, Mishael and Azariah, who were thrown into a fiery furnace.[2] Although The Holy One, blessed be He, could have extinguished the fire and saved them thereby, nevertheless, in order that the miracle might be the greater, He let the furnace become exceedingly hot, and yet not a hair of their heads was singed. A similar miracle occurred in the case of Daniel, who was cast into the den of lions, in the midst of wild beasts. The Holy One, blessed be He, could have killed the wild beasts in the den, but He let them live and sent His angels to shut their mouths, that they should not hurt Daniel: thus the wonder was the greater. For the purpose of showing His wonders, the Holy One, blessed be He, wrought miracles in the wilderness. He divided the Red Sea: then He brought the people to Marah, where from days of old the waters were sweet; but He caused them to become bitter that Israel could not drink thereof. Then He wrought a miracle, and told Moses to cast a bitter tree into the waters and they became sweet again. God did all these in order to try Israel to see whether they trusted in Him. The same applies to the Manna; He gave them Manna day

85

by day, and not for several days at once, that the people might learn to trust Him day by day and pray for their daily bread. The Hazzekuni says that the Holy One, blessed be He, led Israel not by way of the land of the Philistines, lest the Philistines think Israel came to avenge the death of the children of Ephraim, who misunderstood the duration of the Egyptian bondage, and left before the day of redemption and had been exterminated by the Philistines.[3]

ALTHOUGH THAT WAS NEARER. Another reason the Holy One, blessed be He, did not lead Israel through the land of the Philistines, was that Abimelech, king of the Philistines, was a near relative of Pharaoh, and when the Egyptians pursued the Israelites, the Philistines would have come to aid their friends, and would have made war against Israel. But Abraham had sworn not to fight against the children of Abimelech. The Lord wished to avoid a war with the children of Abimelech, for that might have encouraged the Egyptians to pursue after Israel.

18. *AND THE CHILDREN OF ISRAEL WENT UP ARMED OUT OF THE LAND OF EGYPT.* The Israelites went out of Egypt armed with bows and arrows and spears, like warriors, although they had no need to fight, since the Holy One, blessed be He, fought their battles. The Torah teaches us that man should always do his duty, and the Lord will help him in it, for it is written "the horse is prepared against the day of battle, but victory is of the Lord." [4] The Midrash says that the word חמשים [5] signifies that only one-fifth of the people went out of Egypt and that the rest died during the plague of darkness, because of their refusal to leave Egypt; and they died during the darkness that the Egyptians might not see, and say the Israelites were smitten as they were. Another interpretation of the word חמשים is that Israel went out of Egypt to receive the Torah, which was given on the day of Pentecost, fifty days after the Passover.

19. AND MOSES TOOK THE BONES OF JOSEPH WITH HIM TO BURY THEM IN THE PROMISED LAND, FOR

JOSEPH HAD STRAITLY SWORN THE CHILDREN OF ISRAEL THAT THEY CARRY UP HIS BONES WITH THEM. And when all Israel went to ask for gold and silver from the Egyptians, the righteous Moses busied himself with the performance of a good deed and fulfilled his oath. And because Joseph buried his own father with great honour, he merited the privilege that Moses, who was greater than he, should attend his burial. To Moses, however, was given the unique honour that God Himself attended to his burial; and no one knows the place of the sepulchre, because the Holy One, blessed be He, buried him. The Red Sea was divided in honour of Joseph, for as soon as the ark in which lay the bones of Joseph was brought to the sea, the waters divided themselves and ran backwards, because Joseph once ran away from his master's wife[6] and refused to lie with her. The merit of Joseph made the waters of the Red Sea run away before him and divide themselves. 21. AND THE LORD WENT BEFORE THEM BY DAY IN A PILLAR OF CLOUD, TO LEAD THEM IN THE WAY: AND BY NIGHT IN A PILLAR OF FIRE, TO GIVE LIGHT TO ISRAEL AND CONSUME THE EGYPTIANS.

THAT THEY MIGHT GO BY DAY AND BY NIGHT, and receive the Torah as soon as possible. The pillar which led them in the day was with them until the evening, when the pillar of fire appeared; and the pillar of fire was with them until the pillar of cloud appeared. Now when Moses wished to bury Joseph, he went to the river, for the Egyptians had buried Joseph in an iron coffin in the River Nile, so that he could not be removed. But Moses called to the river "Joseph, Joseph, appear. We want to fulfil the oath to remove you to the Promised Land. If you do not appear, we are relieved of our oath." And some sages say that he wrote the Holy Name on a silver plate, and nearby wrote עלי שור which means "Go up, Joseph," who was nicknamed ox. Hereupon, the coffin containing Joseph appeared and Moses took Joseph with him to the Promised Land.

CHAPTER XIV

1. *AND THE LORD SPAKE UNTO MOSES, SAYING,*
2. SPEAK UNTO THE CHILDREN OF ISRAEL, THAT THEY TURN BACK IN THE DIRECTION OF EGYPT, TOWARDS THE CITY OF PITHOM.
3. AND PHARAOH WILL SAY, THEY ARE ENTANGLED IN THE WILDERNESS AND KNOW NOT WHITHER TO GO. The Holy One, blessed be He, commanded Israel to encamp before the god Ba'al-Zephon, to make the Egyptians believe that it was the mighty god which held up Israel from running away. The Egyptians worshipped the strange god, and the Lord turned the heathens' superstitions to their own destruction. The Egyptians would say that no one can run away from the idol, and would take courage to pursue after Israel. Although previously the Egyptians were glad to let Israel go, they would now say that the Israelites were lost in the wilderness, which had shut them in, and they knew not whither to go. And Israel did as the Holy One, blessed be He, commanded them, and turned back towards Egypt, although they did not wish to return into the hands of their enemies.
5. AND ON THE THIRD DAY IT WAS TOLD THE KING OF EGYPT THAT THE PEOPLE FLED. At the beginning, the children of Israel told Pharaoh in Egypt that they were going for a three day journey into the wilderness, and that they would return afterwards. Pharaoh then sent messengers to accompany them into the wilderness, to make sure of their return after three days, but Israel refused to return. The messengers then returned home, and because they were few in numbers, they covered in one day the distance which took Israel two days. They reported to Pharaoh that the children of Israel refused to return to Egypt. And Pharaoh, who took many people with him, travelled two days, a distance which was covered in one day by Pharaoh's messengers. And, although the Israelites retreated towards Egypt, they still were at a distance of a two days' journey, because the Israelites' retreat was only a

little distance, in order to create the impression that they were coming back. Another explanation is that God has performed a miracle for Israel that, although they were numerous, they covered in one day the distance which took Pharaoh two days. And on the seventh day of the Passover, in the evening, they reached the Red Sea, and gave thanks to God. It is, therefore, customary among Israel to recite the Song of Moses on the seventh day of the Passover.

6. *AND HE MADE READY HIS CHARIOT*. Pharaoh himself made ready his chariot, in order to strengthen the determination of his people to pursue after Israel; he also wanted to be right in front of them, and not like other kings who followed safely behind. He also promised to share with them equally the spoil they might take from the Israelites. Pharaoh opened all his treasures, and also those amassed by his royal predecessors, and gave to the pursuers gold and silver, which they took with them in the pursuit after Israel.

7. AND PHARAOH TOOK WITH HIM SIX HUNDRED CAPTAINS, all mighty lords, and he took excellent horses from Egypt. Notwithstanding the fact that the hail had killed all the beasts in Egypt, there were still some left with those Egyptians who, fearing the Lord, took their beasts into shelter, when Moses warned them of what was to come. And, although the people who listened to Moses' warning showed a sense of piety and fear of the Lord, nevertheless, they offered their beasts for war against Israel. From this we learn that the piety of heathens, even of one of the best, is not very worthy.

8. *AND THE LORD HARDENED THE HEART OF PHARAOH*. Pharaoh was undecided whether he should pursue after Israel or not, so the Holy One, blessed be He, hardened his heart to pursue after them.

AND THE CHILDREN OF ISRAEL WENT OUT OF EGYPT TRULY FREE AND WITH AN HIGH HAND.

9. *BUT THE EGYPTIANS PURSUED AFTER THEM*. And

the Egyptians found Israel encamped near Ba'al-Zephon, and, although all the gods of Egypt had been destroyed, nevertheless the Lord left Ba'al-Zephon untouched, that He might lead the heathens to their destruction by means of their strange gods, as already stated above.

10. *AND WHEN PHARAOH DREW NIGH*. Pharaoh, in person, caught up with Israel near Ba'al-Zephon. Another explanation of the word "drew" is that the wicked Pharaoh made the hearts of Israel draw nigh to God in prayer. When the Holy One, blessed be He, wants to cause Israel to be pious, He sets up wicked people to hurt Israel, as in the case of Haman, who planned to destroy Israel, and caused them thereby soon to repent and become pious. Pharaoh likewise, by his pursuit after Israel, caused them to fear greatly and to become pious, and he made their hearts draw nigh, in intercession to God.

AND, BEHOLD, THE EGYPTIANS MARCHED AFTER THEM. The word נוסע is written in the singular form and not in the plural, because they all went, united as one man, in their determination to make war against Israel. The Midrash, however, says that the word נוסע is written in the singular because the angel over Egypt, named Aza, joined in the pursuit against Israel, and for that reason the children of Israel feared so greatly.

11. *AND, THEY SAID UNTO MOSES, BECAUSE THERE WERE NO GRAVES IN EGYPT HAST THOU TAKEN US AWAY TO DIE IN THE WILDERNESS?* Bahya says that the people of Israel divided themselves into four groups: one group cried to God, another group said, "Let us fight the Egyptians," a third group said, "Let us return to Egypt," and the fourth group prayed to God with a loud voice.

14. *THE LORD SHALL FIGHT FOR YOU*. Moses said, the Lord Himself shall fight for you. When the Holy One, blessed be He, smote the first born in Egypt, the Egyptians saw that God him-

90

self was smiting them, and yet they did not repent. Now war against Israel was war against God, therefore, "the Lord will fight for you and you hold your peace." Another explanation is "Ye, Israel hold your peace," that ye come not under divine punishment, because ye too worshipped idols in Egypt.

15. *WHEREFORE CRIEST THOU UNTO ME?* God said unto Moses: "There is no time for lengthy lamentations, when Israel is in great trouble." Another explanation of the verse is that God said: "Why criest thou unto me, I know well that all depends on Me."

SPEAK, THEREFORE, TO THE CHILDREN OF ISRAEL THAT THEY GO FORWARD into the sea and the waters will divide themselves in front of them, because of the merits of their fathers and also because of their faith in Me, which they will show in the wilderness.

16. AND THOU, MOSES, LIFT UP THY ROD AND SMITE THE SEA. The Imre No'am and the Midrash say that Moses first spoke to the sea and said, "Divide thyself," but the sea talked back and said: "Thou hast no authority over me, go to thine own river Nile." Moses reported the same to the Lord, and the Holy One, blessed be He, said that, when a servant disobeys his master, he is smitten with a rod upon his head; therefore, "Lift up thy rod and smite the sea that it divide itself." And Moses did according to the commandment of God, but the sea still refused to obey. Then the Lord Himself appeared, and when the sea saw the Lord, it divided itself immediately and retreated backwards. And Moses asked the sea, "Why runnest thou backward?" The sea replied: "Moses, thou art mistaken, if thou thinkest I run away from thee, which is not the case; but I run from before the face of the Holy One, blessed be He, the creator of the universe." Bahya says, "Lift up thy rod" means that the Lord said unto Moses: "Drop the rod out of thy hand, for the people think thou canst do nothing without it; therefore, let the rod go for awhile and speak to the sea, that it divide

itself." This is also the interpretation of the Hazzekuni.

20. *AND THE ONE CAME NOT NEAR THE OTHER ALL THE NIGHT*. The Israelites and the Egyptians, although they were near to one another, did not come to grips the whole night. For in the night in which the Egyptians caught up with the Israelites, the Holy One, blessed be He, made the pillar of fire, which used to go before the Israelites every night to lighten their way, go behind them instead of before them. Now the Israelites could not flee before the Egyptians, because without the pillar of fire before them it was dark. All this took place in the night in which the Israelites reached the sea at nightfall.

21. *AND THE WATERS WERE DIVIDED*. All the waters of the world were divided when the Red Sea was divided. Ten miracles happened at the Red Sea. First, the sea was divided. Second, the water became like a cave and like a roof over Israel, and Israel walked in the midst. Water was beneath, and on both sides and above Israel. Third, underneath the water became dry and solid, so that the Israelites should not soil their feet, nor sink into the mud. Fourth, for the Egyptians the bottom of the sea became very muddy and dirty, and they sank into it. Fifth, the water became frozen and hard as stone. Sixth, the whole sea did not become frozen solid at once, but partially and by degrees, forming a multitude of peaks in the water like huge hard rocks, against which the Egyptians knocked their heads. And these same peaks lay one on top of the other, just like a high wall. Seventh, the sea was divided into twelve parts, that every tribe might cross by a different path. Eighth, the water became transparent like glass, so that one tribe could see the other in the nearby path in the sea. Ninth, the water of the sea became sweet like sugar, that the children of Israel might drink thereof. And when they took of the water to drink, it became fluid and soft, but as soon as they ceased to drink thereof it became solid again, that the children of Israel neither wet their feet, nor walk in the dirt. The tenth miracle, according to the Hazzekuni,

was that less than one-third of the water became solid for the people to walk thereon, for if the waters had dried out to the bottom, it would have created a deep chasm and would have made it difficult for the people to get down and come out again, therefore the water was like a bridge under their feet on which it was easy to walk. Bahya says that God made all kinds of fruit to grow in the sea, and when a child cried the mother gave it an apple or a pomegranate, for the Holy One caused good fruit to grow in the sea.

22.   *AND THE WATERS WERE A WALL UNTO THEM.* The waters became to the Israelites as a wall protecting them from all sides. The Midrash says that Israel carries religious merits on every side: on the right side they have the Torah, on the left side they have the merit of the phylacteries, on the front the merit of circumcision, and behind the merit of the tassels of the ritual four-cornered garment.

25.   *AND HE TOOK OFF THEIR CHARIOT WHEELS.* With the pillar of fire the Lord consumed all the wooden utensils the Egyptians had in their chariots, and their guns and spears. And the pillar of cloud turned the ground into clay, and the pillar of fire made the clay so hot that it took off the hoofs of the horses.

27.   *AND THE SEA RETURNED TO ITS STRENGTH WHEN THE MORNING APPEARED.* When the early morning appeared and the children of Israel safely crossed the sea, Moses stretched out his hand towards the sea and the sea returned to its strength. Then the Egyptians wanted to withdraw and run away, but God confounded them that they rushed against the waves. Bahya says that the words "to its former strength" refers to a condition which God made with the sea when He created it, namely, that it should divide itself when Israel will go out of Egypt, and remain still, although it is natural for the sea to flow. A similar condition God made with the sun, that it should stand still in the days of Moses in the wilderness, and with both the sun and the moon to stand still in the days of Joshua, although it was natural for them to move on

93

their course. But the Lord had made an agreement with the sun and the moon that they should remain still when such need arises.

AND THE EGYPTIANS FLED AGAINST IT. The waters rushed against the Egyptians and dragged them into the sea. The Hazzekuni says that the Egyptians pursued the Israelites into the sea in expectation of crossing it, because the water was solid as stone, but when they reached the middle of the sea the solid walls of the water melted, and at this point the Egyptians wanted to withdraw, but the water prevented them.

30. *AND ISRAEL SAW THE EGYPTIANS DEAD UPON THE SEASHORE.* The sea gave up the dead on the side out of which Israel came out, so that the children of Israel could see them. This visible proof banished the Israelites' fear that the Egyptians too might have crossed the sea. The sea gave up the dead that every Israelite might see his former master dead. Then the Israelites rejoiced, for they realized that they could no longer be punished by their masters; for a runaway slave was always in fear of his master's pursuit. Another reason why the sea gave up its dead was that the Israelites might spoil the dead Egyptians and take from them the gold and silver they carried with them.

31. *AND ISRAEL SAW THE GREAT WORK.* Israel saw that at the Red Sea God smote the Egyptians with His whole hand, because the magicians called only a "finger of God," [1] the plagues which God sent upon Egypt. We infer that if with one finger God brought ten plagues, then at the Red Sea, where God smote them with His whole hand, He must have inflicted upon them fifty plagues.

CHAPTER XV

1. *THEN SANG MOSES AND THE CHILDREN OF ISRAEL THIS SONG.* Even babes at their mothers' breasts and babes within their mothers' wombs sang and said: "The Lord is our God, we shall sing His praise: the Lord is above all lords."

THE HORSE AND HIS RIDER HATH HE THROWN INTO THE SEA. The Lord bound the rider to his horse and the waves threw both into the sea, tossing them up and down. Bahya states that the Midrash says that the rider said to the horse, "Why is it that yesterday I led you to the River Nile to drink and you did not want to go there, and now you drag me to the water?" Thereupon the horse answered: "I seek the Lord in the sea; therefore, must I run into the sea."

2. *THIS IS MY GOD, AND I WILL PRAISE HIM.*[1] This is my Lord and I will magnify Him with praises. Bahya says that man must compare his deed with the deeds of the Lord. As He is merciful, so man should be merciful. As the Lord provides raiment for people, so man should do likewise towards his fellow man. As the Lord takes care to bury the dead, so man should take care of his fellow creatures.

3. *THE LORD IS A MAN OF WAR, THE LORD IS HIS NAME*. The Lord fights for Israel; He also sustains the whole world with His holy name. An earthly king when he makes war is preoccupied with it to the extent that he can do nothing else, unlike God who, when He makes war, He still does good and sustains the whole world. Another interpretation of the text is that the Lord does not fight with sword nor gun, but with His holy name.

4. *SUNK IN THE RED SEA*. The Egyptians sank in the Red Sea. The bottom of the sea turned into clay, because the Lord repays deed for deed. The Egyptians forced the Israelites to make bricks out of clay, therefore the Egyptians sank into clay.

5. *THEY WENT DOWN INTO THE DEPTHS LIKE A STONE*. The wicked among the Egyptians were like straw upon the waters, which lie on the surface for a long time. They died a lingering and painful death. The Bible, therefore, says, "It consumeth them like stubble." The less wicked went down like a stone and soon died, as our text says, "They went down into the depths like a stone." The best of the Egyptians were like lead, which is

much heavier than stone. They met instant death.

7. *THOU OVERTHROWEST THEM.* Thou confoundest thine enemies. They who hate Israel are like those who hate God Himself. And God confounds them and destroys them.

8. *THE WATERS WERE PILED UP.* The waters rose as though they were high walls. Another interpretation, according to Bahya, has it that the waters became wise,[2] for they were solid for Israel and fluid for the Egyptians, whom they caused to be drowned.

9. *THE ENEMY SAID.* Pharaoh said to his people, "I will pursue Israel, and I will divide the spoil with you."

11. *WHO IS LIKE UNTO THEE, O LORD, AMONG THE GODS, WHO IS LIKE THEE GLORIOUS IN HOLINESS?* Who is a God as slow to anger, as Thou art, to punish the wicked for his evil deeds, and who dost not act impatiently?

FEARFUL IN PRAISES. It is fearful to praise God in case one fails to do it rightly and as well as He deserves it.

12A. *THOU STRETCHEST OUT THY RIGHT HAND.*[3] The earth refused to receive the dead Egyptians, on account of the curse it bore for receiving the blood of Abel. Therefore the Holy One, blessed be He, swore that He will not curse the earth for receiving the dead Egyptians. The Imre No'am says that the words "Then sang" teaches us that God will raise the dead in the days of the Messiah, for the word ישיר is in the future tense and means "will sing," i.e., in the days of the Messiah. The Gemara, tractate Taanith,[4] says that there are three keys in the hands of the Holy One, blessed be He, which He never entrusts to any angel: one is the life of a woman, when she gives birth to a child; second, is rain; and third is the resurrection from the dead.

The Imre No'am, referring to the words "they sank like lead" says that many Egyptians knew magic, and by magical device rose from the sea and flew towards the skies. Then the angels Gabriel and Michael came and struck them over the heads and they went down like lead into the water.

12B. *THE EARTH SWALLOWED THEM.* They merited a burial place, because they acknowledged their wickedness and said "the Lord is a righteous God." Bahya says that the Egyptians merited a burial place, because they accompanied Joseph, when he went to bury Jacob, his father, in the land of Israel, and the Lord pays deed for deed. Because the Egyptians paid homage to Jacob at his burial, they merited a burial place.

14.[5] *THE PEOPLES HAVE HEARD, THEY TREMBLE.* All nations heard of the great wonders and trembled. The Philistines feared that Israel might avenge the death of the many hundreds of the children of Ephraim, who left Egypt thirty years before the time of the Exodus and were destroyed by the Philistines. And the rulers of Edom feared that Israel might avenge the evil which Esau did to Jacob; the rulers of Moab feared that the Israelites might take vengeance, because the herdsmen of Lot quarreled with the herdsmen of Abraham, and the rulers of Moab were descendants of Lot; the rulers of Canaan feared, because they knew that the children of Israel were to conquer the land of Israel. The verse[6] mentions by name the Philistines, the Edomites, the Moabites, and the Canaanites, because of their great fear.

16. *TILL THY PEOPLE PASS OVER, O LORD, TILL THE PEOPLE PASS OVER WHICH THOU HAST PURCHASED.* O God, help us to cross the rivers Arnon and Jordan and to enter the Promised Land. At the crossing of the Jordan, the priests stood barefoot with the ark in the midst of the Jordan, and then the stream halted and the river became dry until all people passed through. We repeat twice in the "Shirah," "Till thy people pass, O Lord! Till thy people pass which thou hast purchased," because of the two rivers, the Arnon and the Jordan.

WHICH THOU HAST PURCHASED. The people thou hast purchased unto thyself to receive the Torah. For when Israel received the Torah they were purchased by God to serve Him forever, as slaves serve their master.

17. *THOU SHALT BRING THEM IN, AND PLANT* THEM in the land of Israel. In his prayers to God, Moses did not say "bring us in," but "bring them in," because through prophecy he foresaw that he would not have the privilege of entering the Promised Land.

18. *THE LORD SHALL REIGN FOR EVER AND EVER.* The Lord shall reign over us forever, in the way He reigneth now over us. Like at the dividing of the Red Sea, the Holy One, blessed be He, was doing good to the righteous and destroying the wicked. So may He rule over us for ever. It is, therefore, written ימלך (will reign) without the letter ו to show that the Lord lays not heavy burdens upon His people, but He speaks quietly and gently to His people. Bahya says that the song of Moses contains eighteen verses corresponding to the eighteen vertebrae forming man's spine, and that these will all revive in the day of the resurrection when the Messiah will come, and they will sing unto the Lord. It is not said אז שר (past tense), but אז ישיר referring to the future time when Moses will sing at the coming of the Messiah.

19. *FOR THE HORSES OF PHARAOH WENT IN.* Israel sang when the Egyptians went down into the sea and when they themselves came out dry.

20. *AND MIRIAM, THE PROPHETESS, THE SISTER OF AARON, TOOK A TIMBREL IN HER HAND.* The verse tells us that she was the sister of Aaron, though she was also the sister of Moses, because Aaron is not named even once in the whole "Shirah"; therefore, he is mentioned here. Another reason advanced by the Midrash is to show that Miriam was already a prophetess before Moses was born; she had then prophesied that her mother would bring forth a son, who would deliver Israel out of the hands of Egypt. Bahya says that one should not wonder that women prophesied, because women are sometimes equal to men, since the woman was made of man. Sarah, for instance, was a greater prophetess than her husband, Abraham, was a prophet. Now when

Miriam sang "Shirah," all the women sang with her and praised the Lord. Bahya further says that one should not belittle women, for they are as worthy as pious men, or prophets. We read in the Torah that Abigail was a prophetess and foretold plainly that there is a world to come, although the Torah says nothing definitely about it. Likewise, Hannah spoke of the resurrection from the dead, of which no previous prophet spoke. We, therefore, infer that women should be held in honour, because when they are pious there is no limit to their piety. The Gemara, tractate Megillah[7] says that there were seven prophetesses; Sarah, Miriam, Hannah, Deborah, Huldah, Abigail, and Esther.

WITH TIMBRELS AND WITH DANCES. Miriam took a timbrel into her hand and beat on it, and all the women danced with one another joyfully. Miriam took a timbrel and no other instrument, because the drumming drowned the women's voices from being heard by the men; for it is sinful for a man to hear the voice of a strange woman, as much as it is sinful to commit adultery with her. It is, therefore, customary when women sing at weddings that they clap their hands, in order to prevent the men from hearing their voices. Women, even when they pray aloud, confuse the men in their prayers and provoke them to evil thoughts towards the same women. They should learn from Hannah, who prayed quietly. Only her lips moved but her voice was not heard, nevertheless the Lord heard her prayer immediately. From this our sages inferred that in prayer one should not raise one's voice.

22.**AND MOSES LED ISRAEL.* Moses had to force Israel away from the seashore, because they tarried in spoiling the dead Egyptians of their gold and silver, for there was more gold and silver on the shores of the Red Sea than in Egypt. Now the Bible says[8] that when the Israelites left Egypt they spoiled the Egyptians of their gold and silver; whence then did the Egyptians get more gold and

---

*Verse 22 occurs in the text after verse 12 and was transposed.

silver? The answer is that the Israelites borrowed only the gold and silver which the Egyptians had in their homes, but later Pharaoh opened his royal treasures and took out all the gold and silver amassed by former kings, over a long period, and distributed the same to his troops, in order to induce them to pursue after Israel.[9]

THEY WENT THREE DAYS IN THE WILDERNESS AND FOUND NO WATER TO DRINK. That was in the month of Nisan, when it was very warm and difficult to be without water. This God did to try the people and see whether they would rebel against Him or not.

23. *AND WHEN THEY CAME TO MARAH, THEY COULD NOT DRINK OF THE WATERS OF MARAH, FOR THEY WERE BITTER*. Bahya says the waters were previously sweet, but that the Lord made them bitter in order to try Israel; therefore the people murmured. Expectant mothers and children suffered badly without water. For on the third day Israel had already consumed the water which they had taken with them from the Red Sea. Therefore they cried unto God.

25. AND THE LORD SAID UNTO MOSES, TAKE A BITTER TREE AND CAST IT INTO THE WATERS AND THE WATERS WILL BECOME SWEET. The Holy One, blessed be He, works one miracle within another. He commanded to cast a bitter tree into bitter water and the waters were made sweet, to teach men to trust in God, who can provide all man's needs.

THERE HE MADE FOR THEM A STATUTE AND AN ORDINANCE. Moses ruled like a king over Israel and made statutes regulating the behaviour of one Israelite to another. And since many heathen sold all kinds of food and fruit to the Israelites, Moses also made laws governing Israel's behaviour toward the heathen, that they may not deal dishonestly. Bahya says that Moses showed the Israelites every herb which is good for healing and every herb which makes people ill; therefore, it is said "there they proved Him"; namely they tried the herbs to see whether what Moses told

100

them was true or not. The next verse says, therefore:

26. *IF THOU WILT DILIGENTLY HEARKEN TO THE VOICE OF THE LORD THY GOD.* Though the herbs be good for charms סגולות and cures רפואות thou shalt not put thy trust in them, but in God, who can help thee and heal thee of thine infirmities. Thou shalt, therefore, not abandon thy prayers, but rather pray to God and He will heal thee.

FOR I AM THE LORD THAT HEALETH THEE from the infirmities and not the herbs. Hezekiah, King of Judah, preserved the book of cures in which all the herbs were written down, and he hid it that the people rely not too much on the book but that they pray to God who would heal them. The Midrash says that the Tree of Life stood near the water, but Satan removed the tree in order to cause Israel to murmur against God. However, the Lord soon showed the Tree of Life to Moses, who, when he cast it into the water, freed the water from Satan's spell: and God made Satan small that he could not incite Israel, otherwise it would have been difficult for them to withstand him.

IF THOU WILT DILIGENTLY HEARKEN TO THE VOICE OF THE LORD THY GOD. If thou wilt obey God's commandments, thou wilt never be sick with any kind of sickness, which comes from eating certain food, or from respiratory causes. The Ba'al Hatturim says that the word מחלה (disease) contains the same number of letters as the word הלחם or as the word המלח[10] to teach us that the human body is exposed to eighty-four forms of מחלה , disease (plus one), which is the numerical value of the word and that all these diseases can be prevented by means of bread, salt and water. The Torah, therefore, records the case of the twelve springs, to teach the people that the above mentioned diseases can be prevented through bread, salt and water.

27. *AND THEY CAME TO ELIM, WHERE WERE TWELVE SPRINGS OF WATER*, that every tribe might have its own spring.

AND THREESCORE AND TEN PALM TREES, that every

101

one of the seventy elders might have a palm tree. And the water was very sweet, because wherever palm trees grow, the water is sweet.

CHAPTER XVI

1. *ON THE FIFTEENTH DAY OF THE SECOND MONTH.* The children of Israel ate of the dough which they brought out of Egypt for thirty days, until the fifteenth day of the month of Iyar, and when the dough was exhausted they cried and said:

3. IT WAS BETTER FOR US TO STAY IN THE LAND OF EGYPT WHEN WE SAT BY THE FLESH POTS, THAN TO DIE OF HUNGER HERE IN THE WILDERNESS.

4. And the Lord sent Manna from Heaven on the sixteenth day of Iyar; on a Sunday began the Manna to come down. AND THE LORD SAID, BEHOLD I WILL RAIN BREAD FROM HEAVEN FOR YOU. The Torah calls the Manna bread, because bread was made out of the Manna, and it was like coriander seed, white and sweet, like honey. Rabbi Eliezer said that the Manna fell sixty cubits high, and that it fell at night time, when the children of Israel were asleep upon their beds. In the morning they arose and gathered the Manna, for the Holy One, blessed be He, pours His goodness upon the righteous when they are still asleep upon their beds. Likewise, in the days when the Holy Temple stood, during the rainy season, it used to rain always on Saturday nights and on Wednesday nights, and it never rained in the day time, in order not to disturb the people in their work. King Hezekiah prayed and said: "O Lord of the universe, I have no strength to smite the heathen, neither can I pursue after them, nor have I the strength to sing unto thee. I can lie down to sleep upon my bed for a long time, and Thou Lord, do what Thou canst do so well." And the Lord said: "I will do according to Thy will." He sent His angel by night and smote the camp of the Assyrians while Hezekiah was asleep upon his bed,

as the Scripture says, "for so He giveth unto His beloved sleep." [1] The Lord poureth goodness upon his beloved, the righteous, while he is still asleep upon his bed. The sinner, however, profiteth little from his early risings. And the Manna was consumed by the digestive organs without having the need for returning the refuse, as it is written, "man did eat the bread of the mighty." [2]

A DAY'S PORTION EVERY DAY. The Manna came down day by day to provide food for the day. The Lord could have sent Manna enough for several days, but He did not do so in order to try Israel, that they may learn to trust Him day by day, and that Israel might pray daily and have confidence in God's provision. Rabbi Eliezer says that who has enough food for the day, and asks what he shall eat the next day he has no faith in God, for the Lord provides to everyone his portion in time. Rabbi Simon says that the Manna fell daily and not at once, for a whole year, in order that the Israelites, with their wives and children, might lift up their eyes unto God and pray for Manna. A second reason for the Manna coming daily was that the children of Israel might eat fresh Manna every day. A further explanation for the daily occurrence was that, if Manna had been provided for a year at a time, it would have proved a burden in carrying the provision on the journey through the wilderness. For the righteous the Manna fell in front of their tents, that they might have it ready at once; the compromising type of people had to walk a little for their portion of Manna, but the sinners had to walk for it a long distance.

THAT I MAY PROVE THEM, WHETHER THEY WILL WALK IN MY LAW OR NO. God said, I will give Manna to Israel in order to prove them whether they will keep my commandments; i.e., whether they will leave any Manna from one day to another, whether they will go out to gather Manna on the Sabbath Day, whether they will gather a double portion on the sixth day. For on the sixth day they gathered the usual portion, but when they brought it home they found it was twice as much.

5. *AND IT SHALL COME TO PASS ON THE SIXTH DAY,
THAT THEY SHALL PREPARE THAT WHICH THEY BRING
IN.*[3] Moses told the children of Israel to prepare on Friday, which
was the sixth day after the Sunday when Manna first came down.

6. *AT EVEN, THEN YE SHALL KNOW THAT THE LORD
HATH BROUGHT YOU OUT FROM THE LAND OF EGYPT.*
Moses and Aaron said to the children of Israel: "Ye shall know
that the Lord has brought you out of Egypt and not we, Moses
and Aaron, against whom you murmur and say, 'Ye have brought
us forth into the wilderness to kill us.' Behold, 'The Lord shall give
you in the evening flesh to eat.' " Because the Israelites asked for
meat, which was not indispensable, the Lord gave it to them at night
time, but the Manna which was indispensable, the Lord gave in the
morning, that they might have time to prepare it, according to one's
need. Bahya, commenting on the words, "I may prove them," says
that Manna was given to the children of Israel that they might
have enough to eat in order to study the Torah. For the same
reason tithes, gifts, and meat offerings, were given to the priests and
to the Levites, in order that they might have enough food and devote
their time to the study of the Torah. And the Lord tries people to
see whether they would walk according to the law. Though the
Lord has foreknowledge of what man will do, and has no need to
try any one, He nevertheless tries man, in order that the people may
see the righteous withstanding trials and learn to do likewise, without murmuring against God. The Lord also afflicts the righteous as
it is written, "The Lord trieth the righteous";[4] that men may learn
from the righteous to withstand trials and learn to praise God and
serve Him, even in tribulation. The Lord likewise tries the rich and
the poor. He tries the rich to see whether he will use his wealth for
charity, and He tries the poor to see whether he would accept
poverty without murmuring. The Lord likewise tries the soul within
the body, whether it will go after the Torah and good inclinations,
or after earthly things and evil inclinations. The Lord tries all men,

and he who withstands the trials is richly rewarded.

8.* *MOSES SAID TO THE CHILDREN OF ISRAEL, YOUR MURMURINGS ARE NOT AGAINST US, BUT AGAINST THE LORD.* From this we infer that he who murmurs against his teacher or against a sage is like unto him who murmurs against God.

12. *IN THE MORNING YE SHALL BE FILLED WITH BREAD: AND YE SHALL KNOW THAT I AM THE LORD YOUR GOD.* From this our sages infer that it was commanded by Moses to give thanks to God after a meal, for he said: "Ye shall know that the Lord has sustained you and ye shall bless His name." However, some sages maintain that thanksgiving after a meal was ordained by the Torah, but the blessing of bread before a meal was ordained by the Rabbis. They reason that, if after having had a good meal, one is commanded to praise God, the more so should one praise God before a meal and say, "Blessed art thou, O Lord our God, King of the universe, who bringest forth bread from the earth."

13. *AND IT CAME TO PASS AT EVEN, THAT THE QUAILS CAME UP.* Many good birds, called quails, came to the children of Israel at night and provided meat for them. This was repeated throughout the forty years in the wilderness. The quails came at eventide and the Manna came in the morning. The Torah only says that the Manna fell for forty years in the wilderness, but does not say that the quails came nightly during the forty years. The Torah is explicit about the Manna, because it was a new creation which came into being by many miracles. But quails were not a new creation, therefore the Torah does not elaborate the point.

AND IN THE MORNING THE DEW LAY AROUND THE CAMP. The Midrash says that the Manna came down in the following manner; first came the dew which softened the ground, after-

---

*For missing passage, see verse 5.

wards came the Manna and then again dew, to cover the Manna. It is customary, therefore, on the Sabbath Day to cover the table with a tablecloth and to place the cakes on the tablecloth, and cover them with another tablecloth as a reminder of the Manna. And the children of Israel called it Manna, meaning a gift from God in Heaven.

16. *GATHER YE OF IT EVERY MAN ACCORDING TO HIS EATING.* Our sages say that Moses told the children of Israel not to say that the strong men from among them will gather much by force and the poor will gather little. He said, therefore "every man according to his eating," i.e., every man will satisfy his appetite with his portion of an omer.

AN OMER A HEAD. He who will eat that measure shall be healthy, but he who will eat more than his portion is a glutton and he will be sick.

EVERY MAN FOR THEM WHICH ARE IN HIS TENT. Every man shall gather for his wife, who is called "ohel" (tent), because she stays at home and should not run around. From this we learn that a man is bound to provide for his wife, and for his children when they are young.

21. AND THEY GATHERED IT ON THE MORNING. The Manna lay until the fourth hour of the day. When the sun came out, the Manna melted away like water. If a man was too late for gathering his portion, he was given some in the way of charity, that he might have food for the day. And many miracles were wrought through the Manna, for it revealed secrets as a prophet reveals to people secrets by his prophecy. When, for instance, a slave ran away from one Israelite to another, and each claimed to be the rightful owner, the truth was revealed through the Manna. The slave belonged to him who had the extra portion of Manna; for everyone received according to the size of his household, an omer per head, regardless of the number of children and the number of male and female servants. He who had the extra omer, to him belonged the

slave. Likewise, when a woman quarreled with her husband and returned to her father's house, and when the husband blamed his wife and the wife blamed her husband, Moses said that the truth would come out in the morning. And in the morning, if the omer fell to the husband's portion, it showed that the woman was to be blamed, and if it fell to the woman's father, it proved that the husband was at fault. In the same manner, if a woman remarried within three months of her husband's death or within three months of being divorced from her previous husband, and she gave birth to a child after six months or so, and it was not certain whether the child was a nine months' baby from the previous marriage, or about a seven months' baby from the second marriage, the matter was then decided by the Manna. If the baby's portion fell before the house of the previous husband, it proved that the child belonged to the previous husband, but if it fell to the latter husband, it proved that the child was of the latter marriage. The Ba'al Hatturim says that rivers of water flowed from the melted Manna and the beasts drank thereof: and when the heathen tasted the meat of the beasts, they wondered why it tasted so good, and said that the Lord wrought great benefits to the children of Israel by giving them Manna in the wilderness.

24. *NEITHER WAS THERE ANY WORM THEREIN.* During week days, if any Manna was left over from one day to another, it became infested with worms, but any Manna left over from Friday to Saturday was without worms. From this we learn that on the Sabbath the dead rest from the worms, like the Manna that was not touched by the worms on the Sabbath. That is the opinion of Bahya.

25. *AND MOSES SAID, EAT THAT TO-DAY: FOR TO-DAY IS A SABBATH UNTO THE LORD: TO-DAY YE SHALL NOT FIND IT IN THE FIELD.* Bahya, commenting on this passage, says that the verse contains three times the word "to-day" to show that one should eat three meals on the Sabbath; one on the Sabbath eve, one on the Sabbath morning, and one on the Sabbath

evening, and the observance of the three meals is considered an important precept.

29. *SEE, FOR THAT THE LORD HATH GIVEN YOU THE SABBATH.* The Midrash says that everything pertaining to the Sabbath was double. The Manna gathered on Fridays was double:[5] the Sabbath offering was double [7] and the punishment for breaking the Sabbath was double, as it is written "everyone that profaneth it shall surely be put to death." [6] And he who keeps the Sabbath receives a double reward; man also receives a double soul for the Sabbath.

32. *THAT THEY MAY SEE THE BREAD.* A portion of Manna was preserved in a glass for the time when the Messiah will come, to show the bread which our forefathers ate in the wilderness. Also the rod of Aaron, the ark with its bars and many vessels from the Temple were hidden in a cave beneath the Temple. And the glass filled with the Manna always stood in the Temple until King Josiah came and hid the glass in a cave beneath the Temple. When the prophet Jeremiah reproved the children of Israel for not studying the Torah, and they replied that they had to work for their daily bread, he took the glass filled with the Manna and showed it to them as a proof that God was able to provide food, and that he who studies the Torah should not be over anxious about what he shall eat.

35. *AND THE CHILDREN OF ISRAEL DID EAT THE MANNA FORTY YEARS.* Bahya says that, although the forty years were short of one month, since they began to eat Manna in the middle of the month of Iyar and ceased in the middle of the month of Nisan, it is nevertheless counted forty years, because one month makes little difference. And the Manna continued thirty-eight days after the death of Moses. For Moses died on the seventh day of Adar and the Manna continued for another thirty-eight days, until the middle of Nisan, owing to the merits of Joshua, who succeeded to the leadership over Israel. Rashi is of the opinion that

the Manna ceased immediately after the death of Moses, but that the Manna that was gathered the day before Moses died lasted until the middle of Nisan; hence the children of Israel did eat Manna fully forty years. Rashi endeavours to strengthen his position by adding that the unleavened bread which the children of Israel brought out of Egypt tasted like Manna; and thus they ate unleavened bread from the middle of Nisan to the middle of Iyar.

36. *NOW AN OMER IS THE TENTH PART OF AN EPHAH.* The Torah tells us how large an omer of Manna was, which the children of Israel received daily in the wilderness; namely, one-tenth of an ephah. An ephah was large enough to contain four hundred and thirty-two eggs. A tenth of an ephah was the size of forty-three eggs and one-fifth. The size of the dough subject to t'rumah should not be less than the size of forty-three eggs.[8] And for the unleavened bread of the Passover no portion of dough mixed for matzoh should be larger than the aforesaid size.

CHAPTER XVII

3. AND THE PEOPLE THIRSTED THERE FOR WATER. When the children of Israel came to the town of Rephidim they cried for water, for there was no water to drink.

AND THEY MURMURED AGAINST MOSES AND SAID, WHEREFORE HAS THOU BROUGHT US OUT OF EGYPT TO KILL US WITH THIRST?

4. AND MOSES CRIED UNTO THE LORD, SAYING, THEY BE ALMOST READY TO STONE ME.

5. *AND THE LORD SAID UNTO MOSES, PASS ON BEFORE THE PEOPLE*, and see if they stone thee, for I can save thee. Moreover thou shouldest not suspect them that they will stone thee.

AND THY ROD, WHEREWITH THOU SMOTEST THE RIVER in Egypt and turned it into blood. Until now thou hast per-

109

formed with thy rod evil things, but from now on thou wilt perform with it good things; for plenty of good water will flow from the rock by means of thy rod.

6. AND WITH THE ROD THOU SHALT SMITE THE ROCK AND THERE SHALL COME WATER OUT OF IT. Bahya says that no prophet had ever had that rod in his hand to perform miracles; not even Joshua, the disciple of Moses. Joshua had a spear in his hand, when, after the death of Moses, he led the Israelites in battle. A rod speaks of lordship, which princes and kings have in their hands, but a spear portrays a man of war who takes part in battle, and it is not a sign of lordship. And the Lord commanded Moses to take the rod with him, because the children of Israel said that the rod was an instrument by which to bring evil, and plagues; therefore the Lord commanded Moses to take the rod and smite the rock that water come out of it, to show the children of Israel that goodness also can be wrought with the rod. Bahya further says that the rock which was at Rephidim later followed to Kadesh, and that the rock was the well which accompanied the children of Israel for forty years in the wilderness, and supplied them with enough water to drink.

8. THEN CAME AMALEK AND FOUGHT AGAINST IS-RAEL: Because the children of Israel spoke evil and committed sin by saying that the Lord was not always with them, for the Lord is always near the Israelites when they are in distress. Therefore, the Holy One, blessed be He, caused Amalek to come up against Israel; and when the children of Israel [1] cried to the Lord, He came to their help and then they realized that the Lord was always with them.

9. AND MOSES SAID UNTO JOSHUA, CHOOSE OUT MEN, FOR US TWO. We infer from this verse that a master should honour his disciple like himself. Bahya says that Amalek was a great astrologer and sage, and he chose for the battle men who were destined to live through the year, so that the children of Israel could not kill them. Moses therefore ordered Joshua to choose out such

men who could defeat Amalek's ruse and destroy his men. The text says, "Joshua discomfited Amalek." [2] He only weakened his men, but could not kill them, because they had been destined to live through the year. Rashi says that Amalek had many great sorcerers, and therefore Moses told Joshua to "choose out men" who could bring to nought the work of the sorcerers, and the men Joshua chose had to be pious and righteous so that their religious merits might help them in the battle.

AND GO OUT, FIGHT WITH AMALEK. "Go out of the cloud and fight against Amalek:" for the children of Israel were surrounded by a cloud, so that no man could do anything against them, but the sinners among Israel were thrown out, outside the cloud, that Amalek might smite them.

10. *AND MOSES, AARON AND HUR*, the three went up to the top of a high mountain, for they fasted and did penance, and then they went up on the mountain to pray.

11. *AND IT CAME TO PASS, WHEN MOSES HELD UP HIS HAND, THAT ISRAEL PREVAILED: AND WHEN HE LET DOWN HIS HAND, AMALEK PREVAILED.*

12. BUT MOSES' HANDS WERE TOO HEAVY TO BE LIFTED UP TOWARD HEAVEN, THEREFORE AARON AND HUR TOOK A STONE AND PUT IT UNDER MOSES AND HE SAT THEREON, AND THEY STAYED UP HIS HANDS, THE ONE ON ONE SIDE, AND THE OTHER ON THE OTHER SIDE. Moses' hands were heavy because he failed to lead Israel in battle himself, but left it to Joshua and thus had sinned, so his hands grew heavy. And he sat upon a hard stone without placing a pillow upon it, because the children of Israel were in great straits and he wished to identify himself with their hardship.

UNTIL THE GOING DOWN OF THE SUN. Moses held his hands toward Heaven until the sun and the moon changed their course, for there were many astrologers among the Amalekites who knew the hour that was favourable for battle. Therefore Moses changed the course of the sun and the moon, that the Amalekites could be guided neither by the sun nor by the moon.

13. *AND JOSHUA DISCOMFITED.* Joshua smote all the mighty men of Amalek and left only the weak.

14. *AND THE LORD SAID UNTO MOSES, WRITE THIS FOR A MEMORIAL IN A BOOK.* Write in the Torah that Amalek did evil unto the children of Israel, that Israel might never forget to avenge themselves. The Hazzekuni says that the Lord told Moses to write a special book about Amalek, but that the book is now lost.

THAT I WILL UTTERLY BLOT OUT THE REMEMBRANCE OF AMALEK. God says, "Blot out his name from off the earth." And many nations shall come in the days of the Messiah to be converted to Judaism, and they shall participate in serving the Lord in true fashion, but Amalek and Esau will never have a part in God; and when God will take just vengeance on Esau and Amalek, at that same time will God's throne be established and become sanctified. As the verse says: "And Saviours shall come up on Mount Zion, to judge the Mount of Esau; and the kingdom shall be the Lord's." [3] The verse means to say that when Esau will be called to justice, then the Lord will be King of all the nations and reign visibly over the whole earth.

CHAPTER XVIII

1. NOW JETHRO HEARD. King Solomon says, "A wholesome tongue is a tree of life." [1] The verse means to say that a wholesome tongue is an excellent cure to the soul, for when a soul commits sin the tongue helps to restore it, but the sins of not believing in God rightly are sickness unto the soul. The tongue is a cure to the soul, when it praises the Lord as the only true God, above all gods, who rewards everyone justly, as we find it in the case of Abraham. Our sages say that a precious pearl hung around Abraham's neck, and when a sick person looked at it the same was cured. Later, when Abraham died, God hung that pearl in the skies on the sun. Our

sages tried to convey by the story that kind and precious words, like pearls, came out of Abraham's mouth,[2] for he brought people to a knowledge of the true God. When Abraham died, he left no one to teach the heathen to worship the true God; therefore God hung the precious stone on the sun, that any man desiring to know whether there be a God may look at the sun rising in the east and going down in the west, and be convinced that there must be a God, who everlastingly controls the movements of the sun. Likewise, through the good reports of Moses, Jethro became converted, for Moses told him of all the wonders the Holy One, blessed be He, wrought for the children of Israel. Thus, the text says, "And Jethro heard of all that God had done, for Moses and for Israel, his people." He heard about all the wonders the Lord had done, for Moses and for Israel, and therefore he became a proselyte. Bahya says that some sages are of the opinion that Jethro came to Moses after Israel had received the Torah, and the support for such opinion may be drawn from the words, "I make them know the statutes of God and His laws." [3] The words, "I make known to Israel the laws" would imply that the Torah had already been given. Morever the Scripture also says "Moses let his father-in-law depart," [4] and it is inconceivable that Moses would have let him depart without first witnessing the event on Mount Sinai, and seeing the Lord appear in wonder. But if the Torah was already given, then Jethro's departure would raise no problem. However, Bahya dissociates himself from the aforesaid opinion for the reason that if Jethro came after the giving of the Law, why then did not Moses tell him anything about the marvels, the smoke, and the fire, which accompanied the giving of the Torah on Mount Sinai, which events might have influenced Jethro to be converted? But he told him only about the miracles the Lord wrought in Egypt. Therefore Bahya and the Rabban say that Jethro came before the Torah was given on Mount Sinai. Moses told his father-in-law nothing about the marvels which would take place on Mount Sinai, because the latter might or might not believe them. But the miracles, which took place in Egypt, were known all over the world, for at the dividing of the Red Sea, all the waters in the world divided themselves; and in the battle against Amalek, when the sun stood still, everybody saw what happened. Rashi says the words, "Now Jethro heard" meant that Jethro believed what happened at the Red Sea, and in the battle against Amalek, because the things were known all over the world. Jethro saw those marvels with his own eyes and became converted. Now, regarding the passage in which Moses tells his father-in-law that he was teaching the Torah, which was not yet given, to the children of Israel:[5] this refers to such precepts, which were in observance before the Torah was given on Mount Sinai, as, for instance, the laws concerning the Sabbath and a few others. These laws Moses taught before the Torah was given on Mount Sinai. Now, the reason why Moses let his father-in-law depart before the event which took place at Mount Sinai was, because Jethro went home only for a little while, but soon returned and found the children of Israel waiting at the foot of Mount Sinai. The Parashah which refers to Jethro stands near the Parashah dealing with Amalek, to show us that Amalek, who was a descendant of Esau and a blood relation of Israel, did evil unto them, but Jethro, who was a complete stranger, joined himself to Israel and did much good unto them. The Torah, therefore, contains many kind words about Jethro, but concerning Amalek, it is said: "Let his name be blotted out from Heaven and from the face of the earth." Another reason for the closeness of the two Parashiyyoth is the known fact that Esau was vicious to Israel at all times throughout the generations. The first battle ever fought against Israel was waged by no one but Esau, who was Amalek. And as Israel's first battle was against Esau, so Israel's last battle in the days of the Messiah will also be against Esau; and as in the first battle Israel was led by Moses and Joshua, so in the last battle Israel will be led by Elijah and by the Messiah ben Joseph. Now Elijah, like Moses, was of the tribe of Levi, and the Messiah ben Joseph is of the tribe of Ephraim, like Joshua. And as in the first battle, many became converted to the God of

Israel, so in the days of the Messiah many heathen will become converted. Now this Parashah is not far removed from the one containing the account of the giving of the Torah on Mount Sinai, to show that when the Messiah will come the Torah will then be a great enlightenment to the children of Israel, and that afterwards comes the Day of Judgment. The Parashah ואלה המשפטים follows therefore the Parashah וישמע יתרו to show that when the Messiah comes, God will dispense justice and judgment to all people. The Torah says that Jethro had seven names. He was called first Jether, but later when he became converted, the Lord added the letter ו (vaw) to his name, and changed to Jethro.

FOR MOSES AND FOR ISRAEL. The Torah teaches us that Moses with his merits was as meritorious as the whole people of Israel.

2. *AFTER HE HAD SENT HER AWAY.* When the Holy One, blessed be He, first commanded Moses to leave Midian and Egypt, Moses took his wife Zipporah, and their two sons with him. But on the way Aaron met him and asked who they were, and on learning that they were the wife and children of Moses, he asked why they were going to Egypt, when there was sorrow for the women and children who were there already. Why then add more to their number? Moses thereupon immediately sent back his wife and children to Midian, to Jethro his father-in-law; and now Jethro brought them back to Moses in the wilderness.

3. *THE NAME OF THE ONE WAS GERSHOM; FOR HE SAID, I HAVE BEEN A SOJOURNER IN A STRANGE LAND.*

4. AND THE NAME OF THE OTHER WAS ELIEZER; FOR MOSES SAID, GOD WAS MY HELP AND DELIVERED ME FROM THE SWORD OF PHARAOH. Moses did not call his first son Eliezer because Jethro required of Moses that the first child should follow the heathen religion of his mother. Moses therefore refrained from mentioning the name of the Holy One, blessed be He, at the birth of his first son, and for the same reason he did not circumcise him, because he feared his father-in-law. Later, on the

way to Egypt, when the angel sought to kill the boy, Zipporah circumcised him, and her father later forgave her that she had circumcised him. The verse says, "For he said, I have been a sojourner in a strange land." This is to say that Moses excused himself for not calling his first son Eliezer and for not circumcising him, because he was a stranger in Jethro's house and the latter forbade him to circumcise his son. But, with regard to Eliezer, the words, "For he said," are missing,[6] because he refused to say why he called his second son Eliezer and so reveal that he was a fugitive, who escaped the sword of Pharaoh, fearing he might be reported to Pharaoh. The Hazzekuni says that the words of the verse are, "And the name *of one* was Eliezer" and not "The name of the *second*," [7] although he was the second, because the first son had to be called Eliezer, owing to the miracle, which God performed in saving Moses from the sword of Pharaoh. The verse therefore says, "The name of one," because he was equal with the first son, for he was named after the first miracle.

6. *AND HE SAID UNTO MOSES, I THY FATHER-IN-LAW JETHRO AM COME UNTO THEE.* How could Jethro come to Moses, when it was almost impossible to make contact with the children of Israel, because a cloud surrounded them and no one could come near them? The answer is that Jethro attached a letter to an arrow and shot it through the cloud, and Moses read the letter in which was written, "I thy father-in-law, Jethro, am come unto thee. Come and meet me. If thou will not come for my sake, come for thy wife's sake, come for the sake of thy children." And Moses went out of the cloud, and when he went out, Aaron, Nadab and Abihu also went with him. Now, when the people saw that Aaron and Moses went out, many notables followed after them to meet Jethro, and thus paid great homage to him, for many important people went out to greet him.

7. AND MOSES DID OBEISANCE TO HIS FATHER-IN-LAW AND KISSED HIM.

9. *AND JETHRO REJOICED FOR ALL THE GOODNESS WHICH THE LORD HAD DONE TO ISRAEL*; although he was sorry for the many heathen that perished. From this we learn that one must not shame a heathen in the presence of a convert, because the convert might feel sorry, for he at one time was a heathen.

11. *NOW I KNOW.* Jethro said, "Now I know that the Lord is in heaven and on earth, he is above all other gods." Jethro worshipped all other gods and therefore he could say, "Now I know that the Lord is above all gods."

YEA, IN THE THING WHEREIN THEY DEALT PROUDLY AGAINST THEM. The Holy One, blessed be He, repaid the Egyptians in kind for the things they had done against Israel. The Egyptians drowned the Hebrew infants, but God delivered them and later caused the Egyptians to drown in the Red Sea.

12. *WITH MOSES' FATHER-IN-LAW BEFORE GOD.* Jethro made a feast on the occasion of his circumcision and baptism. He made a feast to cause his body to rejoice in order that the Shekinah might rest upon him, since the Shekinah does not rest upon a sad person; as we find in the case of Isaac, when he wished to bless his son, he asked for savoury meat that he might rejoice in order that the Shekinah might be with him at the blessing of Jacob. The verse therefore says, "Before God," to teach us that one who eats in the fellowship of learned men is like unto one who rejoices in the fellowship of God.

13. *AND IT CAME TO PASS ON THE MORROW.* It was one day after the Day of Atonement, when Moses sat to judge the people and the people stood before him as before a king.

14. AND WHEN JETHRO SAW ALL THAT. Jethro was grieved to see Moses treating the honour of Israel so lightly and, therefore, he said unto Moses, "Why sittest thou and all the people stand before thee?" The Hazzekuni asks why Jethro asked, "Why sittest thou?" when it was customary for a judge to sit, and for the contending parties to stand. Moreover, the Hazzekuni marvels how

117

Jethro dared to reproach Moses, who was great among Israel. The answer is, that Jethro asked Moses why he was sitting alone, when it would have been better to appoint judges to help him judge the people. He did not say "Moses, why sittest thou?" but, "Why sittest thou alone?" For he knew that a judge was supposed to sit and the people to stand. Moses, however, did not understand him at first and thought he asked why the people stood, and therefore replied that it was because "the people come unto me to enquire of God," and therefore they ought to stand.

FROM MORNING UNTO EVEN. The people stood from early morning until late in the evening. Rashi asks: "How could Moses have spent the whole day judging the people? When did he teach Torah to Israel?" The answer is, that when one judges rightly, even for an hour a day, it is like teaching Torah the whole day. Also, when a judge judges rightly, he is like God in his good deeds, and he is as if he helped God to create Heaven and earth, for with justice has He created the world.

18. *THOU WILT SURELY WEAR AWAY*. Jethro said to Moses: "Thou wilt not be able to endure alone to judge the people, thou wilt fade away, and Heaven forbid, Israel will fade away with thee. Even if Hur were alive and were with thee, he would not have been of much help, the more so when Hur is not available, since he died a long time ago, at the making of the Golden Calf.[8] Moreover, it is also hard on the people to wait one after the other all day long, until the disputes are settled." Bahya states that Moses said: "Many Israelites come to me, some ask me to pray for the sick, some ask me where they can find the things they have lost, and others ask me to do them justice." Then Jethro said unto Moses: "Thou canst pray for the sick and teach Torah to the people, but thou canst not dispense justice all alone; thou must get help from the sages among Israel."

21. *MOREOVER THOU SHALT PROVIDE*. Thou shalt provide wise men to sit with thee and judge the people. Bahya says that

it is written "thou shalt provide" and not "thou shalt choose," because the word תחזה implies prophetic insight; and the selection of wise and pious judges cannot be made quickly with prophetic insight. The meaning of the term "thou shalt see" is thou shalt look in the people's faces and see who was pious and who was not; the verse implies to say that Moses was a sage and could read people's faces. It is said ואתה תחזה meaning: "Thou alone, Moses, must in thy wisdom look into the faces of men and discern who among them are pious."

ABLE MEN. Men of good character. At all times they should feel the burden of responsibilities hanging like a sword over their necks and as if hell were open behind them. He who would judge righteously would be saved from both, but he who would judge unrighteously would die by the sword and then fall into hell.

MEN OF TRUTH. A judge must be a man of absolute truth.

HATING UNJUST GAIN. A judge should despise money, even his own money, and he must fear no man. When a defendant threatens the judge with burning down his house, if he be not acquitted, the judge should not fear, but choose to lose his possessions and judge what is right.

*RULERS OF THOUSANDS. Moses appointed one judge over a thousand people, and as the number of the children of Israel was six hundred thousand, he appointed six hundred judges. Then again, Moses appointed one judge over a hundred people: this meant six thousand more. Then he appointed one judge over fifty people, and that meant twelve thousand more. Finally he appointed one judge over ten people and that meant sixty thousand more. The Hazzekuni asks if that account be correct, then there must have been at least seventy-eight thousand and six hundred judges among the people, and the number of the children of Israel, which was considered

---

*In our text this section comes after Verse 22, but was transposed to its Biblical order.

to have been six hundred thousand, must have been minus the number of the judges. The answer to the query is that the number of the children of Israel was always more than six hundred thousand. Moreover, the judges were all over sixty years old, and the "over sixties" were not numbered among the six hundred thousand; only the people between twenty and sixty years old were counted. Another explanation, according to the Hazzekuni, may be that the judges were among the six hundred thousand and were numbered with the groups over which they had charge.

22.[9] *AND LET THEM JUDGE THE PEOPLE AT ALL SEASONS.* The other judges can judge the people at all times, but thou, Moses, thou hast not always time to do so, since thou hast often to speak with the Shekinah. Moreover, the people are too numerous to be judged by thee alone.

CHAPTER XIX

1. *IN THE THIRD MONTH.* In the first day of the month of Sivan, the children of Israel came into the desert of Sinai. The same day they travelled from Rephidim to the wilderness of Sinai and camped before the mount. The Scripture says ויחן (he camped) and not ויחנו (they camped) to show that they camped with singleness of heart and mind like one man, ready to receive the Torah. But other campings were disturbed with diversity of opinions and strife and therefore the Scripture used the term ויחנו. Bahya says that the first day of the month of Sivan was a Monday; on Tuesday the children of Israel came to the mount and the Lord gave them a few precepts; on Wednesday, Moses reported to the Lord that the people were ready to receive the Torah with all their heart; on Thursday Moses instructed the children of Israel not to come near a woman during the next three days, i.e., Thursday, Friday, and Saturday. Saturday was the sixth day of Sivan and the Lord gave the Torah on that day. The children of Israel, therefore, say on the Sabbath וישמח מושה[1] because the Torah was given through Moses on a Sabbath day.

3. *THUS SHALT THOU SAY TO THE HOUSE OF JACOB.*
The Lord said unto Moses: "Speak gently to the women of Israel
and give them only a few precepts." The Lord told Moses to speak
first to the women because they were light minded about receiving
the Torah. He therefore commanded Moses to give the women only
a few precepts, since they had not the good sense of the men to
study the Torah. Another reason suggested by Bahya is that women
are of great help in the study of the Torah: they influence their sons
when they are young to study the Torah, more often than do their
husbands; and with gentle words they lead their sons to the rabbis.
Unlike men, women are always at home and show compassion to
their sons. Therefore, when a woman lights the candles on the Sabbath eve, she should pray that God may give her children who would
shed light upon the Torah to her. And prayers of that nature are
more rapidly accepted than the prayers of men, with deeds of
righteousness. Therefore, the verse commands to speak first to the
women and to give them a few precepts, and afterwards speak to the
men.

4. *YE HAVE SEEN WHAT I DID UNTO THE EGYPTIANS.*
The Lord first said that he rewards every man according to his
merit. He, therefore, exhorted the children of Israel to keep His
commandments that He might reward them well: "Now those who
transgress my commands I will punish," said the Lord. "For ye have
seen how I delivered you out of the land of Egypt, that ye may
receive the Torah, and how I punished the Egyptians for their evil
deeds."

AND I BORE YOU ON EAGLES' WINGS. I bore you in my
hand like an eagle bears her offspring. All other birds carry their
fledglings from nest to nest, between their legs, because they fear to
carry them on their wings in case another bird, which can fly higher,
may snatch them away. But the eagle carries her offspring on her
wings, because no bird can fly higher than the eagle and snatch
away her offspring; and she does not carry them between her legs,
because she might be shot at from beneath, by some hunter. The

mother eagle prefers to expose her own body to the danger of a flying arrow, rather than that of her young. The Holy One, blessed be He, likewise bore the children of Israel like an eagle. He surrounded them with clouds and said: "If arrows be thrown, let them enter into the cloud and not into the children of Israel": for the cloud carried the Israelites like a mother eagle carries her offspring.

5. *YE SHALL BE A PECULIAR TREASURE UNTO ME.* Ye children of Israel shall be most precious of all nations unto me, and the verse uses the word סגולה, which is like unto a treasure of precious stone, which a king keeps hidden near him. Likewise, shall Israel be near to God, for He is Israel's protector. But the heathen are in the hands of angels in Heaven, and not in the hands of God.

FOR ALL THE EARTH IS MINE. The Holy One, blessed be He, says: "You should serve me; I can reward you with a good reward; the whole earth is mine to do good to him who serves me well."

7. AND MOSES CALLED THE ELDERS OF THE PEOPLE AND TOLD THEM ALL THE WORDS WHICH THE LORD HAD SPOKEN, namely to give them the Torah.

8. AND THE PEOPLE ANSWERED TOGETHER AND SAID, ALL THAT THE LORD HATH SPOKEN WE WILL DO. AND MOSES REPORTED UNTO THE LORD THAT THE CHILDREN OF ISRAEL WERE READY TO RECEIVE THE TORAH. Bahya asks how could the Gemara* say that the Lord had lifted up a big mountain over the children of Israel, and had said: "If they accept not the Torah, I will let down the mountain on them and cover them up," when it is plainly stated here that the children of Israel received the Torah willingly? The answer is that the Torah (the five books of Moses) they accepted willingly, but the Gemara which Moses received by word of mouth, they were unwilling to accept, because of the many hard and difficult precepts

_____

*Appendix II, 13.

t contains. The Holy One, blessed be He, therefore threatened to et down the mount on them, if they refused to accept also the Gemara.

9. *AND MOSES TOLD THE WORDS OF THE PEOPLE UNTO THE LORD.* Bahya says the verse means that the children of Israel desire of Moses to hear the words spoken by God themselves, which is the same as saying, we want to see the Lord.

LO I COME UNTO THEE IN A THICK CLOUD. The Lord said: "I will appear unto thee in a thick cloud, that all Israel may see and recognize me, but thou alone, Moses, shalt enter into the cloud of fire, and so let all Israel hear thee speak unto me. All Israel will thus be prophets, when they hear me speak unto thee, and they will fear me forever, and will believe that God speaks to man. And, if any man will arise and say that he is a greater prophet than thee, Moses, then all Israel will bear witness that there is no prophet like Moses, for they saw clearly that thou, Moses, hast entered into the pillar of fire and spoken closely to God, a privilege no man has merited, and all will forever believe that God does speak to man and he remains alive." The Lord, therefore, told Moses to enter alone into the cloud, that all Israel might believe him to be a true and trusted prophet and they will hearken to his prophecy.

10. *SANCTIFY THEM TO-DAY AND TO-MORROW.* Let Israel be separated from their womenfolk and let them wash their clothes and immerse themselves in water.

13. *NO HAND SHALL TOUCH HIM.*[2] Bahya asks, why should the verse here say, "No hand shall touch him," when it already said in the previous verse, "whosoever toucheth the mount shall be surely put to death?" The same answers the query by saying that it means to say, that whosoever will touch the mount, let no man touch him; he shall not be put to death by strangulation, nor decapitation, but by stoning.

WHETHER IT BE BEAST OR MAN.[3] Let no one draw nigh unto the mount. Bahya says the Scripture means to say that neither

123

the sinner, who is likened to a beast, nor the righteous shall draw nigh unto the mount to touch it. Whosoever touches the mount with a hand shall be stoned to death; therefore set a sign around the mount to show the people how far away they may go.

WHEN THE TRUMPET SOUNDETH LONG, THEY SHALL COME UP TO THE MOUNT. The blowing of the trumpet signalized the departure of the Shekinah, after which the people could draw nigh to the mount. The trumpet was made of the horn of the ram which Abraham sacrificed in lieu of Isaac. Bahya asks, "How could the trumpet on Sinai have been made of the horn of that ram, when the same ram, flesh, skin, horns and all, was burned completely on the day it was sacrificed?" The answer, he says, is that out of its ashes the Lord made another ram. The same is maintained by the Pirque de Rabbi Eliezer; namely, that there was not a piece of that ram wasted, out of which was not made some sacred object. First, from the bones of the ram was built the foundation of the altar in the Temple, from the veins were made ten strings for the harp upon which King David played, from the skin was made the girdle which Elijah wore on his loins, the left horn was blown at Mount Sinai, and the right horn will be blown at the coming of the Messiah. The right horn is bigger than the left one, and therefore it is said in the Scripture, "In that day the great trumpet shall be blown." [4] In the day of the Messiah a great trumpet will be blown.

16. *AND THERE WERE THUNDERS AND LIGHTNINGS.* There were many voices coming from the angels, which accompanied the Lord on Mount Sinai; also great lightnings of fire from the angels which are flames of fire; and the Lord separated the people from the angels with a great cloud that they might not see the angels and be afraid of them.

17. AND MOSES BROUGHT FORTH THE PEOPLE TO MEET GOD. Moses brought forth the people before the Lord of the host of angels near the mount. Twenty-two thousand angels were near the Holy One, blessed be He, to compare with the twenty-two thousand Levites which were close to the Tabernacle, near the

Shekinah. The Midrash says that on the day when the Torah was given, the sun remained still and many rose from the dead, for many among the children of Israel died of fear, and the Lord revived them. Five times the sun remained still in the days of Moses. First, at the going out from Egypt; second, at the crossing of the Red Sea; third, in the battle against Amalek; fourth, at the giving of the Torah; fifth, at the crossing of the river Arnon. All of this took place in the days of Moses.

AND THEY STOOD AT THE NETHER PART OF THE MOUNT. The children of Israel remained within the limits, which Moses assigned them, and the Holy One, blessed be He, was on the top of the mount; and Moses entered into the cloud, even into the thick cloud, wherein God Himself was.

18. *AND MOUNT SINAI WAS ALTOGETHER ON SMOKE.* The smoke was not coming from the fire in which the Lord appeared, for that fire was without smoke. It was a bad smoke that came not out of fire.

AND THE SMOKE THEREOF ASCENDED AS THE SMOKE OF A FURNACE.[5] When the Lord came down upon Mount Sinai, there was much smoke which rose to the very skies and there were heavy clouds and mist, and a heavy rain, and Mount Sinai shook and trembled. And many other mountains leaped and danced so that the children of Israel became frightened because the earth beneath them trembled; and in great fear of the fire, the thunder and the lightning, they kept far away from Mount Sinai.

19. *MOSES SPAKE, AND GOD ANSWERED HIM BY A VOICE.* It was marvelous that the children of Israel, who covered a distance of three miles long and three miles wide, heard clearly every word which Moses spoke on the mount, and that although the trumpet sounded aloud all the time, it did not overpower Moses' voice, for the Lord gave him great strength to speak very loudly, that all Israel could hear what he said to the Holy One, blessed be He.

20. *AND THE LORD CAME DOWN UPON MOUNT SINAI.*

A great fire came upon the mountain when the Lord descended upon it.

21. AND THE LORD SAID UNTO MOSES, GO DOWN, AND CHARGE THE PEOPLE NOT TO TOUCH THE MOUNT THAT THEY DIE NOT.

22-23. AND THOU SHALT ALSO CHARGE THE PRIESTS that they draw not nigh to the mount and that they rely not upon their privileged position. And Moses answered, "I have now warned them for three days, surely they will not touch the mountain." However, the children of Nadab and Abihu did draw nigh the mountain and gazed through the cloud where the Lord was; a thing no man was to do on the penalty of death. However, the Lord wished not to punish the offenders and disturb the rejoicing at Mount Sinai, for it would have been a great grief to Aaron and Moses. Therefore, the Lord waited until the month of Nisan, when the two brought sacrifices before the Altar, and the Lord cut them down and consumed them with a thread of fire which entered their nostrils and burned their bodies.

24. * LET THEM NOT BREAK THROUGH. The Lord said unto Moses: "Charge the children of Israel and the Priests not to gaze at me in the cloud."

CHAPTER XX

1. AND GOD SPAKE ALL THESE WORDS, SAYING. The Lord uttered all the Ten Commandments to the children of Israel. Our sages said that the Lord uttered only the first two Commandments, and the rest were spoken by Moses and not by the Lord in person. The reason for this was that, although the Lord indeed uttered first all the Ten Commandments, and not only the first two, the children of Israel understood only the first two, but did not

---

*For missing passage, see Verse 18-B.

understand the rest; therefore Moses repeated them clearly and made the children of Israel understand them.[1]

2. *I AM THE LORD THY GOD*. The Lord said: "Know thou and meditate over it in thy heart that 'I am the Lord who brought thee out of the Land of Egypt.' " The Lord said: "Thou shouldest worship me, for thou hast seen with thine own eyes the signs I did in Egypt." The Lord did not reveal Himself to them as the Creator of heaven and earth, because they were not eyewitnesses of the creation, but the signs which He did in Egypt they saw with their own eyes. From the wonders they saw the Lord do in Egypt, they ought to have been able to understand that the Lord created the universe, and that He takes care of His creatures and rewards those who serve Him. The Lord greatly rewarded Israel that they receive the Torah and He punished Pharaoh because he sinned against Him.

OUT OF THE HOUSE OF BONDAGE. It is right that ye be my servants, for I brought you out of the house, where you were servants.

3. *THOU SHALT HAVE NONE OTHER GODS*. Thou shalt not worship angels, nor any star in the heavens. The verse calls the other gods אחרים because they are strange to those who serve them; for when they are called upon for help, they can do nothing, neither can they help themselves. Another explanation why they are called "strange" is because various people make them in various ways. For instance, a man makes an idol of wood, then he changes his mind and makes another one of gold or silver. It is written לך (unto thee) and not לכם (unto you), although God spoke to a multitude of people. The reason for the use of the singular form was that Moses might later excuse the children of Israel for making the Golden Calf, and might say to the Lord that when He had said, "Thou shalt have no other gods," He forbade Moses personally to worship other gods, but not the children of Israel.

BEFORE ME. As long as I live let no one serve other gods, and let not Israel think that the prohibition referred to the generations

127

which were present at Mount Sinai, but not to the generations to come. The verse therefore says "before me" in order to lay down the rule that as long as the Lord liveth no other gods shall be served.

4. *THOU SHALT NOT MAKE UNTO THEE A GRAVEN IMAGE.*[2] Think not thou that when I said "Thou shalt have no other gods" I only meant thou shalt not have in thy heart to serve other gods, but I say thou shalt not even make them. Perhaps thou wilt reason in thy heart that it is no sin to make an image of the sun or of the moon or of an angel, because thou mayest excuse thyself and say that the sun speaks of God the Creator, who rules the universe; for the sun which rises in the East and goes down in the West may lead thee to believe that there must be a God who guides the course of the sun. Thou mayest further say that as the Tabernacle reminds thee that God has brought us out of Egypt, and the Matzoth remind thee that the Lord has redeemed us out of Egypt, so a graven image or a painted idol might remind thee of some divine precepts. Nevertheless, I say, "Thou shalt not make unto thee any graven image," even with no purpose of worshipping it, for in the end thou wilt do so.

THAT IS IN HEAVEN. "Thou shalt make no image of the things in heaven" refers to the angels which are in heaven.

OR THAT IS IN THE EARTH BENEATH. By this is meant man, animal, beast, or bird which are upon the earth.

OR THAT IS IN THE WATER UNDER THE EARTH. By this are meant demons which live in the abyss of the waters. There are three kinds of demons. Some are in the air, and at night cause bad dreams to people; some are on the earth and dwell among people and cause them to sin; and some are in the abyss of the water, and if they had power to come out, they would destroy the world.

5.* *A JEALOUS GOD.* God holds to account forever the offender who serves other gods, and He does not pardon that offender.

---

*Verse 5 comes before verse 4 in our text, but was reversed to the Biblical order.

VISITING THE INIQUITY OF THE FATHERS UPON THE CHILDREN. God holds the children accountable for the sins of the fathers and punishes the children for their fathers' iniquities. If they follow in their fathers' footsteps, and work the iniquities of their fathers, they receive double for their sins.

5. *AND SHEWING MERCY UNTO THOUSANDS.* The Lord remembers the merits of the fathers, if they were pious, to the thousandth generation. From this we learn that the Lord's compassion is far greater than His anger. For the iniquity of the fathers is remembered only to the fourth generation, but their piety is remembered to the thousandth generation.

7. *THOU SHALT NOT TAKE THE NAME OF THE LORD THY GOD IN VAIN.* Thou shalt take no false oath in the Name of the Lord. Bahya asks why is it not said "Thou shalt not take *my* name in vain," when the Lord Himself was the speaker? Nachmanides answers the query by saying that only the first two commandments, "I am the Lord" and "Thou shalt have no other gods" were uttered by God in person, because the principal thing in all the commandments is to worship God alone and no one else. The rest of the commandments were spoken by the mouth of Moses, and therefore it is not said "my name" because Moses was the speaker and not the Holy One, blessed be He. The commandment against taking the name of the Lord in vain stands next to the commandment against worshipping strange gods to show that he who takes the name of the Lord in vain is likened unto one who serves strange gods; for he who says, "as the Lord is just, so am I," makes also God a liar, if he has lied, and he denies the existence of God. Thus we find[3] that Saul wished to kill his son, Jonathan, because he broke an oath of which he had no knowledge, and yet his father wished to put him to death. However, the people rescued him on account of his unawareness of the same; otherwise he would have had to die like an idolater. To take the name of God in vain is as bad as to lie with another man's wife, for in both instances the Scripture says, "The Lord will not hold him guiltless." We also find that the Lord

brought a severe famine upon the land of Israel, because Saul broke the oath which the children of Israel gave to the forefathers of the Gibeonites; and as soon as the guilty were put to death the famine ceased.[4] No reward or punishment is attached to the observance of the Ten Commandments, except in the case of honouring father and mother, where it is said "that thy days may be long." [5] In the case of taking the name of the Lord in vain, severe punishment is mentioned to teach us that the taking of the name of the Lord in vain is as bad as idolatry, although many people do not think so. But as a matter of fact it is worse than any other transgression. Murder or adultery may at certain times not be committed because of the fear of other people, but one may take the name of the Lord in vain a thousand times and fear nobody. Had there been no other sin in Israel, but the one of taking the name of the Lord in vain, this alone would be of sufficient reason for delaying the coming of the Messiah. For, when a man commits murder, he does so out of vengeance and obeys his lust; likewise he who commits adultery desires to lust, and he who steals seeks money; and he who bears false witness does it out of revenge. However, he who takes the name of God in vain does not derive pleasure from it, but desecrates God's name.

8. *REMEMBER THE SABBATH DAY TO KEEP IT HOLY*.
The Holy One, blessed be He, having first commanded to honour him and to serve no other gods, now commands the people to remember to rest one day a week, because He created the world and also because He did many wonders for us in Egypt.

TO KEEP IT HOLY. Thou shalt keep the Sabbath holy, Thou shalt not labour and neither think of thy money, nor of the body, but do holy things on the Sabbath day and study the Torah; for he who keeps the Sabbath rightly has forgiveness of sins. A story* tells us that the tyrant Turnos Rufus, once met Rabbi Akiba on a Sabbath day, and asked him why the Sabbath was above any other day of

---

*Cp. Ginzberg: *The Legends of the Jews,* Vol. V, III.

the week. Rabbi Akiba replied by asking the inquirer why he considered himself more important than some other people. "The king* has exalted me," replied Turnos Rufus. "Well," said Akiba, "the same is true of the Sabbath. The Holy One, blessed be He, is our Lord and He exalted the Sabbath." Turnos Rufus further asked, "Why then does God work on the Sabbath, if He exalted it above other days? Why does He give rain on the Sabbath day, and why does He guide the distant clouds on the Sabbath?" Rabbi Akiba replied and said, "Thou art well versed in the Torah of Israel. Now then, when two proprietors share one yard, the law forbids them to carry anything across the yard on the Sabbath without having set up an 'erub,' [6] but if the yard belongs to one proprietor, even though it be three miles long, he may carry things across it without an 'erub.' The same is true of God. The whole world belongs to Him alone, and to nobody else. He may, therefore, send across His domain clouds to carry water on the Sabbath." Rabbi Akiba further pointed out that the children of Israel did not gather Manna on the Sabbath, nor did it fall on the Sabbath, and that river Sambatyon[7] remains still on the Sabbath, although it flows the rest of the week. But the tyrant retorted and said that it was useless to cite examples like the Manna or the Sambatyon, for he had not seen either of them. Rabbi Akiba then said, "Go to thy father's grave and let the sorcerers try to call him up on the Sabbath, and see whether he will come, but in week days he will come.** Even sinners in hell are given respite on the Sabbath; for on the Sabbath eve a voice from Heaven calls on the angel Domah, who is in charge of punishing the wicked, to let them rest on the Sabbath. But as soon as the children of Israel have finished the ויהי נועם and ואתה קדוש [8] the same angel calls the sinners back to hell. Therefore, it is customary not to say ויהי נועם and ואתה קדוש until it is well dark, and not

---

*lord.

**Same story recorded by the author in his comments on Genesis II, verse 3.

to say it hastily in order not to send the sinners back to hell hastily.

9. *SIX DAYS SHALT THOU LABOUR.* Let the Sabbath be unto thee as though thou hast completed all thy labour and thou shalt think no more of it, for the Holy One, blessed be He, can well provide for thee, that thou wouldst have no need to labour.

12. *HONOUR THY FATHER AND THY MOTHER.* The Lord first commanded us to honour Him who is the Father of mankind, and then to honour our earthly parents for their share in bringing us into the world. And as man is bidden to acknowledge God, the first Father of mankind, so should one acknowledge one's father and mother and not deny them; and, as it is forbidden to swear falsely in the name of God, so it is forbidden to swear falsely in the name of one's father or mother. One should not honour one's father and mother for the sake of what one may inherit from them; in the same way, one should not serve God for the sake of reward. One is also bound to assist one's father and mother with one's money and provide them with food, shelter and clothing, as one is bound to honour God with one's money and give alms and tithes. And why in the Ten Commandments did the Torah say, "Honour thy father and mother that thy days may be long"? The answer is given by Rabbi Saadya, who says that long life was promised to him who honours father and mother; but no promise of reward is made for keeping the other nine commandments, because in the case of parents it often happens that they live to an advanced old age and become a burden to their children; therefore the Torah says, "Honour thy father and thy mother, that thy days may be long upon earth." It means to say: "Grudge not their long life, otherwise thou wouldest run the risk of grudging against thine own life, for thou wilt live only if thou honourest them." The Toldoth Yitschak explains the commandment "Honour thy father and mother" by saying that, if thou honourest thy father and mother, thou wilt likewise be honoured when thy turn comes; people will stand up before thee and do thee homage, which is due to old age. Therefore, the Torah

132

says, "Honour thy father and mother that thy days may be long," that thou live to a good old age.

13. *THOU SHALT NOT KILL.* Bahya, commenting on the following commandments, explains them this way. Thou shalt not diminish human life, even if the population of the world be very numerous.

14. *THOU SHALT NOT COMMIT ADULTERY.* Think not thou that it is forbidden only to diminish life, and that there is a merit to increase life, even if by illicit means. The Lord, therefore, said, "Thou shalt not commit adultery, not even to increase the population of the world."

15. *THOU SHALT NOT STEAL.* Thou shalt not steal a man and sell him. Think not that it is forbidden to kill people, but not forbidden to steal and sell them into a foreign land, where at least they would remain alive. The Torah therefore says, "Thou shalt not steal," meaning thou shalt not steal a man and sell him. Nor shalt thou think that it is forbidden to harm only a man's body but not his property, and that his money may be taken away by false witness; the Scripture therefore says:

16. *THOU SHALT NOT BEAR FALSE WITNESS AGAINST THY NEIGHBOU*R: Thou shalt not even harm thy neighbour with thy mouth. Bahya asks why does the text not say, "Thou shalt not bear false witness against thy brother?" The reason is that the Lord wants to teach us not to bear false witness even against a heathen, who is not a brother. The more so is it forbidden to bear false witness against a neighbour. Another reason why it is not said "Against thy brother" is because it is self-evident that a man would not bear false witness against his brother. Moreover, a man should bear no witness at all, not even favourable witness, for a brother or relative. Now, if one might think that it is forbidden only to speak falsely against a neighbour, but to entertain evil thoughts against a neighbour is permissible, the Scripture forbids.

17. *THOU SHALT NOT COVET.* Thou shalt not covet even in

thy heart what belongs to thy neighbour. The sin of coveting money or goods lies in the human heart, and it is a great sin indeed. The whole world suffers from that sin. There is no commandment against robbery, because it is self-evident that it is wrong. If it is forbidden to covet, it is much more blame-worthy to take by violence. However, one kind of covetousness is permissible; namely one may covet a neighbour's zeal for the study of the Torah, for doing good, and for winning the world for the Torah. One may covet these things and practice them. A man may also covet his neighbour's daughter to marry her to his son.

HONOUR THY FATHER AND THY MOTHER [9] is the fifth commandment, because man is begotten of five elements in nature; namely, father and mother, earth, water, air and fire. Then follows a period of nine months, when an infant is confined in his mother's womb. God endows the infant with a soul, intelligence, and with the power of speech. The father contributes the white cells and the mother the red cells. Out of the white cells come veins and bones; and out of the red cells come flesh, hair, and the eyeballs. Also five kinds of creatures have been created in the world: man, beasts, the fowls of the air, fish, and the creeping things.

UPON THE LAND. This term is used in connection with the commandment to honour father and mother, because there are five kinds of husbandry on land. There are fields for corn and other crops, fields for vineyards, fields for vegetables, fields for fruit, and fields for forests, where trees grow. There are also five kinds of metals in the earth; iron, gold, silver, copper, and lead.

THOU SHALT NOT KILL is the sixth commandment, because of the six reasons which may tempt man to commit murder. These are envy, passion, hatred, anger, frivolity and drunkenness. Another reason why "thou shalt not kill' is the sixth commandment, because man was created on the sixth day.

THOU SHALT NOT COMMIT ADULTERY is the seventh commandment, because there are seven kinds of adultery prohibited

134

by the Torah, such as to lie with another man's wife, to have inter-course with a woman during her period of menstruation, with a widow, with a virgin, with an animal, male with male, and with a stranger.[10] There are seven kinds of prohibitions in connection with the same. One must not behold a strange woman; one must not hear her voice, one must not be in the selfsame room with her, one must not speak too much to her, one must not touch her with one's hand, one must not kiss her, and one must not lie with her.

THOU SHALT NOT STEAL is the eighth commandment, be-cause there are eight kinds of theft, such as falsifying accounts or short changing anyone, false measures, false weights, finding and not returning, kidnapping and selling a victim, stealing money, stealing ideas or affections, as for instance pretending to be hospitable by inviting a person to dinner, knowing beforehand that the person could not come. The eighth is when a guardian marries his wealthy ward to his own son, that her wealth may remain in the family, and then keeps the money for himself. This is called stealing.

18.   *AND ALL THE PEOPLE SAW.* All the people were healed of their infirmities; the blind regained their sight; the deaf heard, as it is written, "All that the Lord hath spoken will we do." [11] The dumb spoke, as it is written, "ALL THE PEOPLE ANSWERED."

AND WHEN THE PEOPLE SAW IT, THEY TREMBLED. When the people saw the thunder and lightning they trembled and retired twelve miles from the Mount, but the angels brought them back to the Mount.

19.   *AND THEY SAID UNTO MOSES, SPEAK THOU WITH US, AND WE WILL HEAR, BUT LET NOT GOD SPEAK WITH US, LEST WE DIE.*

20.   AND MOSES SAID UNTO THE PEOPLE, FEAR NOT, FOR GOD IS COME TO PROVE YOU, AND THAT HIS FEAR MAY BE BEFORE YOU FOREVER.

21.   AND THE PEOPLE STOOD AFAR OFF, AND MOSES DREW NEAR UNTO THE THICK CLOUD AND RECEIVED

THE TORAH.

22. AND THE LORD SAID UNTO MOSES, SAY UNTO THE CHILDREN OF ISRAEL that since they were present when I spoke to thee, they shall therefore guard themselves against worshipping angels.

23. YE SHALL NOT MAKE UNTO ME GODS OF SILVER. Ye shall not choose unto yourselves a judge or a community leader, because he happens to have silver and gold. Another interpretation of the verse is that ye shall not call upon me when all goes well with you and neglect me when things are not so well with you. In prosperity or in adversity ye shall call upon me and praise my name.

24. *AN ALTAR OF EARTH THOU SHALT MAKE UNTO ME.*[12] Bahya says that a great miracle was apparent at the altar, for notwithstanding the fact that the altar was covered with a thin layer of copper, as thin as a gold florin, the fire did not burn through the copper to destroy the wood and the earth beneath it. Moses, however, feared that the fire might burn through the copper but the Lord reminded him, saying: "When thou wert on Mount Sinai, where there was much fire, thou wert not consumed because I was with thee. I will likewise be with the altar and safeguard the copper and the wood, and the altar will not burn down."

25. WHEN THOU MAKEST AN ALTAR UNTO ME THOU SHALT NOT BUILD IT OF HEWN STONES, FOR IF THOU LIFT UP THINE IRON HAMMER UPON IT THOU WOULDST POLLUTE IT. Iron shortens human life, for people make of it instruments of destruction; therefore thou shalt not lift up iron upon the altar, which is for the protection of human life. Another reason is that the altar is destined to make peace between the Holy One, blessed be He, and Israel, and since iron is used for war purposes and for killing people, it shall therefore not be lifted upon the altar. We infer from this passage that if God forbids the use of iron on the altar because the altar makes peace between God and man, the more so will a man enjoy peace, if he makes peace between a hus-

band and his wife, between families or between friends; he will never be touched by evil. Bahya says: "God forbade to hew the stones of the altar in order to avoid having pieces of the sacred stones scattered on the streets." The Imre No'am says it is better to make an earthen altar rather than a stone one, in order to avoid pride and haughtiness. For if one builds an altar of dressed stones, it may be costly, and when one finds himself short of money, one may be tempted to rob and lift up the sword against other people and thereby pollute the altar of God, and the Lord hates a sacrifice or an altar of robbery. The verse, therefore, says, "If thou lift up thy sword upon it, thou wilt pollute it." It means to say that thou mayest well have to lift up thy sword in robbery, in order to build an altar of dressed stones.

26. *NEITHER SHALT THOU GO UP BY STEPS.* When thou buildest an altar thou shalt build no steps thereto, because in raising thy legs to ascend the steps thou mayest expose thy nakedness before the altar. And, although the priests wore trousers, it was nevertheless forbidden to build steps to the altar, but a smooth and gradually sloping path. From this injunction our sages inferred that if it is forbidden to expose one's nakedness before stones, the more so before men, who have intelligence and who have been created in the image of God.

CHAPTER XXI

1. *NOW THESE ARE THE JUDGMENTS.* King Solomon, may he rest in peace, says, "These things also belong to the wise. It is not good to have respect of persons in judgment." [1] It is not good to flatter anyone in judgment, for he who judges rightly establishes the throne of God, and he who judges falsely removes the throne of God from its place. Righteous judgment brings peace upon earth, as can be seen in the counsel of Jethro, who said, "All these people also should go to their place in peace." [2] The world can exist and be firm when there is peace within it. True judgment was therefore com-

mended to friends, who have the peace of the world at heart. And it is not right to bring judgment before heathens, but only before the sages of Israel. Therefore, it is written "and these are the judgments that you should set before them." The Gemara, in the treatise "Gittin," [3] emphasizes the words "before them," meaning before Israel and not before the heathens, and more so before the sages of Israel, and not before the untutored. The verse does not use the word להם but the word לפניהם, meaning that it is a great sin to bring a fellow Jew before an ignoramus or before a heathen judge, though the heathen judge may be as completely impartial as a Jewish judge. Nevertheless, it is a greater offence than murder, and murder is a serious offence, for he who destroys a man is like one who has destroyed the entire world. One has to understand that murder and robbery are very serious crimes, nevertheless there could be repentance in one case and a redress of the things taken away in the other case. But in the case of desecration of the Holy Name repentance avails little. Let a Jew, therefore be warned not to bring his fellow Jew before a heathen judge, because this offence is as great as the desecration of the Holy Name and robbery put together. By going to a heathen court, a Jew is in danger of paying homage to the heathen gods and thereby desecrates the holy name of God. He is also in danger of committing robbery, because the heathen judgments are full of robbery.

WHICH THOU SHALT SET. This means the judge shall give the defendant in writing the reason for his verdict. The Parashah dealing with judgments, stands nearby to the Parashah dealing with the building of an altar to show that the seat of judgment should be in the Temple. Rabbi Eliezer says that when there is righteous judgment on earth, there is no judgment in heaven; but when there is no judgment on earth, there is judgment in heaven. Our sages say that the children of Israel were taken away from their land because there was no Torah and justice among them. The word תשים means to say that righteous judgment is like a tonic, and that false judgment is like deadly poison.

138

2. *IF THOU BUY AN HEBREW SERVANT:* The Torah begins this chapter with "If thou buy an Hebrew servant," because the first commandment of the Decalogue says, "I am the Lord thy God which brought thee out of the land of Egypt," that thou be my servant and not sell thyself unto the service of another servant. And as we rest on the Sabbath day, because the Lord rested on that day, after the six days of creation, so shall a servant serve his master six years and go out free in the seventh year, in remembrance of the seventh day in which the Lord rested.

SIX YEARS SHALL HE SERVE. The verse refers to a servant who was sold by a court of justice to make restitution for things he stole, and could not repay. However, his master must not work him too hard, nor employ him in dishonourable work, and he shall work in daytime but not at night.

HE SHALL GO OUT FOR NOTHING. If the servant becomes ill and cannot work, the master shall not charge the servant with the medical expenses, neither for the time lost during the illness, nor for the board while convalescing; but if the servant be ill for over three years, he must repay all expenses.

3. *IF HE COME IN BY HIMSELF, HE SHALL GO OUT BY HIMSELF.* If the servant comes unmarried, the master must not give him a wife while he serves him.

IF HE BE MARRIED, THEN HIS WIFE SHALL GO OUT WITH HIM.[4] Rashi asks why the Scripture has to order the wife's release, when she never came into servitude with her husband. The answer is that the Scripture emphasizes the fact that if one buys a Hebrew servant, one has to feed the servant's wife and children, as long as the servant is in servitude.

3-4. IF THE SERVANT BE MARRIED, the master may give him a Canaanitish servant for a wife to have children with her, and the children shall belong to the master.

5. BUT IF THE SERVANT SHALL SAY, I LOVE MY MASTER, MY WIFE, AND MY CHILDREN, I WILL NOT GO OUT FREE FROM MY MASTER.

6. THEN HIS MASTER SHALL TAKE HIM TO COURT AND BEFORE THE JUDGES BORE A HOLE THROUGH THE SERVANT'S EAR INTO THE DOORPOST, AND HE SHALL SERVE UNTIL THE JUBILEE, WHICH OCCURRED EVERY FIFTY YEARS, AND THEN HE MUST GO OUT FREE. The servant had his ear bored because with their ears the Israelites heard the Lord saying on Mount Sinai that they were to serve Him and none else, because He had redeemed them from Pharaoh's bondage. Yet now when a servant chooses to remain in servitude, and not heed what his ear has heard, he shall have his ear pierced. The ear was bored against the doorpost because the doorposts were witnesses to the Lord's passing over the houses of the children of Israel, in the night when He smote the first born in Egypt, and spared the first born of Israel and commanded the children of Israel to be His servants; therefore if an Israelite sells himself into servitude, he shall have his ear bored against the doorpost.

AND HIS MASTER SHALL BORE HIS EAR. The master himself had to bore the servant's ear, and he could not commission his son or a messenger to perform the task, because the master himself had to put the slave to shame before the judges, for the servant has committed sin. The Scripture uses the term "Hebrew servant" and not "Israelitish servant" because the latter is an honourable name given to the children of Israel, after they had been redeemed from the Egyptian bondage and received the Torah. But when they had been slaves in Egypt they were called "Hebrews," as it is written the "God of the Hebrews." Now he who sells himself into slavery is called an "Hebrew servant" because he is not worthy to be called by the name of Israel. His ear was made to bleed because he refused to remember the blood which was sprinkled on the doorposts when the Lord redeemed Israel out of the Egyptian bondage. The Midrash maintains the Holy One, blessed be He, said: "I have opened a door by which a servant could get out free after six years, but when the same refuses to go out, let his ear be bored against the door."

7. *HIS DAUGHTER TO BE A MAIDSERVANT*. The Torah

permits a father to sell his daughter, when she is young, to an Israelite for a maidservant; but she shall not be set free in the same way as a Canaanitish woman, who is set free, if the master knocks out her tooth or an eye. A daughter of Israel shall receive compensation for such bodily injuries, and shall continue her service to the end of her time.

8. *IF SHE PLEASE NOT HER MASTER.* The Law permits a man who buys a daughter for a servant to marry her; however he is not obliged to give her a piece of silver as a monetary token of marriage. The purchase money which he paid to her father may be counted as such. But if he refuses to marry her, he shall help her to be redeemed from her servitude by reducing her selling price. For instance, if she was bought for a price of twenty-four gulden to serve for a period of six years and then go free, the cost to the master was four gulden per year, and if she had served two years, he must deduct eight gulden from her price.

TO SELL HER TO A STRANGE PEOPLE, HE SHALL HAVE NO POWER. He may not sell his daughter to a stranger. Although it was permissible to sell a Hebrew manservant to a stranger, it was forbidden to sell a Hebrew maidservant to a stranger, because he might commit fornication with her. The Toldoth Yitschak asks why the Torah says that if the servant be single his master shall not give him a Canaanitish woman for a wife, but if he be married to an Israelitish woman the master may give him a Canaanitish woman, and her children be her master's, when an Israelite was not supposed to marry a strange woman at all. Also, how come that a father should sell his own daughter into servitude? The answer is that we are dealing with a case in which an Hebrew was sold into servitude by judicial authorities, to make restitution for the things he stole. Now, if the same servant be married to a Jewish woman, he has less chance of finding a buyer than if he be single, since a master who buys a Hebrew servant must feed the servant's family, from whom little can be expected in return, since they could not be compelled to work. Few, if any, would buy such a servant, and he would have little chance to repay what he stole. Therefore, the Torah permits a master to give a Canaanitish woman to such a servant for a wife, though he be married and has a family, that he may beget children for the master and thus encourage prospective buyers. However, in the case of a single man such problems do not arise, and there would be no difficulty in finding a buyer; therefore the Torah forbids a master from marrying a Hebrew slave to a Canaanitish woman, nor may the master marry the servant to a Jewish woman, because he can lay no claim on the children that may come forth of the marriage although the master would be responsible for their welfare, and thus the master might suffer a loss. Another reason why a married slave may be given a Canaanitish woman is that a married man is less likely to exchange his first wife for a Canaanitish woman forced upon him by his master, and he would finally rid himself of her. Moreover, it also seems more natural for men and women to be more in love with the mates of their first marriages than with the mates of subsequent marriages. But an unmarried man, to whom the Canaanitish woman would be his first wife, is in danger of falling in love with her and keeping her as his wife, and becoming influenced by her evil deeds;[5] therefore, the Torah forbids a master to give a Canaanitish woman to an unmarried Hebrew slave. Now, concerning the question, "How can a father sell his daughter into slavery?" The answer is that the father did so in the hope that the master who paid for the girl would take advantage of the opportunity to marry the woman, or to marry her to his son, without having to pay for her; thus the father would have sold his daughter into marriage rather than into servitude.

The Toldoth Yitschak asks why, if the reason for boring a servant's ear was his disobedience to the commandment of the Lord, who said, "Israel shall be my servant," then was not the slave's ear bored at the time he sold himself, without waiting until the servant desired after six years to remain in servitude. The answer is that he did not sell himself, but was sold by judicial authorities for an offence. He was *guilty of stealing* at first, and not of selling himself into slavery. But if the master was willing to retain him after six years of service, this was a proof that the culprit had become honest. Therefore, the master leads him to the door to show that he is no longer a thief. When a door is open a thief may enter and steal from a house, but when a door is well bolted, no thief can enter. The servant, who is now a changed man, is no longer a thief but is brought to the door, because the human ear may be compared to a door which should be opened at times for listening to goodness and shut at times against evil. Our sages say that the reason why the whole ear is hard as a bone and the lobe is soft is that when one hears evil things, one should place the soft lobe into the ear and shut it off from listening.

9. *HE SHALL DEAL WITH HER AFTER THE MANNER OF DAUGHTERS.* If the master's son marries a slave girl, he shall treat her like a wife, taken from her father's home; and the master shall give her a dowry as he would have given to his own daughter.

10. AND IF THE SON TAKES UNTO HIMSELF ANOTHER WIFE, HE SHALL NOT DIMINISH HER CONJUGAL RIGHTS NOR HER FOOD, NOR HER CLOTHES. Nor shall he honour the second wife more than the former, on account of the former having been a slave girl. Bahya says that it was customary in those days in the land of Persia that a man slept in his clothes with his wife. Therefore, the verse emphasizes the conjugal rights of the women that the man should observe the accepted custom and undress.

11. AND IF HE DOES NOT OBSERVE ONE OF THE THREE DUTIES TO HER, and neither the master nor his son married her, nor did the father redeem her, she shall go out free.

12-13. IF A MAN KILLS ANOTHER MAN BY ACCIDENT, OR AS BY AN ACT OF DIVINE JUDGMENT, HE SHALL BE BANISHED TO THE CITIES OF REFUGE AND NO HARM SHALL BE DONE TO HIM. Here the question arises, "What wrong did the man do when he killed a man, if God willed it, and why must he flee to a city of refuge?" The answer is that if one kills his friend deliberately, and there were no witnesses, then he cannot be put to death. However, an instance may occur when a man accidentally kills his friend, and does not flee to a city of refuge, then God makes the two murderers come to justice. God brings the two together to an inn and leads the one who killed his friend accidentally to climb a ladder and the one who killed intentionally to stand behind the ladder, then the one on the ladder falls upon the other beneath the ladder and kills him, and there are witnesses present. Thus the Lord rewards each one according to his deeds. The one who committed murder wilfully was punished with death, and the one who killed accidentally was banished into the cities of refuge. But when the children of Israel dwelt in the wilderness where there were no cities of refuge, then if a man who killed another man by accident fled to the camp of the Levites, no vengeance was wrought against him.

14.   AND IF A MAN COME PRESUMPTUOUSLY UPON HIS NEIGHBOUR TO KILL HIM, or if death occurs accidentally as in the case where a medical man causes the death of a patient; or when the synagogue sexton, in giving a person forty lashes less one, causes the death of the same; or when a father punishing his son, or a teacher in punishing a pupil, or a master in punishing his servant causes him to die, they shall not be guilty of death. But a murderer shall be taken from the altar, even if he be a priest engaged in the midst of sacrificing, he shall be taken away and be put to death. The same applies to one who was not a priest, but fled for safety to the altar, as Joab did when King Solomon ordered his execution. He fled to the tabernacle of the Lord in search of refuge at the altar, but the altar was no place of refuge for a culprit, for he was taken from it and put to death.

15.   AND HE THAT SMITETH HIS FATHER OR HIS MOTHER AND INFLICTS WOUNDS UPON THEM SHALL SURELY BE PUT TO DEATH.

16. AND HE THAT STEALETH A MAN AND SELLETH HIM SHALL SURELY BE PUT TO DEATH.

17. AND HE THAT CURSETH HIS FATHER OR HIS MOTHER SHALL SURELY BE STONED TO DEATH. Bahya asks why the Torah places the law against stealing a man between the laws against smiting and cursing father and mother, when logically the law against stealing should come after them? Rabbi Saadyah answered the question, by saying that the law against stealing a man was intended primarily against the kidnapping of children, who are an easier prey than grownups; and it might so happen that a stolen child, when he has grown up, would unknowingly curse or smite someone who was his or her father or mother; therefore the Torah placed the law against the stealing of human beings between the laws against smiting and cursing father and mother, to show that he who steals children may cause them later to smite or curse their own parents. Rabban says that the reason why the law against kidnapping a man follows the law against smiting father or mother is that one and the same penalty is attached to both laws, namely, in both cases the culprit will be put to death by strangulation. But for cursing father or mother, the law prescribes the penalty of stoning, which is a more painful death, in order to deter people from being too hasty with their tongues. Another reason for the severe punishment for cursing father or mother is that the offender also takes the name of God in vain.

18. *BUT KEEP HIS BED.* If a man smites another man with his fist or with a stone, and the victim be laid up because of the injury and cannot go to work, the offender shall be imprisoned until the victim has recuperated, and the offender shall also pay compensation for the days the victim could not work. If the offender caused the victim to lose a hand or a foot, payment shall be made for the loss. The loss sustained by the plaintiff is estimated by deducting his personal value after having been injured from his assumptive value on the slave market before the injury was inflicted upon him; and the compensation for the loss of time during the recovery period

is estimated as being equivalent to the earnings, say, of a watchman of a garden during the same period of time.

19. *AND SHALL CAUSE HIM TO BE THOROUGHLY* HEALED. He shall engage a physician to attend the injured man. But if the injured person recuperating from his injuries prefers money to medical care, the guilty party is not compelled to give money. Thus says Rabban. Bahya calls attention to the fact that in the whole Torah the letter פ in ורפא always contains the daggesh; but the פ in the word רפואה as coming from God is without the daggesh. The reason for this is because that which comes from man is hard and painful; therefore the letter פ contains the daggesh, signifying hardness, but the רפואה which comes from God is easy and without pain, therefore the letter פ is written without a daggesh. Rashi, commenting on the verse, says that the offender must pay the doctor's bill, and if he brings a doctor who is willing to undertake the case without payment, or if the offender himself be a physician, the injured party may refuse to be treated by either. He may mistrust a physician who offers his services freely; and he may mistrust the offender, if he be a physician and say to him: "Thou art my enemy and I do not wish to see you."

20. AND IF A MAN SMITES HIS SERVANT OR HIS MAID WITH A ROD AND HE DIE UNDER HIS HAND, HE SHALL BE PUT TO DEATH BY THE SWORD, EVEN IF THE SERVANTS BE CANAANITES.

21. IF HOWEVER, HE SURVIVES A DAY OR TWO AND DIES AFTERWARDS, THE MASTER SHALL NOT BE GUILTY OF DEATH.

22. IF TWO MEN STRIVE TOGETHER AND HURT A PREGNANT WOMAN AND CAUSE HER A MISCARRIAGE, THE GUILTY PARTY SHALL PAY SUCH FINE AS IMPOSED BY THE WOMAN'S HUSBAND AND AS APPROVED BY THE JUDGES. The fine is imposed by the husband and not by the woman, because the child belongs to him and not to her. The

woman is only a temporary custodian of the child. If the husband demands too great a fine, the judges shall judge what is right.

23. BUT IF THE WOMAN DIE AS A RESULT OF THE INJURY, some sages say the guilty shall be put to death. Others say that because it was only an accident a fine shall be imposed by the judges.

24. *EYE FOR AN EYE.* If a man knocks out an eye of another man he shall make restitution for it.

26-27. IF A MAN KNOCKS OUT AN EYE OR A TOOTH OF HIS CANAANITISH MANSERVANT OR MAIDSERVANT, HE SHALL SET THE INJURED SERVANT FREE FROM SERVITUDE. Bahya says that the Canaanites were destined to servitude because Ham, their forefather, sinned with his eye by looking at his father Noah's nakedness and covering him not, then he sinned with his mouth in telling what he saw to his two brothers.[6] But when a Canaanite suffers the loss of an eye or of a tooth, the pain atones for the sin of Ham, and the servant shall be set free.

28. AND IF AN OX GORE A MAN AND HE DIE, THE OX SHALL BE STONED TO DEATH AND HIS FLESH SHALL NOT BE EATEN.

29. BUT IF THE OX WERE WONT TO GORE IN TIME PAST AND HIS OWNER WAS WARNED THREE TIMES AND HE HAD NOT KEPT HIM IN, AND HE KILLS A MAN OR A WOMAN, THE OX SHALL BE STONED AND HIS OWNER SHALL DIE. Bahya says that the Scripture uses the word יגח when the ox gores a man, and יגוף when he gores a beast, because man has a lucky star in heaven, and it is not easy to gore him; the ox must make a strong effort and, therefore, the term יגח is used. But in the case of a beast, which has no lucky stars, no great effort is required; therefore the term יגוף is used. The Gemara, in the treatise of Ta'anith [7] says, when three persons die in one day, it is not considered an epidemic, but when three die in three days, one after the other, then it is an epidemic. Likewise, if an ox gore three

people in one day, he is not considered to be an habitual killer, and the owner is not guilty of neglect, but if the ox kills three people in three consecutive days, he is to be considered an habitual killer and the owner is guilty, if he did not keep him under lock and key. Nowadays, although a man is not condemned to death if his ox gores a man, nevertheless, he is responsible for any harm done by an ox or a mad dog. Moreover, the people are also warned against throwing unclean things in places where people walk and may stumble and hurt themselves or get soiled. The ancient Hassidim used to pick up broken glass from the streets and bury it in the ground so that no one would get hurt by it. There is a story about a man who cleared his field of stones and rocks and dumped them into a public place through which people used to cross. A Hassid came forth and asked the man why he cleared a stranger's field to dump the rubbish into his own field, but the man mocked the public-minded Hassid for his interference. Not many days after, the man was compelled to sell his field and crossed the public field, and hurt himself against the stones. He came to his senses and said: "Truly the Hassid was right, for the street belonged to him, inasmuch as he was part of the public. The streets all over the world are free for everybody." We learn from this story that a man must not pour out unclean water on the streets where people walk for fear they may slip and hurt themselves. Surely God will severely punish the offenders, as He punished the man in our story and brought poverty upon him so that he had to sell his field.

33-34. AND IF A MAN SHALL OPEN A PIT, OR IF A MAN SHALL DIG A PIT ON A PUBLIC PLACE AND NOT COVER IT AND AN OX FALL THEREIN, HE SHALL MAKE RESTITUTION TO THE OWNER.

CHAPTER XXII

1. IF A MAN SHALL STEAL AN OX OR A SHEEP, HE SHALL PAY AN INDEMNITY OF FIVE OXEN FOR THE

OX AND FOUR FOR THE SHEEP. Rashi says that Rabbi Yochanan says that the reason for paying fivefold for an ox and only fourfold for a sheep is that it is easier to steal an ox than a sheep. A thief can take an ox by the horns and lead him away, while a small animal he would have to carry away on his shoulders and risk being shamed. The Holy One, blessed be He, is always eager for man to preserve his dignity and that he be not put to shame. A second reason for the higher indemnity imposed for stealing an ox is that an ox is a beast of burden, and the thief deprived the owner of its usefulness; therefore he shall pay an indemnity of five to one. Bahya says that if a thief breaks into a house and steal clothes, or silver and gold, he shall make twofold restitution, but if he steals a beast from the field which moves about freely and is unguarded, he shall make fourfold restitution. The Lord imposes greater fines for transgressions which require less effort and less risk, in order to deter people from transgressing. Oxen, for instance, are easy to steal, because the herdsmen cannot keep them together in the field; therefore, the penalty for stealing an ox is fivefold. The Rabban says that a thief pays a twofold indemnity, but not a robber, because a thief fears man more than God and steals when man does not see, while a robber fears man no more than God; therefore a robber does not pay double indemnity. The Midrash says that the sin of making the Golden Calf, which resembled an ox, was like the sin of stealing an ox, and Israel paid a fivefold indemnity and many of them died. There were five forms of death and punishment: (1) Death by the sword, when the sons of Levi fell upon the people: (2) Death by pestilence, when the Lord smote the people and many of Israel died: (3) Many people became green and yellow in the face through the water which Moses made them drink in the manner prescribed for women suspected of infidelity: (4) The Temple was destroyed because of the sin of the Golden Calf: (5) The Lord visits every generation of man for that sin.

FOUR SHEEP FOR A SHEEP. The Israelites were four hundred years in Egypt because of Joseph, who is called "a sheep," whom his brothers stole and sold.

18. *THOU SHALT NOT SUFFER A SORCERESS TO LIVE.*
Bahya says that sorcery was forbidden because the children of Israel
learned it in Egypt, and the Lord forbade it that they return not to
Egypt. The Torah says, "Thou shalt not suffer her to live," meaning
that any manner of death thou canst impose upon her may be imposed. The Scripture says "Sorceress" because sorcery is more
common among women than among men. Necromancy, by which
spirits of deceased persons are brought up to unveil future events,
works only if a woman stands at the head of the grave of the dead,
and a man stands at the foot, and a youth stands in the middle of the
grave. The youth has a bell in his hand and rings it loudly, and
thereupon the dead man arises and predicts the future. The Imre
No'am says that it is not said with which death one is to punish a
sorceress, so that she may not know what to expect and may not
avert it through sorcery. Therefore, the Torah says, "Thou shalt not
suffer a sorceress to live," implying that one may punish her with
death in any fashion.

22. *YE SHALL NOT AFFLICT ANY WIDOW OR FATHER-
LESS CHILD.* The Torah forbids to oppress the widow, the orphan
and the stranger, for they have nobody to defend them.

ANY WIDOW.[1] You must not wrong any widow, not even if she
be rich, for widows cry easily, and their tears go not unanswered.
You shall not burden them with community taxes, even if they be
wealthy, for money brings them no happiness. The prophet Jeremiah
therefore compared Jerusalem to a widow and said, "She weepeth
sore in the night." The text therefore says; "She weepeth sore in
the night," because many rich widows can enjoy this world's pleasures during the day and may forget their dead husbands, but at
night they are alone and therefore they cry. Thus writes the Ba'al
Hatturim.

23. AND IF THOU AFFLICT THEM AND THEY CRY
UNTO ME I WILL SURELY HEAR THEIR CRY.

24. *AND I WILL KILL YOU WITH THE SWORD: AND YOUR WIVES SHALL BE WIDOWS, AND YOUR CHILDREN FATHERLESS.* Rashi says that if mothers become widows it is obvious that their children will be fatherless. Why then has the Scripture to say it? The answer is that the husbands will be lost, and it will not be known whether they be alive or dead. Thus the widows will remain in a perpetual state of widowhood, and will be unable to remarry, and the children will be unable to inherit their father's portion.

25. *IF THOU LEND MONEY TO ANY OF MY PEOPLE.* Bahya points out that King Solomon said, "A gift in secret pacifieth anger, and a present in the bosom strong wrath." [2] He who gives charity in secret pacifies the anger of God, but he who takes a bribe brings upon himself the wrath of God. He who gives his money for charity will reap his reward. The Lord will repay him multifold; therefore the Scripture commands us to lend to the poor, saying, "If thou lend money to any of my people with thee that is poor," thou art under obligation to lend to an Israelite. When a Samaritan comes to borrow from thee, and an Israelite comes at the same time, thou shouldst lend to the Israelite. When the Samaritan desires to pay interest and the poor Israelite desires a loan without interest, thou shouldst lend to the Israelite, without interest. If a rich man and a poor man apply for a loan, thou shalt give preference to the poor.

WITH THEE. Thou shalt give preference to the poor within thy community over the poor who come from afar; thou shalt prefer the poor within thine own family to the poor from another family.[3] "The poor with thee": if thou refusest to lend to the poor, thou shalt be smitten with poverty; and if thou dost lend, behave as though the poor owes thee nothing. Thou shalt take no interest on the loan, for to charge interest is a great sin. This can be seen from the story of Obadiah, Governor of King Ahab's household, who was a rich man and who spent his money in feeding one hundred prophets, whom he hid in a cave because Ahab was after their lives. In those days there was a great famine in the land of Israel, and when Obadiah spent all he had, he asked for a loan from Joram the king's son, to whom he had to promise to pay interest on the loan, although in his heart Obadiah felt that it was as wrong to pay interest as to receive it. The Lord later caused Jehu to smite Joram and pierce his heart with an arrow, because the heart lusted after usury.

MY PEOPLE. The poor are called the people of God, as it is written [4] "The Lord hath comforted His people, and will have compassion upon His afflicted." A rich man often denies his poor relatives, but makes a big display over the wealthy ones. God, however, acts otherwise. He loves the poor and hates the rich.

26. *IF THOU AT ALL TAKE THY NEIGHBOUR'S GARMENT TO PLEDGE*, and the neighbour needs it in daytime, thou shalt let him have it for the whole day and keep the pledge only at night. Think not that the poor, who gave his garment for a pledge, is a sinner and that thou art free to refuse to return his pledge without incurring the wrath of God. The Lord says, "*I am gracious*;" "I have compassion even on those who have no merit of their own whatsoever, and I will have pity on the poor."

28. THOU SHALT NOT REVILE THE JUDGE, IF HE GIVE JUDGMENT AGAINST THEE, NOR CURSE THE KING BECAUSE OF IT.

31. AND YE SHALL BE HOLY MEN UNTO ME: THEREFORE YE SHALL NOT EAT ANY FLESH THAT IS TORN OF BEASTS IN THE FIELD: YE SHALL CAST IT TO THE DOGS. When the Lord smote the first born sons in Egypt, the dogs barked against the Egyptians who buried their dead, but they did not bark against the children of Israel, although dogs as a rule bark against people who pass by at night carrying staves in their hands. However, they did not bark against the children of Israel when they left Egypt with staves in their hands; therefore the Torah commanded that any flesh which was torn of beasts in the field should be given to the dogs.[5]

1. *THOU SHALT NOT TAKE UP A FALSE REPORT*. Thou shalt take no oath from an untrustworthy person, nor shalt thou give ear to the defence of one party in the absence of the other, for one may tell falsehoods. But if the other party is present he will deny the falsehoods. Moreover the verse also warns thee against listening to gossip and malicious talk.

2. THOU SHALT NOT FOLLOW A MAJORITY FOR EVIL, though they be a majority. Thou shalt not be influenced by mere numbers and thou shalt not do as they do. From this precept our sages inferred that for condemning an Israelite to death it was necessary to have a clear majority. The Sanhedrin consisted of seventy-one elders, and if thirty-six said "Guilty" and thirty-five "Not Guilty," the verdict was "Not Guilty," because a majority of one was not sufficient, but for a verdict of not guilty a majority of one was sufficient.

NEITHER SHALT THOU SPEAK IN A CAUSE. A judge was not permitted to teach a defendant how to present his case, nor could a judge act as counsel. The plaintiff had to speak for himself, and the defendant to answer the charge.

3. NEITHER SHALT THOU FAVOUR A POOR MAN IN HIS CAUSE.[1] If a poor man comes to thee for justice, thou shalt not justify the poor at the expense of the rich for the sake of providing charity for the poor man.

4. IF THOU SEEST THINE ENEMY'S ASS OR OX GOING ASTRAY AND GETTING LOST THOU ART UNDER OBLIGATION TO TAKE IT HOME TO HIM.[2]

5. *THOU SHALT SURELY HELP WITH HIM*. If thou seest the ass of thy neighbour lying prostrate under its burden, thou shouldest help him to relieve the ass of its burden, even if the owner be thine enemy.

7. THE INNOCENT AND THE RIGHTEOUS SLAY THOU NOT. If a man leaves court condemned to die and there come a

witness claiming to be in a position to prove the man's innocence, the witness shall be given a hearing; but in the case of a man who had been declared innocent and later a witness appears claiming to be in a position to prove his guilt, he shall not be given a hearing. The phrase "The righteous slay thou not" means that if one has been judged righteous thou shalt not put him to death. And the Holy One, blessed be He, says:

FOR I WILL NOT JUSTIFY THE WICKED. I will not permit if one be guilty to go free, and I alone will take the culprit's life, but thou shalt not lay hands on him. The court should not worry for not placing him before a new trial.

19. *THOU SHALT NOT SEETHE A KID IN ITS MOTHER'S MILK.* This precept occurs three times in the Torah, because of the following three prohibitions [3] man shall not eat meat and milk together, he shall not enjoy meat and milk together, he shall not boil meat and milk together. The Torah prohibited the boiling of milk and meat together, but said nothing about eating thereof; nevertheless if one eats meat and milk together, even without enjoying the same, even if one burns one's throat eating it, one is still guilty of stripes. In other breaches of the dietary laws, a man is worthy of stripes only if he enjoyed the prohibited food, but not otherwise. The Toldoth Yitschak says that it was customary among the heathen to seethe meat and milk and pour it under a tree, in the belief that it would make the fruit of the tree grow faster. The Torah therefore forbids the boiling of meat and milk, because it was an idolatrous rite. The Torah placed the injunction against seething a kid in his mother's milk, in the same verse containing the law about the first fruits, to show that it is forbidden to use meat and milk for making the fruit grow; for the Lord Himself will make it grow.

20. BEHOLD, I SENT THEE AN ANGEL. The Lord said unto Moses that the children of Israel would worship a Golden Calf and thus become unworthy of the Shekinah to go with them; and therefore He would send an angel to go with them. But Moses prayed

that in his lifetime no angel but God Himself should go with Israel, and the Lord heard his prayer. Later, when Moses died and Joshua succeeded him, an angel took the place of the Shekinah and accompanied the children of Israel on their journey to the Holy Land. Rabbi Hananeel said that name of the angel was Michael, who went forth with Joshua.

21. *FOR HE WILL NOT PARDON YOUR TRANSGRESSION.* The Lord said: "Ye shall guard yourselves against committing sin before the accompanying angel, because he has no authority to pardon transgressions, since no one but God alone can forgive sin. You shall give ear unto what the angel says to you, that he make your enemies fall before you, and that he bring you into the Land of Israel."

25. *I WILL TAKE SICKNESS AWAY FROM THE MIDST OF THEE.* Bahya says that there are many kinds of sicknesses; some come from overeating or overdrinking; others are caused by germs floating in the air; but if man would study the Torah, he should not fear any sickness, for the Torah is a cure against all sicknesses.

28. *AND I WILL SEND THE HORNET BEFORE THEE.* I will send vicious wasps which will blind the eyes of the Hivites, Canaanites, and Hittites, three nations that inhabited the Land of Israel. Rashi says that the hornets did not cross the Jordan, but attacked first the Hittites and Canaanites who were on the east side of the Jordan and wrought death among them; later they threw their stings across the Jordan against the Hivites living on the west side of the Jordan and afflicted them with blindness and they all died.

29. THE LORD SAID, I WILL NOT DRIVE OUT THE NATIONS FROM BEFORE THEE AT ONCE, FOR THOU ART NOT NUMEROUS ENOUGH TO FILL THE WHOLE LAND, LEST THE LAND BECOME DESOLATE AND WILD BEASTS MULTIPLY THEREIN. I WILL WAIT UNTIL YOU MULTIPLY.

30. AND THEN I WILL DRIVE THEM OUT UTTERLY FROM BEFORE YOU.

CHAPTER XXIV

1. *COME UP UNTO THE LORD, THOU, AND AARON.* This parashah was written before the Ten Commandments were given. In the fourth day of Sivan,[1] Moses went up on Mount Sinai into the cloud; later he came down and told the children of Israel all he had heard from the Lord, and the children of Israel replied that they were willing to receive the Commandments and obey them. Then Moses wrote the books from Genesis to the section containing the Decalogue. In the fifth day of the month, very early in the morning, Moses went and built an altar at the foot of the mount, and the first born from among the children of Israel sacrificed unto the Lord. Bahya says that the first born were all young men and unmarried and were therefore entirely pure. Through the sacrifices offered by the first born, Israel came into Covenant with three rites; Circumcision, Baptism, and Sacrifice. For the same reason these three rites are asked of every proselyte. He must be circumcised, he must be baptized, and he will bring a sacrifice when the Messiah shall come. Every candidate was told about the laws and the precepts in order to caution him against superficial conversions, for proselytes were a stumbling block to Israel. They were, as a rule, superficial in their attitude and lax in observance of the law. They were a bad example to the children of Israel, as were the "mixed multitude" who joined themselves to the children of Israel at the Exodus from Egypt. They incited Israel to make the Golden Calf, which caused the death of many Israelites in the wilderness. They became proselytes and went out of Egypt into the wilderness with the children of Israel and did much evil. Some sages maintained that the reason why proselytes should first be cautioned concerning the laws and precepts is that

they may have no excuse later to say that they had no knowledge that there were so many laws, and had they known of them beforehand they would not have become proselytes. The Gemara [2] says that proselytes, as a rule, are stumbling blocks to Israel not because they themselves are bad, but because when the Lord sees how they forsake father and mother and friends, in order to cleave to the God of Israel, He expects greater piety from the children of Israel.

6. *AND MOSES TOOK HALF OF THE BLOOD.* An angel came and divided the blood into two equal halves. Moses took one-half and put it in a basin and sprinkled it on the children of Israel, and the other half he poured upon the altar.

9-10. *THEN WENT UP MOSES, AND AARON, NADAB AND ABIHU, AND SEVENTY OF THE ELDERS OF ISRAEL. AND THEY SAW THE THRONE OF GOD AND IT WAS AS A PAVED WORK OF SAPPHIRE STONE.* They also saw a brick which the Lord kept there as a memorial of the affliction of the children of Israel, who had been forced to make bricks in Egypt, and from which He delivered them. The Hazzekuni says that there was a woman by the name of Rachel who used to assist her husband in mixing the clay, and while doing so she suffered a miscarriage and lost her infant in the clay. She cried unto the Lord, and the angel Michael came and made a brick out of the clay in which the infant was lost, and placed the same under the name of God; therefore the brick is called לבנת הספיר, which means a brick made out of the membrane in which the infant was kept in his mother's womb. And the seventy elders who had been overseers over the children of Israel in Egypt, and who secretly assisted their unfortunate brethren, now merited to see the brick under the Throne of God, and were also privileged the honour to be elders in Israel.

11. *AND THEY BEHELD GOD.* NADAB AND ABIHU AND THE SEVENTY ELDERS ATE AND DRANK AND BEHELD GOD. To behold God was an offence worthy of death, but the Lord

wished not to upset the joyous occasion and waited until the eighth day of Nisan, and then He caused Nadab and Abihu to die for their sins.[3] The elders, however, He caused to die in the wilderness when all Israel murmured against God and asked for meat to eat.

12. COME UP TO ME INTO MOUNT SINAI. Soon after the Decalogue was given, Moses went up and acquainted himself with the entire Torah and with the six hundred and thirteen[4] precepts. Joshua, his servant, accompanied Moses only to the foot of the mountain, since he was not allowed to go farther. Here he pitched a tent and remained for the forty days during which Moses was on the mountain.

14. MOSES SAID UNTO THE ELDERS, TARRY YE HERE with the people, and exercise judgment among them; and let Hur, the son of Miriam, be included among the judges.

15-16. AND WHEN MOSES WENT UP THE MOUNTAIN A CLOUD COVERED THE MOUNTAIN, until the sixth day in which the Lord gave the Torah, and the cloud rested on the mountain seven days after the giving of the Torah. There Moses remained for forty days and forty nights. The verse teaches us to honour Moses, and to compare him to the angels, who neither eat nor drink. The forty days on the mountain Moses spent in studying the Torah, therefore he merited that for forty years his face shone so brightly that no man could look into it; and Moses had to cover the glow of his face with a veil, and this was a great honour to him. That glow remained with him until his death. Moses lived as many years as the number of days he spent on the mountain. We read that Moses three times went up on the mountain and tarried there for forty[5] days each time; that would make the total number of days one hundred and twenty; and Moses lived one hundred and twenty years. During the whole six days at the giving of the Torah, Moses was covered with a cloud and could not be seen. And on the seventh day the Lord cleared a path in the cloud and Moses drew nigh and spake with God.

2. *THAT THEY TAKE FOR ME AN OFFERING.* King Solomon, may he rest in peace, says, "Receive my instruction and not silver." [1] The verse teaches that a man should strive after learning, and with gladness receive the exhortations of the Torah, rather than strive after money. With the help of the Torah one can acquire this world, as well as the world to come, but the amassing of much wealth may lead to harm and worry. The verse, therefore, says, "receive my instruction," meaning receive it gladly and not sadly. When one does a good deed without the right motive and without joy, the deed is worth nothing. The same applies to charity. If one gives charity because other people do so, or because of compulsion, such motives are not right. [2]

6. *OIL FOR THE LIGHT.* This was a symbol of the Messiah, who will shed light like pure oil, and who will deliver us from the dark bondage, as it is written, "I have ordained a lamp for mine anointed." [3] The Parashah of Terumah teaches us that if the children of Israel in the Diaspora will give offerings and charity, they will be redeemed from their bondage. Rashi says that in the Parashah כי תצא the Torah instructs a merchant to use correct scales, [4] and that the same instruction has its place near the story of Amalek, who killed many of the children of Israel, to show that improper use of money and false scales may cause enemies to arise against Israel and kill many of them and take away their money. The Midrash teaches us that as long as the Tabernacle and the Temple existed they protected Israel against being led away into captivity, but when the Temple was destroyed charity took its place. The Torah therefore recalls all the captivities at the offerings of the Tabernacle.

7. *ONYX STONES, AND STONES TO BE SET.* Bahya says that workmen were not permitted to cut the precious stones but had to use them as they were found; for precious stones possess charms only when they are whole and not cut up. Now, if it be asked, how

letters could have been engraved on the stones without cutting away anything, the answer is found in the Gemara tractate Sotah.[5] The letters were painted with ink over the stones, a small worm called "Shamir" was placed over the letters, and the Shamir engraved them upon the precious stones without cutting anything away. And the precious stones were set in gold to teach us that the Torah is above gold and silver.

8. *AND LET THEM MAKE ME A SANCTUARY.* The Yalkut quotes a saying from the Pesikta [6] to the effect that Moses heard three things from God which made him fear:

(1) When the Lord commanded him to build a Tabernacle that He might dwell therein, Moses said that there was not enough timber and stone in the whole world for building a house wherein God could dwell, since He fills the whole universe. But the Lord said to Moses that it was not so, inasmuch as twenty boards on the North side and twenty boards on the South side and eight boards on the West side would be a house sufficient for Him to dwell therein.

(2) When the Lord commanded Moses to bring sacrifices, Moses said that all the beasts and fowls in the world would not suffice. However, the Lord told Moses that it was not so, but to bring only two lambs a day, and not even then both together, but to bring one in the morning and the other in the evening.

(3) When the Lord said that every man should give a ransom for his soul, Moses feared and said that all the money in the world would not suffice to ransom a single soul, but the Lord said that this was not so, but let every one give only a small coin and it will be enough. This is like unto a parable about a man who had a daughter, and as long as she was small he was not restrained from talking with her on the streets, or in the market, in public, but when she grew up, he was no longer at ease to talk with her, except at home. Likewise when the children of Israel were in Egypt, God spake to them in the open, as it is written "I will go through the land of Egypt." Later He spoke to them at the Red Sea, but when

they had received the Torah on Mount Sinai they became spiritually mature, and the Lord said that it was no longer proper to speak to them in open places; He therefore commanded a Tabernacle be built where He could speak to them. Bahya says that the sanctuary was divided into three parts. The first part, the Holy of Holies. Behind the veil there were the Ark, the Tables with the Ten Commandments, and the Cherubim. The first part symbolized Heaven, where the angels dwell, who are absolute wisdom and understanding; and they are to be compared with the Torah within the Ark, which symbolizes wisdom and understanding. The same can be compared to a man who has a head in which there is a brain containing understanding and a mouth which speaks with understanding, for a man is judged by his words, whether he be wise or foolish.

In the second part of the Sanctuary, in the front of the veil, were the Table, the Candlestick, and the Altar of Incense. These were important objects, but not as important as those in the first part. The objects in the second part can be compared with the solar system, which includes the sun, the moon and the stars, and which, although of great importance, are nevertheless not as important as the angels. The same can also be compared to a man, whose heart is the seat of life, as the sun and the moon with their light are the centre of life for the world.

The third part, the outer court, was the place where the animals were sacrificed. This part can be compared with the world, wherein everything perishes and dies. This part can also be compared with the parts in the human body, the heart and the digestive organs, which consume and digest the food which man eats and drinks. Bahya says that the three divisions in the Sanctuary teach us that if a man be pious he can be compared to the three divisions in the universe; i.e., the angels, the constellations, and the world; and the Shekinah will rest upon him, as she rested upon the Tabernacle.

10. *AND THEY SHALL MAKE AN ARK OF ACACIA WOOD.* Bahya points out that at the making of the Ark it is said

"they shall make," and at the making of the other vessels it is said "thou shalt make." The reason for using the plural "they" in the first instance and the singular "thou" in the second instance is that the first instance deals with the Ark, which contained the Torah. It is therefore said "they shall make," in order that the whole world should have a part in the study of the Torah, and that no Israelite make any excuse that he has no part in the Torah. That is the opinion of the Imre No'am and the Ba'al Hatturim. The making of the Ark is mentioned first, and the rest of the vessels afterwards, to teach us that man should first spend an hour or two in the morning studying the Torah before doing business or work. Bahya adds another reason why at the making of the Ark it is said, "they shall make"; namely, in order to encourage the whole world to support the study of the Torah. He who is not able to study should with his money support scholars, that they may study, and that he may thereby have a share in their study.

11. *THOU SHALT OVERLAY IT WITH PURE GOLD.* The verse teaches us that God provides a defence [7] for the scholars who study the Torah, and for the people who with their money support the scholars, as it is written, "For wisdom is a defence, even as money is a defence." [8] God makes an alliance between him who studies the Torah and him who supports the scholar in the study thereof, as it is written, "She is a tree of life to them that lay hold upon her." [9] It means that the Torah gives long life to him who helps in the study thereof, although he himself does not study. In the making of the Ark half cubits are employed, as it is written, "Two cubits and a half shall be the length thereof, and a cubit and a half the breadth thereof, and a cubit and a half the height thereof." This is to say that a scholar should keep himself humble, broken in spirit, and without pride. The Toldoth Yitschak says that the words "Thou shalt cover it with pure gold within and without" mean to say that a scholar should be inwardly in his heart as he is outwardly with his mouth, Alas, there are many scholars who talk piously with their mouths but vanity is in their hearts. Our sages say that

the Torah can be compared to a pure glass or to a mirror, therefore a scholar should be like a mirror showing his inwardness as much as his outwardness. The Imre No'am says that the Ark was made of wood covered with gold, to teach us that when a scholar is poor he should be covered up with gold. Bahya and the Toldoth Yit-schak say that it is written at the making of the Ark עליו ועשית זהב זר,[10] but at the making of the Table and the Altar it is said זר זהב ועשית לו[11] because the latter symbolized the crown of royalty and wealth; therefore the word לו is used.[12] The same is also true of the priesthood, which is symbolized by the Altar where the priest officiated. There, too, the word לו is used.[13] The reason for the use of the word לו in these instances is that priesthood and kingship are hereditary. If the father be a priest, the son follows him into priesthood; and if the father be a king, the son may inherit the throne. But in connection with the Ark, the word עליו is used because the Torah is not hereditary. A man may be a scholar but his son may be an ignoramus; therefore at the Ark it is said "*Make upon it*" i.e., "Make thou a crown upon it." It means to say that a man should make an effort to study the Torah, for it is not an hereditary privilege. The Midrash says, that at the Ark, which contained the Decalogue, the word ועשית עליו is used to teach us that the Torah is a crown above all crowns, above the crown of kingship and above the crown of priesthood, for neither the crown of kingship nor the crown of priesthood amounts to very much, if there be no Torah.

18. *AND THOU SHALT MAKE TWO CHERUBIM.* Bahya says that the Scripture used the word שנים and not שני to show us that the two cherubim were not identical. One was a male, and the other a female. But in connection with the two Tables containing the Ten Commandments the word שני is used because the Tables were identical.

22. *BETWEEN THE TWO CHERUBIM.* Here the Scripture uses the word שני to teach us that God's love for Israel is like

the love of a male for a female. The Gemara in tractate Yoma [14] says, that at the feasts when the Jews went up to the Temple in Jerusalem, the veil was drawn aside and they were shown the two cherubim as a sign that God loved them as much as a man loves a woman.

23. *AND THOU SHALT MAKE A TABLE*. The Lord commanded Moses to make a Table for the Tabernacle, and place bread upon it, that the priests might eat thereof. And when there were many priests, and one ate a piece of the bread, even a small piece, as small as a lentil, one was filled to satiety. The table is therefore called שלחן, which comes from the verb שלח, meaning "to send," because the Lord sends His blessing from the Table.

SHITTIM WOOD. The verse means to teach us that the letter in the word שטים stands for [15] שלום (peace), טובה (Goodness), ישועה (Salvation), מחילה (Forgiveness). These things come because of the Table. The same was also true of the Ark and the Altar, through which came all blessings upon the earth. The Table was also to be compared with an Altar which made atonement for sin, for when one feeds the poor, it is like offering a sacrifice. It was therefore customary among Jews in France, when a pious man died, to make his bier out of the wood of his table as a sign that man takes nothing with him, except the charity he did in sharing the bread on his table with others.

29. *AND THOU SHALT MAKE THE DISHES*. Iron pans were made for the baking of the Shewbread, and when it was baked, the Shewbread was taken out and placed in golden pans, and stored away until the Sabbath morning when it was placed upon the Table.

31-32. AND THOU SHALT MAKE A CANDLESTICK OF PURE GOLD AND THERE SHALL BE SEVEN BRANCHES. The Lord commanded this in order that man should stand in awe when he sees the beautiful candlestick, and thus respect the Sanctuary. The candlestick was kept on the outside of the veil as an indication that the people are in need of light, but not God. The soul rejoices in light because it comes from Heaven where there is much light. King Solomon compared the soul to a candle, as it is written, "The spirit of man is the lamp of the Lord." [16] The candlestick had seven branches to be compared with the seven stars of the constellation, which govern the course of the universe. The candlestick stood on the south side of the Sanctuary because the people of the south abound in learning and in wisdom which can be compared to light, as it is written, "The Commandment is a lamp; and the Law is light." [17] The Table, which is a symbol of wealth, stood on the north side because gold comes from the north, as it is written, "Out of the north cometh golden splendour." [18] The candlestick stood near the Table to show that one cannot study the Torah without bread to eat. The Ba'al Hatturim says that the Parashah dealing with the candlestick does not contain the letter ס because Satan[19] is afraid of light and an evil encounter avoids light.

Let everyone therefore be warned, so far as possible, to carry a light at night. The Midrash and Bahya, commenting on Parashah Bereshith, say that it is known that Satan has his main power on the eve of the Sabbath. It is recorded in the Gemara, in tractate Nizikin,[20] that Satan used to stir up two neighbours against each other on every Sabbath eve, and that Rabbi Meir used to restore the peace among them. Satan was later heard calling out three times on a Sabbath that Rabbi Meir ousted him out of his dwelling, because he made peace between the quarrelling parties, and Satan cannot dwell in a place where peace abides. Satan has his main power on the Sabbath eve, because, as the Midrash Rabba says, the Lord created the demons late on the Sabbath eve. Jews therefore say the prayer מגן אבות [21] on the Sabbath eve, as a protection against demons. One is exhorted to listen to the blessings recited by the Cantor, and not to talk in the middle of the prayers. Rabbi Hirtz, in his סדר התפלה tells the story of a Rabbi who died and later appeared to his disciple in a dream. The disciple noticed a mark on the Rabbi's forehead and asked the meaning thereof. The Rabbi replied that he got the mark because of his bad habit of talking when the Cantor was reciting the מגן אבות and the קדיש . Another reason for the mark was that he failed to cut his fingernails before the Sabbath and therefore he was put to shame. The "Sefer Haggan" [22] says that one should not cut one's fingernails on a Thursday, because they would begin to grow on the third day, which would be a Sabbath day. Women light candles on the Sabbath eve because women and Satan were created together; women therefore light candles to banish Satan, who was created on the eve of the Sabbath.

40. *AND SEE THAT THOU MAKE THEM AFTER THEIR PATTERN.* The Lord said to Moses: "Make the candlestick according to the pattern which was shown unto thee," because the Lord had shown him a candlestick of fire in order that he might make one of gold, but Moses could not copy the pattern; therefore the Lord ordered him to throw the gold into the fire and the candlestick would fashion itself. Bahya says that it is written כתבניתם and not בתבניתם to show that Moses could not make the candlestick according to the pattern shown to him, because fire in Heaven is not like fire on earth; it is spiritual fire. The Toldoth Yitschak says that the Ark symbolizes the scholar, who believes in his heart what he confesses with his mouth and who trusts in God. He who has true faith in his heart will inherit this world and the world to come, and will be like an angel. The Ark was made of wood, and the Cherubim upon it symbolized angels sitting upon wood, to teach us that man, although he be flesh and blood, can nevertheless reach the high levels of angels. The Table symbolizes earthly goods, and the Candlesticks symbolize the world to come, where there is much light. The boards of the Tabernacle symbolize disciples standing around their master like the boards around the Tabernacle. The curtains symbolize the people who support and protect the scholars as the curtains protected the Tabernacle.[23]

CHAPTER XXVII

20. *AND THOU SHALT COMMAND.* Bahya quotes the saying of King Solomon that "Ointment and incense rejoice the heart; so

doth the sweetness of a man's friend that cometh of hearty counsel," [2] and infers from the same that one should be kind to the stranger and the poor, and feed them. King Solomon compared victuals to ointment and incense, which have a pleasant smell, in order to teach us that the poor should be well fed so that their hearts may rejoice; also that kind words be spoken to them. By "the sweetness of a man's friend," the verse means that one should speak sweetly to the poor as if he were a personal friend and from the bottom of one's heart, as the words "of hearty counsel" would imply, and not like some who invite a poor man to a meal but at heart wish he would not come. The Midrash interprets the words "ointment and incense rejoice the heart" as meaning that the ointment and the incense rejoiced the heart of the Holy One, blessed be He, in the way He rejoiced at the creation of the world, as it is written "Let the Lord rejoice in His works." [3] Likewise the Lord rejoiced after the completion of the Tabernacle, when the oil candles were lighted and incense burned. God created man last of all His creation, because man was the most important act of creation. Likewise, after the Tabernacle was completed, God commanded the High Priest to light the oil candles in the Tabernacle.

AND THOU SHALT COMMAND, to burn olive oil and not oil made from rapeseed nor from nuts. The first flow of oil pressed out of the olives was for the lighting of the oil candles on the candlestick, and the second flow was to be used with the sacrifices.

THAT THEY BRING UNTO THEE. [4] The verse means to say that if thou rightly observest the Torah she will remain with thee in this world and in the world to come; and the Commandments thou observest no one shall take from thee. The Scripture uses the term "UNTO THEE" meaning "Make light unto thyself for the Lord does not need thy light, He has enough light in Heaven." The same can be compared to a parable about a guide who was hired to lead a blind man, and who asked the blind to light a candle for him, but the blind man replied, "I have hired thee to guide me on the right path in the dark, and askest thou me to light thee a candle?"

"Yes," replied the guide, "I ask thee to light a candle for me, in order that people might see that thou also renderest some service unto me." Likewise, the children of Israel were compared to blind people walking in darkness, and the Lord guided them and asked of them that they light a candle for Him, so that they might have an opportunity to serve him and be rewarded with many blessings for doing His will.

BEATEN FOR THE LIGHT. The text indicates that the first Temple lasted four hundred and ten years, and the second four hundred and twenty years, making together eight hundred and thirty years, which corresponds to the numerical value of the letters in the word כתית (beaten). The word כתית was an allusion to the two Temples, which were destined to be beaten and broken by enemies. However, the Temple which will be built when the Messiah comes will remain forever. This is inferred from the word למאור which points to the Messiah, who will lighten us with everlasting light. The Ba'al Hatturim says that Moses' name is not mentioned in this section, because when the Lord was wroth with the children of Israel for having made the Golden Calf, and wanted to consume them, Moses interceded on their behalf and asked that his name be blotted out from the book, if God would not forgive the people their sin. Moses' name therefore is not mentioned here, because the curse of a sage cannot be made void. The Tzror Hamor says that Israel in the Diaspora is compared to an olive which is pressed, because the children of Israel are pressed on all sides, but in the end they shall go forth, and shed light like olive oil lights, and that this is for the sake of the Torah, which is compared to an olive.

CHAPTER XXVIII

4. *AND THESE ARE THE GARMENTS WHICH THEY SHALL MAKE.* The High Priest was like an angel, and when he ministered to God he had to be dressed differently from other people; and he was also to be as pure as an angel, when he sacrificed

before the Lord. Bahya and the Toldoth Yitschak say that the Gemara tractate Erakin [1] maintains that the garments of the High Priest had as much expiatory power as the sacrifice itself.

The Breastplate which the High Priest wore against the heart made expiation for sins coming from neglect of the laws and commandments. The Ephod made expiation for idolatry. The Robe which was an outer garment made expiation for evil talk, and the Coat of chequer work, which was an undergarment, made expiation for murder.[2] The Mitre which was worn on the head made expiation for man's pride. The Girdle made expiation for evil thoughts coming from the heart. The Plate which was of pure gold worn on the forehead made expiation for arrogance. The Breeches made expiation for adultery. Bahya says that the verse [3] enumerates only six of the eight articles of clothing which belonged to the High Priest, and that the reason for this is that the verse counts only the articles with which Moses was to dress the High Priest publicly, but the Breeches which the High Priest was to put on in private by himself are not enumerated in this verse. Nor does the verse count the Plate on the forehead, which was an ornament and not an article of clothing.

6. *AND THEY SHALL MAKE THE EPHOD.* Bahya asks why in verse 4 the Breastplate should be placed before the Ephod, and in this verse the making of the Ephod comes first. The same answers the query by saying that the reason for this is that this verse deals with the making of the clothes, and the Ephod was a larger article of clothing than the Breastplate. But in verse 4 the Breastplate was placed first, because it contained the Holy names. Half of the Breastplate contained the names of the tribes Reuben, Simeon, Levi, Judah, Dan, and Naphtali, and these names were engraved upon a precious stone. The other half of the Breastplate contained the names of Issachar, Zebulon, Gad, Asher, Joseph and Benjamin, which were engraved upon another precious stone; and these two precious stones were made of onyx. The engraving was made by placing upon the stones a small worm called "Shamir," which effected the im-

prints on the stones. And the Ephod was made like a shirt, as wide as the back of a man and as long as to drape down to the sole of the foot. And it had two shoulder straps, and upon each of them was an onyx stone set in gold; and upon each shoulder was engraved the names of six tribes. The Breastplate was made of silk woven with gold, and it had four rows of stones and every row contained three stones; all together they contained twelve stones. Upon every stone was engraved the name of a tribe plus the names of Abraham, Isaac and Jacob, and also other Holy names.

Upon every stone were six letters, and all together the twelve stones contained seventy-two letters corresponding to the seventy-two hours in the six days of the work week, to remind the people that the world was created in six days, and that it is preserved because of the merits of the twelve tribes. Bahya also says that the Breastplate was fixed opposite the heart of the High Priest, and the Ephod against his back and joined to the Breastplate like the Arba Kanfoth.[4] The twelve names of the tribes were in front against the heart of the High Priest and then again they were engraved upon the shoulders. The names upon the Breastplates were called "Urim and Thummim," and when a man desired to inquire of God, he placed himself before the High Priest, who looked upon the Breastplate hanging against his heart; and watching the letters he learned the answer to the enquiry. The High Priest did not use the Breastplate for giving divination to individuals, but only to the King or to the community, when called upon to do so. Bahya says that the twelve stones on the Breastplate were the best among all the precious stones.

The first stone was a ruby, which is red. Upon that stone was engraved the name of Reuben, because Reuben's face blushed when he was shamed before his brethren for defiling the bed of his father Jacob and his stepmother, Bilhah.[5] And the ruby acted as a talisman that if a pregnant woman carried it, she was protected against a miscarriage; or if a woman laboured hard in giving birth to a child, a ruby would also act as a talisman and render the required help. And if a woman finds it difficult to conceive, then a ruby should be ground into powder and the same given the woman to swallow with water, and she should then be able to conceive. The same reminds us of Reuben, who found mandrakes in the field and brought them to his mother Leah, and Leah gave the same mandrakes to Rachel and the latter rewarded Leah with a night's privilege to be with Jacob. And the mandrakes had the effect of making Jacob lustful to unite with Leah. Thus we see that mandrakes help women to conceive and bear children.

The name of the tribe of Simeon was engraved upon a topaz, and the topaz was cut like a prism, and it was of green and yellow colour, because the tribe of Simeon were put to shame and made to turn green and yellow when they committed the sin of whoredom with the daughters of Midian. The topaz possessed a cooling quality which cools down sexual passion, for when the body is hot it lusts for sexual excitement. The topaz is found in abundance in Ethiopia, and because of the hot climate the sexually excited people cool down their bodies with that stone.

The name of the Tribe of Levi was engraved upon a carbuncle. And the carbuncle sparkles like light, and Noah had such a carbuncle with him in the Ark, and it served for a light. The name of the Tribe of Levi was engraved upon the carbuncle because out of that tribe many sages have come, who enlightened the children of Israel with Torah and wisdom; and the carbuncle was a talisman for wisdom.

The name of the Tribe of Judah was engraved upon an emerald. The emerald was green, as Judah's face was green with shame for lying with Tamar, his daughter-in-law. The emerald served as a talisman in war, and caused the defeat of the enemy. The Tribe of Judah won all its wars in the time of King David; and in the days of the Messiah ben-David, Judah will win all his wars.

The name of the Tribe of Issachar was engraved upon a sapphire, and the sapphire was of a transparent white colour, because the tribe studied diligently the Torah which was written on a table of sapphire. Moreover, the two tables upon which Moses wrote the Ten Commandments were hewn out of sapphire, taken from beneath the throne of God; therefore he who studies the Torah will merit that because he studied the Torah which was written upon sapphire, his soul shall rest beneath the throne of God, which is of sapphire. The sapphire is a talisman against sickness and the Torah is a cure for the body.

The name of the Tribe of Zebulun was engraved upon a precious stone called Mother of Pearl [6] which symbolized wealth. The talismanic quality of the Mother of Pearl was that it brought good fortune to the bearer thereof. The same also possessed the charm for bringing sound sleep, and this reminds us of Zebulun at whose birth his mother said, "Now will my husband dwell with me."

The name of the Tribe of Dan was engraved upon a figure which was a turquoise, and it showed the face of a man turned away, to symbolize the tribe of Dan, which turned away from the true God and worshipped strange gods.

The name of the Tribe of Naphthali was engraved upon an agate, which served as a talisman for horse riders against falling off their horses. The name Naphthali means "to cleave," and the stone caused the bearer thereof to cleave to his horse, and not to fall off.

The name of the Tribe of Gad was engraved upon an amethyst which was a crystal, and which could have been found all over the world and was known even to children. Likewise the Tribe of Gad was everywhere and known to everybody, because they were numerous. Their feats in battle were known to all nations, since the tribesmen of Gad used to chop off, with one stroke, the heads and arms of their enemies. The amethyst served as a talisman to strengthen man's heart in battle, and that he be neither afraid, nor torn to pieces in battle.

The name of the Tribe of Asher was engraved upon a beryl. The beryl served as a talisman for digestion; and in the land of Asher grew very digestible food.

The name of the Tribe of Joseph was engraved upon an onyx,

and it served as a talisman for finding favour, like Joseph, who found favour in the eyes of men. A person who wears such a stone has his words accepted by kings and princes.

The name of the Tribe of Benjamin was engraved upon a jasper. The jasper had three colours, red, black and green, and served as a talisman to prevent the shedding of blood. The name of Benjamin was therefore engraved upon the jasper because he refrained from telling his father that Joseph was sold by his brethren. The Hebrew word for jasper consists of two words יש פה, which means there is a mouth, and Benjamin's name was engraved upon a jasper to show that, although he had a mouth, he did not disclose what happened to Joseph. Bahya says that the precious stones had to be kept well polished, otherwise they lost their talismanic qualities. The Toldoth Yitschak also writes about the precious stones and asks of Bahya: "How comes it that the name of Simeon was placed upon a topaz, cut like a prism, on the Breastplate to shame him for his sin, when the purpose of the Breastplate was to expiate sin and bring joy to Israel?" The same answers that the name of Simeon was engraved upon the prism because it did away with adultery, and showed up who committed it. There was a story of a lord who journeyed far from his wife. He took a precious prism and asked of his wife to wear it round her neck, so that she may always remember him while he was gone. She took the selfsame prism and wore it round her neck, but she committed adultery while her husband was gone. When the lord returned he asked to see the prism, and it was split when adultery was committed. When the lord saw the stone split he asked for an explanation. She did not know what to answer, to her shame. Likewise a prism was given to Simeon that he might guard himself against committing adultery, and that he repent that the Lord might forgive him, and thus prevent the prism from splitting in the Breastplate. The Gemara in tractate Sota says that the Shamir was a worm by which the names of the tribes were engraved upon precious stones, and that the worm was as small as a grain of oats, and that it was created at the beginning of the creation. The

Shamir was wrapped in wool and kept in a lead vessel filled with oat bran, and when the Shamir was placed upon stone, iron, or upon any other hard object, it caused it to split.

The Talmud of Jerusalem in tractate Yoma [7] contains the story of a woman named Kamhith, who had seven sons, all high priests in the Temple. Sages inquired of her what she had done to have merited such signal honour, and she related to them, that in all her life she never uncovered the hair of her head before anybody, not even before the ceiling in her house. We find many righteous women, who brought pious children into the world through prayer and chastity; like Hannah, who prayed in the temple at Shiloh, and said: "Lord of the Universe, look upon the pain and miseries of my life and give me a child, and if Thou wilt not hearken unto me and grant my request, then I will hide myself with a strange man, that my husband Elkanah may see and suspect me of committing adultery. Then he will take me to the Temple and place me before the High Priest, who would give me to drink of the 'bitter water,' which was given to a woman suspected of adultery, when there were no witnesses." The High Priest used to say to every woman before administering to her of the "bitter water": "If thou art guilty of adultery let the water make thy body swell, but if thou be innocent and clean of that sin, then may God grant thee pious children." And if the woman had not had previously any children, then after she drank of the water, God blessed the woman with pious children. Therefore Hannah said that she would hide with a strange man, that God might bless her with children, and God heard her prayer and gave her a pious son, Samuel, who was a prophet in Israel.

31. *AND THOU SHALT MAKE THE ROBE OF THE EPHOD*, for the High Priest, and it shall have seventy-two bells on the hem, to give warning when entering into the Holy of Holies; as it is customary among kings not to enter their chambers without first being announced that all might be well. And, although God and the angels know everything in advance without being told, it

was nevertheless necessary for the honour of the angels, which were in the Temple all the time, to warn them that they might leave the place and let the High Priest enter to bring incense before God, and thus avoid the risk of the High Priest being molested by the angels. Likewise, when the High Priest left the Holy of Holies, the bells again signalled that the angels might return to serve God. The bells always rang at the entrance, as if to ask permission to enter, and at the exit, as if to take permission to leave the place.

36. *AND THOU SHALT MAKE A PLATE OF PURE GOLD* for the High Priest to wear upon the forehead, stretching from ear to ear. And at each end of the plate were holes through which silk threads were drawn and firmly fastened behind the High Priest's neck. Bahya says that it was surprising that the priests could withstand the strain of serving daily in summer, and suffering the cold of winter dressed only in one robe, and barefooted. Many scholars were therefore placed at their disposal to see who among the priests were sick and unfit for service, for there were many among them who had intestinal trouble owing to colds and to the fact that they had to dip themselves often in cold water, and walk around barefooted.

CHAPTER XXIX

1. *AND THIS IS THE THING THAT THOU SHALT DO.* Bahya says that the verse uses the term "Dabar" to indicate that when the Temple will be destroyed and no more sacrifices offered, the "Dabar" of prayer will take the place of sacrifices. The Scripture therefore says וזה הדבר, meaning that the "Dabar" will take the place of sacrifices.

The Levites recited every day a different Psalm. On the first day of the week they chanted Psalm XXIV, "The earth is the Lord's and the fulness thereof," because the earth was created on the first day of the week, "for the earth was without form and void and darkness was upon the face of the deep." On the second day of the week they chanted Psalm XLVIII — "A Song, a Psalm of the Sons of Korah," because God separated the Levites from the rest of the people that they might serve Him, as on the second day He separated the waters under the firmament from the waters above the firmament in heaven, which is close to the Holy One, blessed be He. On the third day of the week they chanted Psalm LXXXII, "He judges among the gods," because on the third day God created the Garden of Eden, in which grew all kinds of trees that He might judge man for his sins, as He judged Adam and drove him out of the garden. On the fourth day of the week they chanted Psalm XCIV, "O Lord, thou to whom vengeance belongeth," because God judges the heathen who worship the sun or the moon, which were created on the fourth day. The Holy One, blessed be He, will avenge Himself of their deeds. On the fifth day of the week they chanted Psalm LXXXI, "Sing aloud unto God, our strength." The same chapter also contains the words, "which brought thee up out of the land of Egypt," and also delivered them from the hands of Pharaoh, who was likened to a monster fish, which God created on the fifth day. On the sixth day of the week they chanted Psalm XCIII, "The Lord reigneth; He is apparelled with majesty," because on the sixth day God created man in His own image, and when man walks in the way of the Lord he reigns over all the creatures in the world. On the Sabbath they chanted Psalm XCII, "A Song for the Sabbath day," because God rested on the Sabbath day and therefore we too should rest on the Sabbath. Ibn Shu'aib, commenting on the Parashah, "Remember what Amalek did unto thee," [1] says that our sages have arranged four parashiyyoth; parashath שקלים, [2] parashath זכור, [3] parashath פרה, [4] and parashath החודש [5] the month of Adar. Now parashath שקלים precedes parashath זכור to teach us that the shekels which the children of Israel gave to the Temple had annulled the ten thousand pieces of silver which Haman, a descendant of Amalek, offered to King Ahasuerus for the destruction of the people of Israel. The Holy One, blessed be He, always provides the cure before the plague. The Scripture says, "Remember what Amalek did unto thee," and curse him with thy mouth, because Amalek, although he was separated from the children of Israel by seven kingdoms, he nevertheless crossed them all and slew many Israelites. He had cut off the male organs of his victims and threw them against heaven, telling the Holy One, blessed be He, to take back his circumcisions. That he did in spite of the fact that he saw the miracles which God wrought for Israel, and which caused other nations to fear and refrain from attacking the Israelites. Amalek, however, attacked them, and led others in the same. The Midrash asks why Amalek did not attack the children of Israel before they immigrated to Egypt, when they were few in numbers? In answer to the query several opinions are quoted. Some said that it was due to the fact that Amalek was afraid of Jacob, since Esau with 400 men could not prevail against him; others said that Amalek thought them too insignificant and was ashamed to engage them in battle. Another opinion is recorded as saying that Amalek reasoned with himself that, if he would destroy the children of Israel, prior to their immigrating to Egypt, he himself would run the risk of coming into Egyptian bondage, since God had foretold to Abraham that his descendants would serve Egypt, and Amalek, coming from the line of Esau, was a descendant of Abraham and Isaac. Now when the children of Israel were slack in the observance of the Torah and the precepts, Amalek has the upper hand over them. And a cloud surrounded the children of Israel in the wilderness and protected them against the bows and arrows of Amalek, but the wicked among Israel were thrown outside the camp by the cloud and left to be slain by Amalek.

Haman, who was a descendant of Amalek, likewise gained the upper hand over the children of Israel, because they were sinful and ate of the food at the feast which Ahasuerus made. Another opinion concerning the sin of Israel says that it was idol-worship. In connection with Haman's plans to destroy the children of Israel, the Scripture uses three terms: "to destroy," "to slay," "to perish." [6] "To destroy" means to destroy the souls of Israel, by destroying the

Torah. "To slay" means to slay their bodies; and "to perish" means to take away all their money and their possessions. At the feast of Purim, the children of Israel make therefore a threefold celebration. First, they read the book of Esther, to commemorate the failure of Haman's plan to destroy the Torah; second, they feast to rejoice their bodies, contrariwise to the plan of slaying their bodies; third, they send gifts to the poor as a reminder of Haman's plans to take away everything they had. Ibn Shu'aib asks why our sages make Purim the principal feast for feasting and drinking, while at other feasts wine is not essential? Moreover, how cometh it that our sages should encourage much drinking, which is the cause of much evil, as we find in the case of Noah and Lot, who disgraced themselves and the latter committed incest with his own daughters? How cometh that the Gemara [7] says that one must drink to drunkenness, and Rabban that one must drink till one falls asleep? There is a story that Raba was very drunk on Purim and killed his friend, Rabbi Ze'era; then Raba prayed and revived him. The following Purim Raba invited Ze'era to drink with him again, but he refused, saying, "God does not perform miracles every day, maybe you will kill me again." Another reason for drinking on Purim is that the whole story of King Ahasuerus, from beginning to end, was the result of excessive drinking. The King made four feasts. The first feast was given by the King and his Queen, Vashti, at which the queen lost her life and her crown was given to Esther, who saved the children of Israel from the hands of Haman. The second feast the King gave when he took Esther for his wife, and at which occasion two of his chamberlains, Bightham and Teresh, conspired to poison him. However, their conversation, which was understood by nobody else, was understood by Mordecai, and the latter revealed the plot to Esther, and she in turn reported it to the King on behalf of Mordecai. The two conspirators were hanged, and it was written down in the records that Mordecai saved the King's life. Now, in the night, before Haman planned to hang Mordecai, the book of records of chronicles was read to the King and it was found in them what Mordecai did for the King. And the King was wroth against Haman for daring to hang a good man, who saved his life, and ordered Haman to be hanged instead. All this came through drink at the second feast.

BUT HE THOUGHT SCORN.[8] The Midrash maintains that God, the Holy One, blessed be He, said to Haman: "I have not destroyed the children of Israel in the wilderness when they made the Golden Calf; how then darest thou, O wicked Haman, to plan their destruction now?" The same can be compared to a parable about a bird which had a nest on the seashore, and a gale came and blew it into the sea. In wrath the bird sought to drain the sea. It carried water from the sea to the land and dropped sand into the sea. Another bird came and asked what it was doing, and being told that because the sea drowned the nest, the bird in revenge sought to make the sea dry, the other bird then replied that it was impossible, and that anyone attempting such a task would perish. Haman likewise tried to destroy the children of Israel, but the Lord saved them.

THERE IS A CERTAIN PEOPLE.[9] Haman said to the King that the children of Israel differed from the rest of the world in their religious faith, their Torah, and their festivals. Every seventh day they observe the Sabbath and every thirtieth day they observe the Feast of the Month, and then the Passover, Pentecost, New Year, the Day of Atonement, and the Feast of the Booths [10] and the Feast of Assembly.[11] The Holy One, blessed be He, then said: "O wicked, thou complainest against the many festivals the Israelites observe, and lo and behold, I will add one more, Purim, which they will observe with great joy, and when thou art hanged."

The third feast King Ahasuerus gave when he and Haman sat down to eat and drink, and at which the King took off the ring from his finger and gave it unto Haman to seal with it the decrees for destroying the children of Israel. But as soon as the children of

Israel learned of it, they proclaimed a great fast and did penance and God heard them and delivered them. All these things happened as the result of festivities.

AND FAST YE FOR ME AND NEITHER EAT NOR DRINK.[12] The Scripture seems to imply that Mordecai and Esther have fasted in the days of the Passover. Ibn Shu'aib asks why it was necessary to say "neither eat" when it is said "fast" and it is obvious that to fast means not to eat? The answer to the query, according to the same source, is that the fast was called for the days of the Passover, when the children of Israel were supposed to eat unleavened bread and drink four cups of wine and rejoice. But they were called to refrain from taking any food even for the celebration of the Passover.[13]

The fourth feast was when Esther gave a two days' reception for the King, at which she exposed Haman and hastened his downfall. Rabbi Abraham asks why Mordecai wished to have the Amalekites destroyed; was it not enough for him that the lives of the Jews were spared? The answer to the question is that Ahasuerus told Mordecai to be wise in the matter of protecting the lives of the Jews, since letters had already been sent by Haman in the name of the King against the Jews, and the King's decree could not be altered. Then Mordecai did what the King told him and wrote letters in the name of the King, to the effect that the King's original decree was that the Jews should lay hands on the Amalekites, and not the Amalekites to lay hands on the Jews on the thirteenth day of Adar. Haman misled the King and, therefore, was hanged. It is, therefore, incumbent upon the people to obey the King's original decree and let the Jews lay hands on the Amalekites on the same day. Ibn Su'aib asks why the Gemara[14] says that the sons of Haman were hanged all together and died at once when the Scripture says[15] "And in Shushan the Palace, the Jews slew Parshandatha" and that the sons of Haman died by the sword; and further Scripture says[16] that Esther asked the King that the sons of Haman be hanged? The answer to the query is that the sons of Haman were first slain with the sword but did not die, so Esther asked the King that they be hanged and die. May the Lord grant us the privilege to see our heathen enemies perish in the days of the Messiah.

The story of Haman is recalled in this section because this portion of Scripture is read in the week in which Purim is observed, if it be not a leap year.

CHAPTER XXX

12. *WHEN THOU TAKEST*. Bahya quotes King Solomon as saying, "The fear of the Lord prolongeth days, but the years of the wicked shall be shortened," [1] and declares that the text teaches us that God performs secret miracles for man's sake every day, but man neither thinks nor does he enquire after them. From the verse in Proverbs we learn that the Holy One, blessed be He, performs miracles every day. He prolongs the life of the righteous and shortens the life of the wicked. Fear rather shortens man's life, and yet the Scripture says that the righteous who fear the Lord live long and are not affected by fear. This is what the verse means, "The fear of the Lord prolongeth days." It is also obvious that good food helps to prolong life, and yet the wicked, although he eats well, is nevertheless cut down by the hand of the Lord. True, there are some righteous people whose span of life is short, and there are some wicked people whose span of life is long, but the reason for this is that the righteous are not wholly righteous, and the wicked are not wholly wicked. Another explanation might be that God sometimes shortens the life of a righteous man, that he may enjoy greater bliss in the world to come. Man has to believe that God works miracles for him, of which man is unaware, and he who does not believe in that, does not believe in the Torah, and is not a Jew. Our sages have said that God's blessing does not come upon things which are measured, since God performs miracles only upon the things which are in secret. The same have also said that, if one measures anything and then asks for God's blessing upon it, such prayer is in vain,

because an evil eye comes upon things which are counted or measured. The Lord therefore forbade Israel to be numbered, except through the shekels, which they gave; and by counting the shekels the number of Israelites was determined. Our text says, "they shall give every man a ransom for his soul, that there be no plague among them." If the children of Israel were to be numbered individually, God would look upon every one individually and see his shortcomings and would cut him down. But when the whole community is taken together there would be among them righteous people, whose good deeds would make up for the deficiencies of the others and protect one another.

13. *HALF A SHEKEL.* Moses was a king among Israel and minted his silver coins, as it was customary for kings to mint their own coins. That coin was called "Holy Shekel" because all holy things were weighed according to it. A first born male was redeemed with five shekels, and the shekel was also used in connection with other precepts; and since the precepts were written in the Torah, which is holy, the shekel too was called holy. The language in which the Torah was written is called "holy" because God spoke in that language to the prophets. The seventy names of God and the names of the angels were written in the Holy tongue, and the world too was created in the Holy tongue. Now when the Messiah will come, all the world and all the peoples will speak in the Holy tongue,[2] as it is written, "For then I will turn to all the peoples a pure language, that they may all call upon the name of the Lord";[3] God commanded the children of Israel, that every one of them give half a shekel, because in making the Golden Calf they broke the Ten Commandments, and the half a shekel which consisted of ten gerahs[4] was to make expiation for the breaking of the Ten Commandments. Another reason why God commanded to give half a shekel was that it made expiation for the sin of the Golden Calf, which had been made in the middle of the day. The Tzror Hamor says that the Parashah כי תשא stands near the Parashah קטורת, because incense holds off epidemics which come as the result of numbering the

people, and the same also teaches us that God wishes to save us from peril.

THEY SHALL GIVE EVERY MAN A RANSOM FOR HIS SOUL,[5] in order to prevent the coming of epidemics, on account of counting the people. The verse means that so long as the Temple would stand, incense would prevent epidemics, but that after the Temple would be destroyed, righteousness would take the place of incense, as it is written, "Righteousness delivereth from death." [6] Our sages say, and it is also written in the Parashah, that God forgives sins once a year, on the Day of Atonement; therefore the Parashah began with the words כי תשא [7] meaning: "Thou, God, shalt 'take away' and pardon the sins of the children of Israel," because of the alms [8] they give. And God commanded to give half a shekel to teach us that He does not ask much, but only half a shekel, from the rich and the poor alike. Bahya says that the half a shekel given to the Temple was symbolic, to teach us that man should divide his substance between his physical and spiritual needs. Man should not over-feed his body with meat and drink, but he should eat to be able to serve God with his body as with his soul. Out of the half shekels which the children of Israel contributed were made silver sockets to hold the borders of the Tabernacle, and the silver sockets made expiation for the sin of the Golden Calf. The Scripture teaches us that a repentant sinner should be low in spirit like a socket, over which people trample, and that the children of Israel should see the sockets and repent of their sin.

17-21. The Torah places the Parashah dealing with the laver near the Parashah dealing with the shekels, because the shekels remind us of the need for giving alms by providing food on the table for the poor, and that one remember to wash hands before meals, and that the greatest act of charity is giving food to visitors. Another reason why the two Parashiyyoth are close to each other is that the penalty for not giving alms is poverty, and the same penalty follows for not washing one's hands before eating. Our sages used to say that he who washes his hands in abundance of water will enjoy the abundance of all things. The priests washed their hands and feet under the laver by placing their hands upon their feet and letting the water run on both at the same time. They placed their right hands upon their right feet, and their left hands upon their left feet, and let the water run upon their hands and feet simultaneously. The laver contained twelve spouts for the twelve priests required at the daily sacrifices; for twelve priests occupied themselves with the daily sacrifices. However, the thirteenth priest who slaughtered the animal had no need to wash himself; therefore, there were twelve spouts, and not thirteen in the laver.

31. *THIS SHALL BE AN HOLY ANOINTING OIL UNTO ME.* Bahya, in the name of Nachmanides, asks why our text says "unto me" when the oil was required for the anointing of the priests, and not for God. The answer is that the oil was required not only for the anointing of the priests, but also for the anointing of kings, as it was in the case of King David and others.

35. AND THOU SHALT MAKE A PERFUME. Eleven kinds of spices were mixed into the incense and burned in the Sanctuary. Our sages say that among the sweet spices was mingled one spice called "Galbanum," which smelled like the devil's dung, to show that God is not ashamed of sinners who repent and join themselves to the righteous in fasting and in prayer. Our sages further say that when a congregation fasts and prays, yet has no repenting sinners in its midst, then something is wrong with such a congregation, for the Lord is exalted by the repentance of sinners, and by their numbering themselves among the righteous. However, when no repenting sinners are present in the congregation, the righteous suffer, because all Israel is responsible for one another. For the same reason the "lulab" [9] is joined with four "hoshanoth" [10] which have no sweet smell nor taste, to symbolize the sinners who have neither Torah nor merits. The other things taken together with the "lulab" have some good qualities. The "ethrog" [11] has a pleasant smell and a pleasant taste, and the "haddasim" [12] too have a sweet smell. Upon

the "lulab" grow tasty dates, nevertheless the tasteless and the odourless things are taken together with the good and tasty things, to show that God desires the sinners to repent and be numbered among the righteous.

CHAPTER XXXI

2. *SEE I HAVE CALLED BY NAME BEZALEL.* The verse teaches us that there were no craftsmen in Israel who knew how to handle gold, silver, or silk, for all they had learned in Egypt was to dig clay and make bricks. The verse, therefore, praises Bezalel who was very clever and although he was at that time only a lad of twelve, nevertheless had within him the gift of prophecy and knew how to work in gold and silver, silk and many other crafts, which were necessary in the work of the Sanctuary.

6. *AND WITH HIM AHOLIAB — THE SON OF AHISA-MACH, OF THE TRIBE OF DAN.* God paired up Aholiab of the humble tribe of Dan with Bezalel of the mighty tribe of Judah, to show that man should not think too highly of himself, and if he be of an influential family, he should not disdain the company of humbler families, for in the sight of God all men are equal, whether poor or rich.

10. *AND THE GARMENTS OF SERVICE.* The high priests' garments are called in Hebrew בגדי השרד, which may mean garments of "remnant," to show that thanks to the priestly garments Israel remained in the world. The Gemara in tractate Yoma* tells us a story about Alexander the Macedonian, who had come against the City of Jerusalem to conquer it, and that Simon the Just, who was high priest at that time, came out dressed in his high priestly garments to meet the conqueror. But when Alexander saw the high priest, he rose from his chariot and bowed before the high priest.

---

*Yoma 69-a

When asked by his servants why he had paid such great homage to a Jew, he replied that in every battle which he fought he saw a vision of a man dressed like the high priest, and that the same helped him to be victorious. It was the apparition of an angel dressed like the high priest.

13. *VERILY YE SHALL KEEP MY SABBATHS.* The verse teaches us that, although God commanded the building of the Tabernacle, yet no work was to be done on the Sabbath, not even for the building of the Tabernacle. Our sages say that the word "verily" in the verse lessens rather than adds weight to the commandment, and the reason for it is that in cases involving danger of life the Sabbath might be violated. Remember that the observance of the Sabbath was the first commandment given to the children of Israel before they received the Torah, and that the Sabbath alone is as important as the whole Torah. Our sages further say that Jerusalem was destroyed because of neglect for the Sabbath observance. The same have also said that, if the children of Israel would rightly observe two consecutive Sabbath days, the Messiah would come immediately. They also said, "When an Israelite serves idols, and then observes the Sabbath, the Holy One, blessed be He, forgives his transgression."

14. *YE SHALL KEEP THE SABBATH.* Once more the Torah repeats the commandment to "keep the Sabbath," and that means to say that the observance of the Sabbath should begin early on Friday evening and should be well kept until Saturday evening, when the Sabbath comes to an end.

EVERY ONE WHO PROFANETH IT SHALL SURELY BE PUT TO DEATH. He who profanes the Sabbath, disregarding warnings against doing so, and if there be witnesses, shall be put to death. But if there be no witnesses and the culprit profaned the Sabbath, God Himself will cut off his days on earth.

16. *TO OBSERVE THE SABBATH.* One should prepare before the Sabbath the things needed for the Sabbath, and God blesses

one's money for the sake of the Sabbath. The Tzror Hamor says that the Scripture repeats twice the injunction to keep the Sabbath because of the two important Sabbath days: one is שבת הגדול [1] to commemorate the exodus from Egypt, when the children of Israel were set free from their Egyptian bondage and no longer had to work physically for Pharaoh, since their bodies were set free. The second Sabbath is שבת שובה [2] which comes between the New Year and the Day of Atonement, when the soul is cleansed from the sins man has committed. Now, on account of two Sabbath days, namely the שבת הגדול when the body was redeemed from bondage and the children of Israel no longer had to perform forced labour; and the Sabbath שובה when the soul is redeemed; therefore it is fitting that Israel should remember the signs and wonders which God wrought for them and that they rest from all manner of work on the Sabbath day.

Bahya says that the Gemara in tractate Yom Tob [3] records Rabbi Simeon Ben Yohai, saying that all commandments were given publicly, except the Sabbath, which was given privately rather than publicly, as it is written, "It is a sign between me and the children of Israel." [4] Bahya asks: "How could the Sabbath have been given in private when it is contained in the Ten Commandments, which were given in public?" The answer to the query is that the verse teaches us that the Sabbath was given for the soul, which is hidden in the body, so that not the body only, but also the soul might rest and study the Torah, in which the soul finds rest; because the soul longs to study the Torah and to observe the precepts. Our sages have said that the Sabbath should be divided into half for God and half for man; half to be spent in festivity and rejoicing, and the other half day in studying the Torah and doing good deeds, and thereby to rejoice the soul; and not like some people who spend the Sabbath day in vain gossip or in unnecessary discussions. Our sages have, therefore, forbidden to discuss secular things on the Sabbath day. The Scripture says, "It is a sign between me and the children of Israel," which means that the Sabbath shall be a covenant only between God and the children of Israel, that they speak about divine things. The Scripture commands "To keep the Sabbath," meaning that the Sabbath should be kept as a time for repentance and for studying the Torah, and for thinking of serving the Holy One, blessed be He, because during the week days man is engaged in labour or in business, and has not enough time to think of spiritual things. The Tzror Hamor says that the words "to do" mean, as the Gemara [5] in the tractate of Shabbath and Kiddushin says, that when a man has even a hundred servants he should still occupy himself with the preparations for the Sabbath; as was the case with Rabbi Joseph, who was the head of the community, and a worthy leader; yet he did not mind roasting a calf's head for the Sabbath. The same is also told of Raba, who too was a community leader and possessed many servants, and still used to busy himself salting his fish for the Sabbath.

18. *AND HE GAVE UNTO MOSES, WHEN HE HAD MADE AN END OF COMMUNING WITH HIM . . . THE TWO TABLES OF STONE.* The verse used the term ככלתו [6] to teach us that God gave to Moses the Torah as a gift, like a man gives gifts to his bride. It was too difficult for Moses to comprehend the whole Torah in the short period of forty days, so God gave him special understanding and the strength required for the task. Resh Lakish says that when one preaches the Torah to a congregation and the people find it not to their taste, it were better for them not to have been born at all. When Israel received the Torah they found it as acceptable as a bride is acceptable to her bridegroom. Rabbi Simeon says that as a bride is adorned with twenty-four ornaments, so should a scholar be adorned with the twenty-four books of the Torah, the Prophets and the Writings.[7] The Tzror Hamor maintains that our verse, "When he had made an end of communing with him," means that Moses came down from Mount Sinai with the two tables as soon as God ceased from communing with him, and that the children of Israel were wicked in claiming the delay of Moses

in coming down as their excuse for making the Golden Calf.

TWO TABLES OF TESTIMONY.[8] God gave to Moses two tables to serve as testimony to Israel that the Shekinah should abide among them. The two tables were like the insignia which a King displays to inform the people of his presence in their midst. Bahya says the Ten Commandments were written on two tables, and not on one, because the tables were for a witness, and two witnesses were required. The tables were of stone, which is on earth, and the writing was from heaven; that heaven and earth might serve as witnesses against Israel, if they failed to keep the Torah, as it is written, "Call heaven and earth to witness against them."[9] Now if the children of Israel were to cease from keeping the Torah, the heavens would cease from giving rain and the earth would cease from bringing forth its produce. Another reason why the Ten Commandments were given on tables of stone was because the trespassing of most of the Commandments incurred the death penalty by stoning.

CHAPTER XXXII

1. *AND WHEN THE PEOPLE SAW THAT MOSES DELAYED TO COME.* On the seventeenth day of Tamuz the children of Israel saw that Moses was tarrying on Mount Sinai. For the Torah was given on the sixth day of Sivan, and during the first six days of the month the mountain was covered with a cloud. After the giving of the Torah, Moses returned to Mount Sinai on the seventh day of Sivan, and told the people that he would remain on the mount for forty days and forty nights, and that he would return on the sixth hour of the fortieth day. He did not include the day on which he ascended the mount, and he therefore expected to return on the sixth hour of the sevententh day of Tamuz. The Israelites, however, did count the day on which Moses ascended, and consequently expected him back on the sixth hour of the sixteenth day of Tamuz, and when the time came and Moses did not return, they said כי בשש, meaning, the sixth hour has passed and Moses has not come back, he must be lost.[1] The Midrash says that Satan had

brought darkness upon the earth on that day and made something which looked like a stretcher being carried appear in the skies, that the Israelites might think Moses was dead. Then the Israelites made the Golden Calf on the seventeenth day (after mid-day), and in the morning they sacrificed to it. Moses returned at the sixth hour as he promised, and when he saw the idol which the children of Israel had made unto themselves, he threw the Tables down and broke them. On the eighteenth day he slew those who worshipped the Golden Calf, and he burned the idol with fire. On the nineteenth day he returned to the mount again to intercede for the children of Israel that their sin might be forgiven; and he remained there in continuous prayer for another forty days. After that, at the beginning of Elul, Moses went up again to receive another set of Tables, and tarried there another forty days, until Yom Kippur, the day on which the Lord forgave Israel the sin of the Golden Calf, and Moses received another set of Tables; and after Yom Kippur the children of Israel brought gifts of gold and silver and silk and precious stones for the building of the Tabernacle. We infer from that, that the section recording the story of the Golden Calf should come before the section recording the building of the Tabernacle.

2. *AND AARON SAID UNTO THEM, BREAK OFF THE GOLDEN RINGS WHICH ARE IN THE EARS OF YOUR WIVES,*[3] and I will make you a god that will lead you. Aaron thought that the women would refuse to give up their earrings and thereby spare him from making a strange god, and that meantime Moses would return; for Aaron well knew that Moses would return on the next day, but the children of Israel were sinful and would not listen to him. Aaron was afraid that if he refused to do the bidding of the people they might kill him, as they killed his nephew Hur, a good man, to whom they went first, requiring of him to make them an idol, and when he refused they killed him. Therefore, Aaron was afraid that the same might happen to him. Aaron's intentions in any case were towards God. The women were more God-fearing than the men and refused to give their earrings for the making of an

idol, so the menfolk took off their rings and brought them to Aaron, who wrapped them up in a piece of cloth and threw them into the fire. Then came the sorcerers from amongst the mixed multitude, which joined themselves to the children of Israel at the Exodus, and through their witchcraft they brought a calf out of the fire. Some sages say that there was a man by the name of Micah, who as a child had been saved from the horrible fate of remaining immured in a brick wall in Egypt; for when the Israelites failed to make the number of bricks apportioned to them, the Egyptians punished them by taking their children away from them and immuring them in brick walls. When Moses saw how much the Israelitish children had to suffer in Egypt, he asked God why they should suffer, even if their parents did sin, and the Lord answered and said that the children too will be wicked. And, in order to convince Moses, He told him to save one child from encasement, revive him, and see into what he would grow up. Moses did so and called the name of the child "Micah," which means "Squashed," [4] because he was squashed in a wall. Micah, however, was very wicked, and took the silver plate with which he brought Joseph's coffin out of the Nile, upon which Moses had engraved the sacred name of God, for the Egyptians had placed Joseph in an iron coffin and buried him in the River Nile. Now, at the time of the Exodus, the children of Israel could not locate the coffin, so Moses took a silver plate and engraved on it the words שׁוֹר עֲלֵה [5] ("come up Ox") and he threw the plate into the river, and the coffin came up. Micah took that same plate and threw it into the fire and out came an ox, which the children of Israel took for a god.

4. *AND MADE IT A MOLTEN CALF.* Bahya says on behalf of Rabban that Aaron fashioned the face of an ox because an ox stands at the left side of the Throne of Glory, facing northward.[6] And from the north comes much evil upon the world, especially was it so in the wilderness, where the children of Israel sojourned, and where the land was utter waste and nothing grew there. Aaron therefore fashioned the face of an ox that God might take pity upon

the children of Israel, and send them a soothing wind from the left side of His throne where the ox stands.

5. *AND WHEN AARON SAW THIS HE BUILT AN ALTAR BEFORE IT.* When Aaron saw the Golden Calf alive and leaping around, he could not dissuade the people from worshipping it, "and he built an altar." Aaron still thought in his heart that Moses might return before he finished building the altar, and that was the reason why he undertook to build the altar himself, for if the people were to assist him in the building thereof, it would have been completed in no time. Aaron had to build the altar out of sheer fear that he might be killed like his nephew, Hur, and he feared that if he were killed Israel might perish because of it. Another reason why Aaron wished to build the altar by himself was that if the children of Israel were to build it, they would have had no excuse, no scapegoat. Aaron, therefore, sought to take the blame on himself, in the hope that God would forgive him, rather than to place the responsibility upon all the people. Bahya says that Aaron thought his intentions towards God were good; he was falling short only in breaking one Commandment, "Thou shalt not make unto thee a graven image."

AND AARON MADE PROCLAMATION AND SAID, TO-MORROW SHALL BE A FEAST TO THE LORD. Moses interceded for Israel and said: "O Lord of the universe, if the children of Israel deserve to be thrown into the fire, remember the merits of Abraham, who let himself be thrown into the fiery furnace for Thy name's sake. If they deserve to be killed by the sword, remember the merits of Isaac, who stretched out his neck over the Altar to let himself be slaughtered for Thy sake. If they deserve to be banished into captivity, remember the merits of Jacob, who escaped to Laban, because of Esau, his brother."

6. AND THEY ROSE UP TO PLAY.[7] The children of Israel danced and mocked God. The Tanna Debe Eliyahu quotes* Rabbi

---

*See also Aboth III, 13.

Akiba as saying that mockery and laughter lead men to many trans-gressions; they cause indecent exposure and adultery. The verse in Jeremiah says, "Hear ye the word of the Lord," [8] ye mockers. The Lord said to Israel: "My children, I sat for nine hundred and sixty-four generations before the Creation, and studied and meditated about the Torah, and since the day of Creation I sit on My Throne of Glory and for eight hours of the day I study the Torah, and for eight hours of the day I pass judgment on the world, and for eight hours I perform acts of charity and feed the whole world; but I neither scoff nor scorn, except at the time when the heathens say they will wage war against the Holy One," blessed be His name. As it is written, "He who sits in Heaven mocks." [9] Once more, we find that God laughs at the burning of incense, when people take fine incense and mix it with devil's dung, which smells. Once again, God laughs when the wicked one would swallow the pious one. As the verse in Psalm says, "The wicked plotteth against the just." However, "The Lord shall laugh at him." [10]

And Aaron also knew well what a great merit there was in teach-ing the Torah to the children of Israel, so he taught them. He taught prayers to those who did not know how to pray, and the ignorant he instructed in the Torah. Great merit was given not only to Aaron, but the same is also given to every person who teaches his friend Torah or prayers, and exhorts him to do what is good. God rewards such a teacher with a better understanding of the wisdom of Torah.

Moses went up on Mount Sinai three times for forty days. The first forty days he spent in receiving the Torah, and at that time Israel made the Golden Calf. The second forty days Moses spent in prayer for Israel, that God might forgive them for making the Golden Calf. At that time Israel was like an accursed thing and Moses removed his tent from the Camp of Israel, for he did not wish to dwell in their midst. Then the Holy One, blessed be He, said to Moses that poor Israel had suffered the curse long enough, and that it was time for Moses to move his tent back into the camp of Israel.

In the third forty-day period Moses went up on Mount Sinai to receive another set of Tables. During that period the children of Israel fasted and lamented over their sin, and at the end of that period they fasted day and night, and with tears in their eyes went to meet Moses on the mount. Moses joined them in lamentation, and God had compassion on them and forgave the sin they had committed by making the Golden Calf. And the Lord said unto them: "Your lament shall be turned into joy and gladness, and the day of Yom Kippur will for all times be unto you a day of atonement in which your sins will be forgiven you."

And Moses brought down the second set of Tables, for he had broken the first set because of the Golden Calf. The letters on the Tables disappeared, for the children of Israel through their sin had proved themselves unworthy to receive them, and Moses was speechless. At the time when Moses had broken the Tables, the Holy One, blessed be He, decreed that from thenceforth Israel shall study the Torah in exile, with anxiety, sadness, and grief, wandering from place to place like a repentant sinner. They shall study it in poverty and in want, because riches prevent studies, and in bodily weakness, because study is weariness to the flesh. However, when the Messiah comes they will study the Torah with elation and gladness, and will inherit joy in the world to come. Commenting on this chapter the Yalqut says that when Moses interceded on behalf of Israel, he asked for permission to punish those who served the Golden Calf. He went down the mount and burned the Golden Calf and called on the children of Israel, saying, "Whoso is on the Lord's side, let him come unto me," for the Lord commanded me to destroy all those who served the idol. That he said, in order to create the impression, that what he was about to do was according to a Commandment from God; however, no such commandment was given. After the children of Levi slew those who worshipped the idol, Moses again interceded on behalf of the people and said: "Lord of the universe, only three thousand worshipped the idol with all their hearts, and desirest Thou to destroy six hundred thousand?" And the Lord had compassion on them. Moses' action can be likened to a parable about a king who was wroth with his eldest son, and delivered him to one of his rulers to do away with him and throw him to the dogs. But the ruler let him live and sent the king's son in hiding from city to city, without revealing to the king his whereabouts. After thirty days the king, in high spirits, gave a great feast, and when he noticed his eldest son's absence he became sad, but none of the servants knew the reason for the king's sadness, except the one who hid the king's son. He went and brought the young prince back to his father, and when the king saw him he rejoiced and gave a crown to the faithful ruler. God likewise rewarded Moses, who saved the children of Israel four or five times from death and made intercession for them. He gave him the crown of the Torah, as it is written, "And the children of Israel saw the face of Moses." They looked at his face, and they could not behold it because it shone like the sun and the moon. The light on Moses' face remained with him forever, even after his death, as it is written, "His eye was not dim," * which means that his eyes and his face shone even after he died. It is also said that upon the face of every sage who studies the Torah day and night, God sheds a light in the world to come, as it is written, "The soul of my Lord shall be bound in the bundle of life with the Lord thy God." [11] The soul of the righteous is with God and shines with the light of the Lord.

7.[12] AND THE LORD SPAKE UNTO MOSES, GET THEE DOWN FOR THY PEOPLE HAVE CORRUPTED THEM- SELVES. Moses answered and said unto God: "Now when they have sinned, Thou sayest 'thy people,' but when they were in Egypt Thou callest them 'my people Israel.' "

10. *AND NOW LET ME ALONE*. Rabbi Eliezer says the Scrip-

---

*Deuteronomy XXXIV: 7.

ture should not contain this verse, for it is inconceivable that Moses would have held on to the Lord and said: "I will not let Thee go until Thou pardonest the sin of the Golden Calf."

13. *TO WHOM THOU SWEAREST BY THINE OWN SELF.* Moses entreated God and said: "Thou hast sworn by Thine own name not to destroy the children of Israel; Thou didst not swear by heaven or by earth, nor by the sea, and it is not meet for Thee to break Thine oath." This is like unto a parable about a king, who planted a vineyard with good vines. Later, when the king came and tasted the wine of the first year's fruit and found it sour, he wished to destroy the vineyard, but the wise husbandman restrained him from doing so, and explained to the king that the wine of the first year's fruit is never so good, and that it will improve in the second year. Moses likewise spoke to God in similar fashion to the effect that the children of Israel will improve in piety. Moreover, he entreated God to keep His promise and multiply the children of Israel, as the stars of heaven, and give them the land of Israel; and God heard the prayers of Moses and pardoned the children of Israel their sin.

15. AND HE TURNED AND WENT DOWN.[13] Moses went backwards down the mount with his face turned towards God, as at the conclusion of the "Amidah," [14] when the Jews step backwards as if they were in the presence of God. The Midrash quotes the Yalqut,* saying that when Moses was about to descend the mountain, he was met by demons who wanted to kill him. He was greatly afraid and sought refuge at the Throne of God, and the Lord protected him and covered him with a cloud. From this incident we can see how harmful sin can be, because before the children of Israel committed sin, Moses went up the holy mount without incident, but after the sin of the Golden Calf, he was afraid of five demons. The names of the demons were Aph, Quetzeph, Mashbith, Mashchith, and Hemah. But as soon as Moses mentioned the names

---

*Shemoth Rabbath 42.

of the patriarchs, Abraham, Isaac, and Jacob, three demons ran away and only two, Aph and Hemah, remained, so Moses entreated the Holy One, blessed be He, to withdraw one and leave him to face only one, which he would withstand, as it is written, קומה יי באפך [15] i. e., "Arise and watch the demon," [16] Aph.

* AND THE TWO TABLES OF THE TESTIMONY IN HIS HAND WRITTEN ON BOTH THEIR SIDES. One could read the writing from both sides, and that was a miracle, for otherwise it is almost impossible to read a man's writing from both sides, because on the left side the script appears upside down.

16. *AND THE TABLES WERE THE WORK OF GOD.* This means to say that the Tables were made in God's honour. Another interpretation of the term "the work of God" is that God rejoices in the Torah night and day. Bahya asks why the text praises here the worthiness of the Tables, when it would have been more appropriate to have done so in the chapter dealing with the giving of the Ten Commandments? The answer is that notwithstanding the great worthiness of the Tables, Moses broke them when the children of Israel made the Golden Calf, and therefore the verse praises here their worthiness. Bahya raises another question, namely: "How cometh that Moses on his own authority broke the Tables which contained the writing of God? Even if the children of Israel did sin, and thereby became unworthy of the Holy Tables, he should not have broken them, but rather should have returned them to God and asked what to do with them." The incident can be compared to a king who sends through a messenger a sealed letter to some princes, and if they refuse to receive the letter, the messenger returns the same to the king. Why did not Moses do likewise and return the Tables to God? The answer to the query is that when Israel made the Golden Calf, Moses saw that the letters disappeared from the Tables and it was as if the King's seal had been torn off, and therefore

---

*This passage is found in the text following verse 10, but it is transposed to the Biblical order.

Moses refused to deliver them and threw them away. The letters on the Tables can be compared to the soul, and the Tables themselves to the body; and when the soul goes out of the body, the body has to be buried. Our sages say that the Tables became heavy in the hands of Moses and he could not retain them after the letters disappeared from them, like the body of a man becomes heavy after the living soul has gone out therefrom. Our text uses first the singular form and says, "The two Tables of Testimony were in his hand," and later, after the children of Israel sinned, our text uses the dual form and says, "And he cast the Tables out of his hands" because, before the letters disappeared he held them in one hand, but afterwards he could no longer hold them even with both hands.

17. *AND WHEN JOSHUA HEARD THE NOISE OF THE PEOPLE AS THEY SHOUTED.* Joshua heard the noise which the children of Israel made in dancing before the idol and singing to the accompaniment of eight instruments, but he himself was not in their midst. He lived outside the camp, behind the mountain, waiting for the return of Moses. And during the time he dwelt outside the camp, God let a separate portion of Manna come down from heaven to his place of abode. And Joshua told Moses that there was a great noise in the camp, like to a noise of war, but Moses answered and said that it did not sound like a noise of war, because in battle the victors shout with joy and the vanquished wail aloud, but here there was a noise of derision and laughter. And Moses was wroth and he broke the Tables, for he said to himself: "If idolaters [17] are denied even a share in the Passover lamb, the more so Israel that has become apostate should be denied the Tables of the Lord, which contained the whole Torah:" he therefore threw them down and broke them. The Toldoth Yitschak says that Moses did not break the Tables on the Mount at the time when God told him what the children of Israel had done, because he thought perhaps they would repent; but when he returned and saw them dancing round the Calf, he broke them. The Tzror Hamor says that Moses broke the Tables before the children of Israel to show them that the worthy Tables

198

hewn out of precious stones were being destroyed because of their sins. The same gives another reason: Moses broke the Tables because they were witnesses that Israel had promised to receive the Torah, a thing as binding as a promissory note sealed in the presence of witnesses. Now, therefore, when Israel broke the Commandments contained in the Tables they became worthy of death. Moses broke the Tables as if to tear up the promissory note. Moses burned the idol and ground it to powder and scattered it upon the waters and made the children of Israel drink thereof, that the idol might turn into faecal matter within their bowels. Another reason for making the children drink thereof was to try them like a woman suspected of infidelity was tried and made to drink the Holy Water; and if the water did her no harm she was considered innocent. Moses, likewise, by means of the water found out who among the children of Israel worshipped the idol in secret, since they who worshipped it openly were put to the edge of the sword, but they who only rejoiced secretly turned green and yellow. Our sages say that one who worshipped the idol publicly and was warned against it, but disregarded the warning, was put to the edge of the sword; one who worshipped it publicly, although there were witnesses, but he was not warned against it died by an act of God, during the pestilence; and one who worshipped it publicly, but was neither warned nor were there any witnesses against that person, the same turned green and yellow through the drinking of the water. Although God could have caused the faces of the sinners to have turned yellow without Moses making them first drink of the water, He did not do so, in order that no one could say that the people turned green and yellow because of some sickness.

26.   THEN MOSES STOOD IN THE GATE OF THE CAMP AND SAID, WHOSO IS ON THE LORD'S SIDE, LET HIM COME UNTO ME. AND ALL THE SONS OF LEVI GATHERED THEMSELVES TOGETHER UNTO HIM, FOR THEY DID NOT WORSHIP THE CALF.

27.   AND MOSES SAID, LET EVERY MAN PUT ON HIS

SWORD AND GO THROUGH THE CAMP AND SLAY THOSE WHO WORSHIPPED THE CALF REGARDLESS OF WHETHER THEY BE YOUR FATHERS, MOTHERS, SONS, RELATIVES, OR FRIENDS.

28. AND THE SONS OF LEVI SLEW THREE THOUSAND FROM AMONG ISRAEL. And Moses blessed the sons of Levi that they be worthy to serve in the Temple.

31-32. AND MOSES ENTREATED THE LORD ON BEHALF OF THE PEOPLE AND SAID, IF THOU WILT NOT FORGIVE THEM, BLOT ME, I PRAY THEE, OUT OF THY BOOK WHICH THOU HAST WRITTEN.

33-34. AND THE LORD SAID, I WILL FORGIVE THEM NOW, BUT IN THE DAY OF VISITATION I WILL VISIT THEM INDIVIDUALLY. In all the afflictions which come upon Israel, there is not a single instance which does not contain a measure of punishment for the sin of the Golden Calf.

35. AND THE LORD SMOTE THE PEOPLE who worshipped the idol in public and had witnesses against them, but had not been warned against doing so.

CHAPTER XXXIII

4. *AND WHEN THE PEOPLE HEARD THESE EVIL TIDINGS.*[1] When the children of Israel heard the evil tidings that God had commanded them to take off their ornaments, they became afraid and cried. When they had received the Torah at Sinai, the Lord gave to every one of them two crowns, which they were now commanded to take off. "Therefore, now put off thy ornaments from thee" means that God asked the children of Israel to take off the garments which they wore at Sinai, and which the Lord had let be sprinkled with the blood of the sacrifices as a sign that the wearers thereof had received the Torah. Now the children of Israel were commanded to take off the robes, since they had transgressed

against the Torah, and therefore should no longer wear them. Bahya made the comment on behalf of Rabbi Hananeel, and further pointed out that in verse 4 it is already said, "No man did put on his garments"; why then does verse 5 say that God asked them to put off their garments? The answer to the query is that at first the children of Israel took off some garments of their own accord, as a sign of contrition; but later were ordered by God to do so. Some sages say that the ornaments in question refer to the sign of the Tetragrammaton which descended upon the children of Israel at Sinai, so that even the angel of death had no power over them, because of the Torah, as it is written חרות על הלחות.[2] The children of Israel were set free from the angel of death through the Torah which was written upon the Tables. And Moses took away their crowns of beauty; therefore it is said in verse 7, "And Moses took the "אהל", meaning the light.[3] The Gemara, commenting on the words, "And Moses took the Ohel," quotes Rabbi Johanan as saying that the words mean that all Israel suspected Moses of lying with their womenfolk.[4] And Moses pitched his tent 2000 cubits outside the camp, because the children of Israel were like an anathema.

7. *AND IT CAME TO PASS THAT EVERY ONE WHICH SOUGHT THE LORD*. From the verse our sages inferred that one who went to see Moses was as one who went to see God, because welcoming a scholar is like welcoming God. Every one who wished to study the Law of God went into the tent of Moses.

8. AND IT CAME TO PASS, WHEN MOSES WENT OUT UNTO THE TENT, THAT ALL THE PEOPLE ROSE AND STOOD, EVERY MAN AT HIS TENT DOOR, UNTIL MOSES WAS GONE INTO HIS TENT.

* *AND LOOKED AFTER MOSES*. The Gemara,[5] in the first section of Shekalim, says that the people looked at Moses' big feet

---

*Passage transposed according to Biblical order.

and fat legs, and murmured that he was living on the fat of the land. The Tanhuma says that the words, "Every one which sought the Lord," mean that even the angels from heaven, which came down to minister, had first to go to the tent of Moses and ask for permission from God, who dwelt there. Even the sun and the moon, before setting out on their course of shedding light upon the earth, had first to go to the tent of Moses and ask for permission from God, who dwelt there.

9-10. AND IT CAME TO PASS WHEN THE PILLAR OF CLOUD DESCENDED FROM HEAVEN AND STOOD AT THE DOOR OF THE TENT, THAT ALL THE PEOPLE ROSE UP AND WORSHIPPED, EVERY MAN AT HIS TENT DOOR, WITH FACES TURNED TOWARDS THE PRESENCE OF GOD IN THE CLOUD.

11. AND THE LORD SPAKE UNTO MOSES FACE TO FACE, IN A MANNER THAT EVERY ONE COULD SEE IT, and Moses later brought back the words of the Lord to the children of Israel in the camp and taught them Torah in the way he received it from God. Moses continued doing this daily from Yom Kippur until the month of Nisan, at which time the Sanctuary was ready and the Lord no longer spake to Moses in the tent, but in the Tabernacle. The Midrash [6] says that the Lord said unto Moses: "When I am wroth with the children of Israel, and thou too art likewise, who will comfort them? Move therefore thy tent back to the camp and dwell with them."

12. *SEE, THOU SAYEST UNTO ME, BRING UP THESE PEOPLE: AND THOU HAST NOT LET ME KNOW WHOM THOU WILT SEND WITH ME.* Moses said: "Thou desirest to send an angel before me, but I do not care for angels, I prefer Thy presence to accompany me; Thou hast also said that Thou holdest me in esteem above all people and that I have found grace in Thy sight. Tell me, I pray Thee, what reward givest Thou to them who find favour in Thy sight? Thou hast threatened to smite the children

of Israel with the pestilence and make of me a great nation; but let it not be so, O Lord, because the children of Israel are Thy people of old."

14. *AND HE SAID, MY PRESENCE SHALL GO WITH THEE.* The Lord said: "I myself and not an angel will go with thee," and Moses gave praise for the manifestation of God's love towards His people. Moses prayed that the Shekinah abide not upon the heathen,[7] because he desired Israel to be better than the rest of the nations, and to be separated from idolaters, and the Lord granted the request; and although the Shekinah did reveal herself to Balaam, the latter had to prostrate himself and could not behold the vision. But the prophets of Israel stood upon their feet and with their eyes beheld the Shekinah.

The Ibn Shu'aib, referring back to verses 4 and 5, asks, why was it first said that the children of Israel took off their garments of their own accord, and later it is said that the Lord commanded them so to do? The answer, he says, is that the children of Israel possessed illustrious garments, bright as light, which are worn by angels when they reveal themselves to the pious or to the sages. In heaven, the angels have no need of garments because they are like fire, but when they appear to man they put on garments, like man. Such precious garments God gave to the children of Israel at Sinai, that when they wore them the Angel of Death could not come near them, as it is written חרות על הלחות,[8] i. e., the children of Israel were set free even from the Angel of Death because of the Torah which was written upon the Tables. However, after they had made the Golden Calf, they were ashamed to wear the illustrious garments openly and wore them only beneath their ordinary garments, like a person in mourning, and that is what is meant by the words "and no man did put on his garments." They wore them beneath their ordinary clothes. Later, however, the Lord commanded them to take the garments off altogether; therefore, it is said, "And the children of Israel stripped themselves,"[9] i. e., they took them off altogether, and Moses gathered them up. However, there were still some saints against whom the Angel of Death could not prevail, as can be seen from a story recorded in the tractate Baba Metzia, Chapter VII,[10] about Rabbah Bar Nahmani, whom infidels accused before the king of interfering with the tax collections. This was because he used to gather the people on Rosh Hashanah, and on the Passover, and to preach to them, and for that reason they were absent from their homes, and no taxes could be collected on those days. When Rabbah heard of the accusation he went into hiding, but the king sent a messenger to apprehend him. And when the messenger arrived at a traveller's inn, where the Rabbah was hiding, a table was set before the messenger and he was given two cups of drink, and when he tasted thereof his face became contorted. The innkeepers went to Rabbah, to inquire of him how to cure the stricken messenger, and he advised them to set again the table before the messenger and give him another cup of drink, which they did, and the messenger was cured. The messenger then said that he was sure that Rabbah was there because of the miracle. He searched and when he found him he said that he would let himself be killed rather than hand over Rabbah to the king; nevertheless, if he should be tortured, he would have no alternative but to give him up. He therefore imprisoned Rabbah in a room and locked it, but Rabbah then prayed to God, and the walls crumbled down, and he escaped into an open field and sat down upon the trunk of a tree, and continued studying the Torah. There happened to be a discussion in heaven concerning leprosy, as to whether a person is to be considered clean or unclean before the hair of the affected place turns white. The Lord judged him clean, but the heavenly academy judged him unclean; so the matter was referred to Rabbah Bar Nahamani for a final decision. The heavenly academy sent the Angel of Death to bring Rabbah's soul to Heaven to decide, but Rabbah was immersed in studying the Torah, and the angel could not break in on him. Then the angel caused a tree to rustle, and when Rabbah heard the noise, he thought his persecutors were closing in on him, and he chose death rather than falling into the hands of man. As he was dying he gave final judgment on the disputed case, and pronounced it clean. A voice from Heaven was heard saying, Blessed art thou, Rabbah, that thy soul went out of thee with the word 'clean.'" Later a letter was dropped on the city of Pumbeditha saying: "Let it be known that Rabbah was taken to the heavenly academy." Then Abbaye, together with other Rabbis, went out to search for the place where Rabbah died, in order that they might give him a proper burial and mourn after him, but they could not find him. Then, far away, they saw a flock of birds standing together with their wings spread out, as if they were shading something, and they then understood that Rabbah was there. The Rabbis then mourned after Rabbah three days and three nights, and a second letter came down saying that he who ceases from mourning, let him be an anathema. They then continued to mourn for another seven days, and a third letter came down saying: "Depart in peace." From this story, we learn that the Torah saves man from the Angel of Death.

The Gemara, commenting on the section, "With what may the Sabbath lamp be lighted," [11] tells a story about King David and the Angel of Death, who could not prevail against him because the king continued in his studies of the Torah, behind a tree. Then the angel caused the leaves to rustle and the king was frightened and rose up to see what caused the rustling. As he rose up his foot slipped and he fell and died. But as long as the king was immersed in the study of the Torah, the Angel of Death could not touch him. The Ibn Shu'aib says that a sage can alter a divine decree. There is a story about Rabbi Simeon ben Halafta, who with several other Rabbis, went to the city of Tzepori to attend a circumcision service. At the feast which followed, the father whose son had been circumcised said that he considered it a privilege to drink with the Rabbis at the circumcision of his son, and expressed the wish that it might be granted unto him to drink again with them at the wedding of his son, and they all said, Amen, may your wish be granted. Later, when the Rabbis left the place, they met on the way the Angel of Death looking very sorrowful, and when they asked him the reason for his sorrow, he told them that he had been commissioned to take the child's soul after it was one month old, and now since the Rabbis said Amen to the father's wish, he could not execute his task. Rabbi Simeon then asked the angel whether he had any orders against him and his colleagues; and the angel said: "No, because they occupied themselves with the study of the Torah and with observing God's commandments, and that he had no authority over such people." Then Rabbi Simeon said to the angel, that "As thou hast no authority over our bodies, so mayest thou have no authority over the words to which we have said Amen, and let the child live." It is also said that the righteous have power to annul divine decrees. The Lord has ordained man to dwell upon the earth and angels to dwell in Heaven, but Moses seems to have reversed the decree by going up to Heaven, and causing the Lord with His angels to come down on Mount Sinai. God created the angels in such a way that they need not eat, but when they came down to visit Abraham they obliged him and did eat. God ordained man to live on food; yet when Moses went up to Heaven he did not eat nor drink for forty days. God gathered the waters in the sea, but Moses divided the sea and made a dry path across the Red Sea. God ordained the light to be day and the darkness to be night, but Jacob came and made from night day, and caused that day to be longer than it formerly was.

18. *SHEW ME, I PRAY THEE, THY GLORY.* When Moses saw that the Lord answered all his petitions, he further asked to be shown the divine glory, and the Lord said: "I will let thee have a glimpse of Me, but thou shalt see only as much as I permit thee. I will instruct thee how to intercede before Me, and think not thou that when the merits of the patriarchs have been exhausted, there will be no more hope for the children of Israel: far from it! I will

therefore instruct thee how to pray so that Israel may have hope. Go down into a cave, and I will stand upon a rock nearby, and I will wrap Myself in a Prayer-shawl, like a Cantor before a congregation, and show thee how to pray, and thou in turn shalt teach the children of Israel to say 'The Lord, the Lord, a God full of compassion and graciousness, slow to anger, and plenteous in mercy and truth; keeping mercy for a thousand, forgiving iniquity and transgression and sin.' " The Lord instructed Moses to pray in that manner.

20. AND THE LORD SAID UNTO MOSES, THOU CANST NOT SEE MY FACE, FOR MAN SHALL NOT SEE ME AND LIVE. The Yalkut records a story [12] about King Hadrian, who once asked Rabbi Joshua that if it be true that the God of Israel had made Heaven and earth, why does He not show Himself, say twice a year, so that the people could see and fear Him? The Rabbi replied that man cannot see God and live; and as it was in the middle of the day and the sun was high, he asked the king to look straight at the sun, but King Hadrian pointed out that it was impossible. Well, said the Rabbi, if one cannot look at the sun, which is only one of God's instruments, how could one behold the splendour of God, which is of pure fire and great light? The king was satisfied with the answer. However, when the Messiah will come to destroy all the idolaters,[13] God will reveal Himself to all flesh, as it is written, "And the glory of God shall be revealed." [14] It is also said that when the soul is about to depart from the human body, it sees God. The Yalkut says that God showed Moses many treasures in heaven, and when the latter asked to whom they belonged he was told that one belonged to those who gave alms, another to those who fed the orphans, and so on. Last of all he was shown some special treasure, and when he asked to whom it belonged he was told that out of that treasure God grants rewards to those who have no merit of their own. The Scripture, therefore, says, "I will be gracious unto whom I will be gracious," [15] meaning, I will grant to people free gifts.

CHAPTER XXXIV

1. *HEW THEE.* The Lord said unto Moses in his tent, "Hew thee two Tables" out of sapphire stone, and I will write upon them the Ten Commandments. Our sages say that Moses became very rich through hewing the Tables out of precious sapphire stone. For large pieces of stone were broken off, and Moses sold them for good money and became rich thereby. The verse therefore says "Hew thee," meaning any of the pieces which have been hewn out of the sapphire shall be thine. The Gemara, tractate Shabbath, says that the first Tables were hewn out in heaven by God Himself, but the second Tables were hewn out by Moses. Rashi says that the same can be likened unto a parable about a king who went overseas and heard that his wife became unfaithful in the company of her maidservants. One of his lords tore up her marriage deed[1] so as to save her from her husband's wrath, and to defend her by saying that she was not legally his wife, since she had no marriage deed. When the king returned home, he found out that the queen was free from all blame and that only her maidservants were involved. And the king was reconciled to the queen, and then the lord who tore up his master's marriage deed asked the king to write another one, because the former was gone; but the king replied and said: "Since thou hast torn up the deed, write another one and I will sign it." The king can be compared to the Lord, the servant to Moses, the spouse to the people of Israel, and the maidservants to the mixed multitude among Israel. The children of Israel had a marriage deed, i. e., the Tables which Moses had broken; therefore, the Lord said unto Moses, "Hew thee two Tables" because thou hast broken the first two Tables.

3. *AND NO MAN SHALL COME UP WITH THEE.* The Lord said unto Moses, Come thou alone with me on Mount Sinai and let no man come with thee. At the giving of the first Tables there was a great noise, therefore an evil spell brought about their destruction, but later, at the giving of the second Tables, the Lord said: "I will

give the Tables quietly, that they may abide with you." And Moses hewed the Tables out of sapphire, and early in the morning went up the mount holding them in his hands. And the Lord came down with the cloud and stood near Moses and taught him how to call upon the name of the Lord and say: "The Lord, the Lord God, merciful and gracious," i. e., the Lord is merciful to the children of men before they trespass, and is also merciful unto them after they have trespassed, if they repent.

6. LONGSUFFERING. The Lord is merciful and longsuffering. He does not punish the transgressor soon after he has transgressed, but leaves him time for repentance. And Moses made haste and bowed his head. In the Gemara, tractate Sanhedrin,[2] it is said that when Moses first heard that the Lord was longsuffering, both to the just and to the unjust, he said: "Let the unjust perish." But the Lord cautioned him that one day he might be glad of God's longsuffering. Later, when the children of Israel sinned and made the Golden Calf, as a result of which the Lord wanted to destroy them, Moses interceded on their behalf and prayed that the Lord might be longsuffering with them. The Lord then reminded Moses of his previous saying, but Moses replied: "Yes, Lord, nevertheless Thou hast promised to be longsuffering, even to the unjust." The Scripture therefore says, "And now I pray thee, let the power of the Lord be great according as thou hast spoken,"[3] i. e., deal mercifully with the children of Israel, as Thou hast promised to be longsuffering even towards the unjust. The Jerusalem Talmud,[4] commenting on the words "forgiving iniquity" says that the Lord permits some of men's evil deeds to be taken off from the pan of the scales to lighten it and allow the pan on the other half of the balance, carrying the good deeds, to weigh it down. Rabbi Huna said on behalf of Rabbi Abbahu that, although the Holy One, blessed be He, does not forget, but remembers everything, nevertheless, He lets it appear as if He had forgotten some of man's offences. Some sages say that God permits the lifting up of the pan loaded with sin in order that the

other pan on the scales, loaded with good deeds may balance over.

15. *AND ONE CALL THEE AND THOU EAT OF HIS SACRIFICE*. It is recorded in the Gemara, tractate Abodah Zarah,[5] that Rabbi Simeon ben Eliezer said that the children of Israel who live in the Diaspora serve idols to a degree, if and when heathens make a wedding and Israelites attend the wedding feast, it is as if they had served idols. They must not touch any drink or food, even if Kosher, because they must not enjoy any heathen feasts.

17. *THOU SHALT MAKE THEE NO MOLTEN GODS*. The Gemara, tractate Pesahim,[6] says that he who does not observe the Feast of the Passover, well and according to his means, is like unto an idolater, because the Commandment, "Thou shalt make thee no molten image" stands near the Commandment, "The feast of the unleavened bread shalt thou keep." The close proximity of the two Commandments teaches us that one who works on holy days to make money, or one who withholds from spending any money for holy days, shows himself thereby to be a lover of money, and is like unto a man who puts his trust in it; which is the same thing as putting his trust in idolatry.

23. *SHALL ALL THY MALES APPEAR*. All men were enjoined to go up to Jerusalem for the festivals, and to appear before the Shekinah. Women and blind men were exempted. Bahya says that women and people with bodily defects were exempted from going up to Jerusalem, because the cloud on the Temple was as clear as a mirror, and that one could be seen in it. It was considered improper for a woman or a person with bodily defects to be seen in the holy cloud; they were therefore exempted from the pilgrimage.

27. *FOR AFTER THE TENOR OF THESE WORDS I HAVE MADE A COVENANT WITH THEE*. The sages infer from this verse that the Torah, which God had given in writing, should not be committed to memory but should be maintained in writing, and that the oral words which He gave to Moses by word of mouth should

not be committed to writing, but that the children of Israel learn them by heart. Bahya says that God did not command to write down the oral law, which the Gemara expounds and serves as a commentary on the Torah and as a guide to the understanding of the Pentateuch; and the Holy One, blessed be He, desired the children of Israel to have a better understanding of the Torah than other nations, who did not receive it on Mount Sinai, for only Israel was present at Sinai. However, during the Persian captivity,[7] when the children of Israel suffered much, and were scattered and could not study the oral law, Rabbi[8] summarized the whole tradition and compiled the Mishnah, that Israel might not forget it.

28.   *AND HE WAS THERE WITH THE LORD FORTY DAYS AND FORTY NIGHTS.* Bahya asks how Moses knew it was day or night, when there is only light and no darkness in heaven, and how did he know when the forty days were fulfilled? The explanation is that when the Holy One, blessed be He, studied the Pentateuch with Moses, Moses knew it was day, and when God studied with him Gemara he knew it was night; or when he heard the angels chant "Holy" he knew it was day, and when he heard them chant "Blessed" he knew it was night. Another explanation was that when Moses saw the Manna being prepared he knew it was day, and when Moses saw it being dropped he knew it was night. A still further explanation is that when he saw the sun bowing before God he knew that it was day; and when he saw the moon doing the same he knew that it was night.

30.   *AND BEHOLD, THE SKIN OF HIS FACE SHONE.* When Moses came down from heaven his face shone like the sun or the moon, and no one could behold it because of the light. Bahya says that Moses' face began to shine at the giving of the second Tables, and not at the first, because at the giving of the first Tables Israel was present and saw the signs and the wonders, and there was no need for additional proof that the Tables came from God. But at the giving of the second Tables, no one was present except Moses;

211

therefore, a sign was required to assure the people that Moses was in heaven, and had received the Tables from God. Another reason why God did not cause His light to shine upon Moses at the first giving of the Tables was that He knew the first Tables would be broken, and therefore did not honour Moses by causing His light to shine upon his face; but the second Tables were meant to last, therefore God gave His light to Moses. The Midrash asks how Moses merited to have God's light upon his face, and says that when Moses was in the cave,[9] God covered his face with His hand, and from that time he received the light upon his face. Some sages say that the light came upon Moses' face because he spoke with God face to face; other sages say it was because Moses wrote the Tables, and when he had finished writing some light remained on his pen, and Moses wiped his pen on his face, thereby catching the light on his face.

AND THEY WERE AFRAID TO COME NIGH HIM. Our sages point out how great was the sin of the Golden Calf, that before the children of Israel made it, they could look at the Holy One, blessed be He, on Mount Sinai, through seven walls of fire, without fear; but after the Golden Calf they could not look even at the light on Moses' face, although it was much less than the light which emanated from God.

33. AND MOSES PUT A VEIL ON HIS FACE, that it might not harm the people, but when he entered the Tabernacle he took it off. Likewise, when he went out of the Tabernacle to instruct the people in the Torah and precepts which God revealed to him, he had his face unveiled; but when he finished teaching, he put the veil on again.

CHAPTER XXXV

1. *AND MOSES ASSEMBLED ALL THE CONGREGATION OF THE CHILDREN OF ISRAEL.* The day after Yom Kippur, Moses gathered all the people together. For on the day of Yom

Kippur Moses came down the mount with the new Tables, and that was on a Thursday. The day on which he went up the mountain was a Monday, the first Monday in Elul. The children of Israel therefore fast on Mondays and on Thursdays to commemorate God's forgiveness of their sins in the days of old. On the day after Yom Kippur Moses assembled all the children of Israel, and commanded them to build the Tabernacle. Ibn Shu'aib says that when Moses completed the building of the Tabernacle, he recited the prayer, "Let the beauty of the Lord our God be upon us," [1] that the Shekinah might abide upon the Sanctuary. The Midrash [2] records Rabbi Levi saying that at first the Shekinah dwelt mainly upon the earth, as it is written, "And they heard the voice of the Lord walking in the garden"; [3] but later when Adam ate of the tree of knowledge of good and evil the Shekinah moved away into the first heaven. And when Cain killed Abel his brother, the Shekinah moved into the second heaven. When the generation of Enosh came and worshipped strange gods, the Shekinah moved to the third heaven. When the evil generation came that perished in the flood, the Shekinah moved to the fourth heaven. When the generation that built the Tower of Babel came, the Shekinah moved to the fifth heaven. When Nimrod, the wicked, came, the Shekinah moved to the sixth heaven, and when the people of Sodom came, the Shekinah moved away to the seventh heaven. Later, when Abraham, who was righteous, appeared, the Shekinah moved back to the sixth heaven. When Isaac came, the Shekinah moved back to the fifth heaven. When Jacob came, the Shekinah moved to the fourth heaven. When Levi came, the Shekinah moved to the third heaven. When Kohath came, the Shekinah moved to the second heaven. When Amram came, the Shekinah moved back to the first heaven; and when Moses came, he caused the Shekinah to return upon the earth. Therefore the Holy One, blessed be He, commanded Moses to build a Tabernacle in which the Shekinah might dwell.

2. *SIX DAYS SHALL WORK BE DONE.* The verse says that

in "six days work will be done," *i. e.*, the work will be done by itself, which means to teach us that he who observes the Sabbath rightly will have no need to work at all. The Torah contains the injunction regarding the Sabbath, prior to the injunction about the Tabernacle, to emphasize the priority of the Sabbath, that no one was to work on the Sabbath, not even to build the Tabernacle. The more so should one refrain from working on anything else on the Sabbath. The Ba'al Hatturim says that the Torah places the injunction about the Sabbath near the section which says that the skin of Moses' face shone, to teach us that on the Sabbath day God lights up the face of every Israelite, and endows him with graciousness.

3. *YE SHALL KINDLE NO FIRE THROUGHOUT YOUR HABITATIONS UPON THE SABBATH DAY.* Commentators ask why the Torah forbids the kindling of fire above any other work, and say it is because most work is done by the aid of fire. At the end of the Sabbath, when work may be resumed, the Jews recite the Habhdallah [4] Service over lighted candles. We also find that when the Lord created the world He first created light, which is like unto fire. The Torah forbids the kindling of fire on the Sabbath, also for another reason, because women go to the Synagogue and talk about the meals they cook, and pay no attention to the prayers and thus make void the prayers. The injunction against the kindling of fire on the Sabbath is placed near the section dealing with the Tabernacle, to teach the people, and women in particular, not to talk vainly on the Sabbath in the Synagogues, which is likened to the Tabernacle. The Gemara, in tractate Kiddushin,[5] says that ten measures of speech were given to the world, nine of which were taken by women, but one must not talk during the Service in a Synagogue. Rabbi Huna said it is forbidden to discuss even holy things during the reading of a portion of Scripture from the open scroll, and that superfluous words should not be uttered even outside the Synagogue. The Menorath Hamaor says that our sages told us that one can recognize a person by his talk. The one who talks

much is foolish, but the one who talks little is wise and of good upbringing. As the Gemara, in tractate Kiddushin [6] says, the one who withdraws first from an argument is of better breeding. Rabbi said that the quietness of the Babylonian Jews was a mark of their good breeding. And, although the Torah should be discussed abundantly, nevertheless there are instances when even the Torah should not be discussed; namely, at the reciting of the Shema, at the reciting of the Eight Benedictions, at the reciting of the Hallel and at the reading of the appointed portion from the Scripture during the service. The Gemara [7] says that if a man was guilty of chatting in the midst of his prayers, he was disqualified from military service, for when Israel was at war with other nations, all who had been guilty of transgressions were sent home, in order to avoid causing the children of Israel to suffer defeat because of sin. The same applied to those who were guilty of talking in the midst of their prayers, because it was a great sin. It can be inferred from what has been said that, although it was meritorious to be engaged in discussing the Torah, nevertheless our sages forbade doing so during prayer; the more so is it forbidden to utter vain words during prayer. It is regrettable that people are not sufficiently warned against uttering superfluous words, which is sinful, especially if they are uttered on the Sabbath. The Gemara [8] exhorts the people to keep their conversation holy, especially on the Sabbath day, and the topics of their conversation should not be of the same nature as during weekdays. In the Midrash [9] Va-yikra Rabah it is recorded that the mother of Rabbi Simeon Ben Yohai once talked a lot on the Sabbath, and her son reminded her that it was a Sabbath day, and to cease from talking. The Ba'al Hatturim, commenting on the text, "Ye shall kindle no fire," maintains that the Holy One, blessed be He, said that since fire in hell rests on the Sabbath, let it also rest on earth on that day, which means to say: "You shall not work on a Sabbath day." The Toldoth Yitschak says that the Scripture deals with the offering of silver and gold to the building of the

Tabernacle, and with the gift of silver and gold for the same, before dealing with the laws governing the Sabbath, in order to teach people that the Sabbath is indicative of the world to come, where no work is done. It was also that man might know that this world is nothing to be compared with the world to come, and that he might not regret the gifts of silver and gold which he made to the Tabernacle.

5. *TAKE YE FROM AMONG YOU AN OFFERING*. The verse teaches us that man should not say that when he becomes rich he will give alms and contribute to charity. The verse says plainly, "Take ye from among you," meaning that every man should give what he can afford and what God has put into his heart, as it is written, "Whosoever is of a willing heart, let him bring the Lord's offering."

The Toldoth Yitschak asks why it was necessary to say, "Let him bring" when at the beginning of the verse it is said, "Take ye." He answers his own query by saying that when Moses ascended on Mount Sinai, the Holy One, blessed be He, commanded that the children of Israel give gold and silver to the building of the Tabernacle. Moses first had in mind to appoint trustees to go from house to house and collect the offerings; but when, at the making of the Golden Calf, the people brought of their own volition the silver and gold he changed his mind and asked the people to bring their offerings, without the help of collectors, that they make thereby expiation for the gold and silver they brought for the Golden Calf. If they gladly brought their gifts for a sinful purpose, the more so should they feel refreshed in giving for a holy cause.

20. *AND ALL THE CONGREGATION OF THE CHILDREN OF ISRAEL DEPARTED FROM THE PRESENCE OF MOSES*.[10] Bahya says that the text teaches us that the children of Israel were eager to bring their gold and silver to the Tabernacle, and that the women were even more eager to do so than the men. The Scripture therefore says, "And they came both men and women," which means to say that when the menfolk came, they found the

womenfolk already at the Tabernacle, and that was a great honour for the women. The verse praises the women who were unwilling to give their earrings towards the making of the Golden Calf, but excelled in giving the same for the Tabernacle. The Pirque de R. Eliezer says that, because of their generosity, the women have merited to observe the holiday of the first day of the month, during which they are to refrain from hard work, but wear their good clothes; and in the world to come the Holy One, blessed be He, will reward the women richly and rejoice their hearts.

In Ecclesiastes, King Solomon says, "One man among a thousand have I found, but a woman among all those have I not found." [11] The verse means to say that not a single woman was present at the making of the Golden Calf when the crowd shouted, "These be thy gods"; [12] because the women refused to contribute their earrings towards the making of that idol. The verse may be interpreted in many other ways, as for instance, one pious man among a thousand have I found, but not even a single woman among a thousand have I found. The Gemara, in tractate Gittin,[13] Section Hasholeach, says that the daughters of Rabbi Nahman could skim a boiling pot with their bare hands without the use of a ladle. When Rabbi 'Ilish saw it, he pondered over the saying of Solomon, "One man among a thousand have I found, but a woman among all these have I not found," and wondered why Solomon had said that there was not one pious woman among a thousand, and if so, how cometh that fire has no power over the daughters of Rabbi Nahman? Later it came to pass that the daughters of Nahman were taken captive, together with Rabbi 'Ilish. In prison the latter met another Jew who understood even the language of the birds. A raven came and crowed, so Rabbi 'Ilish asked what it said, and he was told that the raven advised him to break away from prison. But the Rabbi said that a raven may tell lies, and that it could not be trusted. Then a dove came with a similar message, and when the Rabbi again asked what the message was, and was informed that the dove too told him to break away from prison, and that he would escape safely, he took the message to heart and said that Israel is sometimes compared to a dove and that a dove tells the truth; and that the Holy One, blessed be He, would deliver him from prison. However, before breaking away from prison, the Rabbi decided to visit Rabbi Nahman's daughters and see whether they be as pious as they formerly were. He walked up quietly to the place where they were and listened to their talk. He heard them saying one to another not to worry about their husbands at home, since their captors make as good husbands as those at home, and they were not worried about living in adultery with Samaritans. They counselled one another to ask their captors to carry them farther away, to make it more difficult for their husbands at home to find out their whereabouts, in fear that they might redeem them. Then Rabbi 'Ilish made his escape, and the other Jew who was with him in prison, who understood the language of birds, followed him. They came to a large creek and the Lord performed a miracle for the Rabbi to cross it, but his companion remained behind. The Samaritans came and slew him, but Rabbi 'Ilish returned home safely. The daughters of Rabbi Nahman too returned home finally, and resumed their practice hitherto of skimming a boiling pot with their bare hands, a thing they did with the help of witchcraft. Rabbi 'Ilish then said that Solomon was right in saying that there was not a virtuous woman among a thousand. Women, therefore, are exhorted not to move around alone among strange [14] men.

22. *AND THEY CAME BOTH MEN AND WOMEN.*[15] The men followed the women. Rabban says that articles of gold and silver are chiefly a feminine attire; therefore, the text says that the men followed after the women, *i. e.*, the women were first to bring their gold and silver, and the men came afterwards with their rings of gold and silver. The Toldoth Yitschak asks how the authorities could have accepted gold and silver from the women, when our sages forbade anyone to accept gifts from women, except minor things, since it is not lawful for a woman to give away the gold and

silver she brought from her father's house, nor may she give away such things which she got from her husband? The answer is that the wives came together with their husbands when they brought their offerings to the Tabernacle, as the text says, "And they came, both men and women." [16] We also infer from the verse that a woman should not give much alms without her husband's knowledge, except small gifts to the amount of a cent [17] or so, which she may give without his knowledge. The Gemara says that a woman may also give food to the poor or to a visitor, as can be seen from the following story, recorded in the Gemara, tractate Taanith. [18]

* Once upon a time there was a dire need for rain, and the sages sent up two Rabbis to Abba Hilkiah to ask him to pray for rain. When the Rabbis reached his house, they did not find him at home. They went to look for him in the fields, and found he had hired himself out to plow a field. They greeted him, but he did not heed them. At the end of the day's work he carried home chips on one shoulder and his cloak on the other. The whole way along, he did not put on his shoes, but when he had to cross a creek he put them on. When he came across thorns and shrubs, he lifted up his garments, and when he reached his home town, his wife, dressed in pretty white clothes and bedecked with her finery, came out to meet him. When he arrived at the door of his house, he let his wife enter first, then he followed after her, and the visiting Rabbis last. Then he sat down to eat, but did not invite his visitors to join him. Distributing bread to his children, he gave to the older child one slice of bread, and to the younger two slices. After the meal he said to his wife: "I know that the Rabbis came to see me on account of rain; let us go up to the attic and pray, and let them not know that rain came through our intercession." When in the attic, he stood praying in one corner and she in another. The clouds appeared first over the corner where she stood, because her prayer was heard first. Then he came down and asked the Rabbis the purpose of their visit;

---

*Text has been somewhat rearranged in the translation of the story.

and they told him that they were sent to ask him to pray for rain. "Well," replied Abba Hilkiah, "Blessed be the Lord who put you beyond the need of my prayer, for it rains already." They, however, replied: "We know well that this rain has come through you, but be it as it may, we should like you to give us an answer to the following question. Why, when we greeted you, did you not heed us?" He answered: "Because I hired myself out for the day, and did not think it right to interrupt my work." "Why did you carry the chips of wood on one shoulder and your cloak on the other," they asked. He replied: "Because it was a borrowed garment, and it was lent for the purpose of wearing it, and not for the purpose of carrying wood on it." Then they asked: "Why did not you wear your shoes the entire way, but when you had to cross the creek you put them on?" He answered, that on the entire way he could see on what he was stepping, whether it be stone or bone, but in the water it was impossible to see and he had to protect his feet. "Why did you lift your garments when you came upon thorns and shrubs?" they asked. The reply was, because a scratch on the body heals up, but a rent in the garment does not heal up. "Why did your wife come to meet you all dressed up?" "Well," he replied, "in order that I should not cast my eyes upon another woman." "Why did you let your wife enter the house first, and you after her, and we last?" "Because you are strangers and you are unknown to me, so I placed myself between you and my wife." "Why did you not invite us to eat with you?" "Because there was not enough food, and I did not wish to be dishonest in inviting you halfheartedly." "Why did you give one slice of bread to the older child and two to the younger?" "The older stays at home and can eat any time, but the younger goes to school." "Why did the clouds appear first over the corner where your wife was standing?" "Because she gives food to the hungry and they find immediate relief by her action, but I only give alms with which to buy food." From that story we infer that a woman may give food to the poor without her husband's knowledge, for if Abba Hilkiah's wife had asked her husband's consent, he would have had a share in the merit, and the cloud would not have appeared first over her corner. From the same story it can also be learned that even the poor should give something to charity. Abba Hilkiah was poor and had to hire himself to strangers as a day labourer, and yet he gave to charity.

The Gemara in Ketuboth also tells us of Mar Ukba,[19] who had an impoverished neighbour for whom he placed every day four gulden under his door. One day the poor man decided to find out who his benefactor was. When Mar Ukba, accompanied by his wife, placed the money under the door, the man ran after them, but the benefactors, in running away, landed in a burning furnace. The feet of Mar Ukba burned, so his wife asked him to place them upon her feet, which suffered no burn because she used to give to the poor things baked and cooked, which were for immediate relief to them. They ran into the burning furnace to avoid causing embarrassment to the poor man, as it is written, "Better for a man to throw himself into a fiery furnace than to put his neighbour openly to shame." From the story it can be inferred that a woman may give to the poor from the ready things she has in her kitchen. Charity should be given first to a woman in need rather than to a man in need, because a woman is more ashamed to beg than a man. Charity saves from two things, from the Angel of Death and from hell.

24. *EVERY ONE THAT DID OFFER AN OFFERING OF SILVER.*[20] At the silver offering, the Scripture uses the term מרים (to divide up), but at the gold offering the term used is תנופה (to lift up), in order to teach us that when one brought an offering of gold to the Tabernacle it was lifted up that people could see the generous gift.

27. *AND THE RULERS BROUGHT THE ONYX STONES.* The breastplate which the High Priest wore upon his breast was adorned with onyx stones given by the rulers of the people, that the stones might make expiation for the pride hidden in their hearts, since rulers and community leaders are proud people. The rulers have said one to another, "Let the people bring their offerings of

gold and silver first, and then we will supply the rest that may be required." But when the people contributed more than was required, there was nothing left for them to bring but precious stones. The verse, therefore, spells the word הנשאם without the letter י, as a rebuke to the rulers for being last with their contributions, and, although their intention was good, their action was not praiseworthy to the Torah. We infer from this verse that a man should not linger behind with a good deed or with a donation, but that he should be first to help, and his reward in heaven will therefore be the greater. Some of our sages have said that the clouds brought the precious stones, and that without the clouds it would have been impossible to find any precious stones in the wilderness. They maintain that the word הנשאם means clouds. Other sages were of the opinion that the precious stones came down from heaven together with the manna, and that the children of Israel collected them.

31. *AND HE HATH FILLED HIM WITH THE SPIRIT OF GOD.* The Lord endowed everyone with the gift of prophecy, so that one understood how to make the things one was asked to make, even if one had no previous experience in such work. The verse teaches us that God grants understanding to every person who desires to work for Him, even if the person has no experience in the work. He granted understanding even to the beasts that were employed in the building of the Tabernacle.

CHAPTER XXXVI

5. *THE PEOPLE BRING MUCH MORE THAN ENOUGH.* The Scripture tells us that the children of Israel gave in one day more gold and silver than the whole work required. The workmen, by reporting the same to Moses, demonstrated their honesty in the work, and Moses, desiring no surplus of gold and silver, commanded that it be proclaimed to the people to refrain from bringing any further gifts of silver or gold.

1. *AND BEZALEL MADE THE ARK*. Bezalel made three arks. The first was made of gold, the second of wood, which was placed into the golden one, and the third ark again was made of gold and placed within the wooden one, and then the edges were covered with gold. The layer between was of wood to illustrate the need for respecting the poverty-stricken scholar, and to supply his needs as if to cover him with gold, like the wooden ark. For the same reason, the two Tables of the Lord which Moses broke were put into the ark to teach the people the need for respecting a poverty-stricken scholar.

CHAPTER XXXVIII

8. *THE MIRRORS OF THE SERVING WOMEN*. The women of Israel gave to the Tabernacle mirrors made of pure copper, but Moses refused to accept them. He thought the mirrors to be unbecoming to be placed in the Tabernacle of God, because women used them for looking in when they made themselves up, and the mirrors could have been a cause of bringing lustful desires to men. Our sages have, therefore, forbidden men to dress themselves before mirrors, but women may use mirrors for adorning themselves. When Moses first refused to accept the mirrors, the Holy One, blessed be He, advised him to accept them, since, thanks to the mirrors, the number of children of Israel increased greatly in Egypt. For when the men of Israel laboured and were very tired, and had no sexual lust, the women thought of a way by which to make themselves desirable to their husbands. Every woman had a mirror with her and teased her husband, saying; "Look in the mirror and see that I am prettier than you." In that way, the women aroused their husbands' passion and caused them to unite with them and the women conceived and bore children. The Lord therefore commanded Moses to take the mirrors and make lavers of them for

the washing of hands. And when a woman was suspected of infidelity to her husband and there was no witness against her, she was given to drink water from that laver, and if she was guilty her body swelled up. Bahya says that the mirrors were given by the older women, who were no longer interested in them, because their lust had left them and they preferred to spend their mornings and evenings in prayer. Ibn Shu'aib says that the goats came of their own volition to the women in order that they might weave of the hair on their backs curtains for the Tabernacle. However, the goats did not come on the Sabbath days, or on the first days of the months. The skilled women spun the curtains of the hair while it was still on the backs of the goats, but that showed special talent. The women, therefore, have merited to enjoy the New Moon holidays. Bahya says that great merit is attached to the reading and studying of the structure of the Temple; its length, its width and the number of things that furnished it. And, although the Temple had been destroyed, our sages nevertheless said that people who sincerely study the laws which governed the sacrifices are like unto those who actually bring sacrifices, and they will receive God's rewards. The Lord rewards those who study the structure of the Temple as if they had helped in the building of the same; and they shall merit that the Lord will again build them a Temple wherein the Shekinah will dwell. Amen, so be it.

21. *THIS IS THE SUM*. Bahya comments on the verses "Better is little with the fear of the Lord, than great treasure and trouble therewith. Better is a dinner of herbs where love is, than a stalled ox and hatred therewith," [1] and says that to gain a little money with the fear of the Lord is better than fortunes acquired by unlawful means. It is better to live humbly and be loved by people than to live high at the expense of others, and be hated by them for usury or unlawful gain, which is like robbery, and this is one of the great-

*Translation of commentary somewhat rearranged to improve style.

17.   AND IT CAME TO PASS IN THE FIRST MONTH THAT MOSES ERECTED THE TABERNACLE. The Midrash says that Moses erected the Tabernacle three times. The first time he erected it for the morning sacrifice, and then dismantled it again. The second time he erected it for the dedication service, and the third time for the evening sacrifice. The Midrash also says that all the skilled men who worked at the building of the Tabernacle could not assemble it, but brought the parts to Moses, who often grieved that he had no time to take part in the actual building of the Tabernacle. The Lord, however, had comforted his servant, and promised him that no one would be able to assemble the various parts and erect the Tabernacle except Moses himself, who by touching the parts caused them to assemble themselves together, and the people saw that Moses erected it. The Yalkut says that many miracles occurred at the Tabernacle. First, the court of the Tabernacle, although not larger than fifty cubits,[1] accommodated six hundred thousand worshippers, and when they prostrated themselves they were four cubits apart from one another. Second, the people saw the fire coming down from heaven descending upon the Tabernacle and proceeding from thence to the Tent of the meeting,[2] and from there to the altar to consume the sacrifice, and finally remaining upon the altar.

Bahya says that God said to the children of Israel: "I caused to-day my Shekinah to abide with you, but if you sin the Shekinah will depart from you again." However, in the latter days, when the Messiah comes, then the Shekinah will abide with the people forever. Moreover, at present the Shekinah is seen only through fire; but when the Messiah comes it will be seen face to face, as it is written, "For they shall see, eye to eye, when the Lord returneth to Zion." [3] Amen.

---

*The "Tzeenah U-Reenah" omits Chapter XXXIX.

APPENDIX I

1. The river Sambatyon referred to in the text is supposed to be situated in the same locality as that in which the lost Ten Tribes had settled themselves, and Jewish traditions are full and precise in affirming that this river flows with great noise and violence during six days of the week, but that it comes to a standstill on every Sabbath.[1]

2. TEKUFAH תקופה means circle or circuit of the year or seasons. There are four Tekufoth: (1) Nisan (April); (2) Tamuz (July); (3) Tishre (October); (4) Tebeth (December); corresponding to the Vernal Equinox (March 21); Summer solstice (June 21); Autumn Equinox (September 23); and Winter Solstice (December 22). There are two different calculations of the Tekufah; namely, that of Samuel and that of Ada bar Ahava. Jewish tradition has accepted Samuel's Tekufah.[2]

APPENDIX II

Rabbinical sources mentioned in our text of the
"Tzeenah U-Reenah"

1. Now there arose a new king, etc. Rab and Samuel (differ in their interpretation) one said that he was really new, while the other said his decrees were new. (Sotah 11-a)
2. R. Hiyyab ben Abba said in the name of R. Simai; There were three in that plan, viz., Balaam, Job and Jethro. Balaam who devised it was slain, Job who silently acquiesced was afflicted with sufferings; Jethro who fled merited that his descendants should sit in the chamber of Hewn Stones. (Sotah 11-a)
3. R. Avira expounded that through the merits of the righteous women who lived in that generation were the Israelites redeemed from Egypt. (Sotah 12-b)
4. R. Hanina said, he entrusted them with a significant sign; viz., if it is a son his face is turned downwards and if a daughter her face is turned upwards (at birth). (Sotah 11-b)
5. R. Hanan said, he entrusted them with an important sign, and told them, when a woman bends to deliver a child, her thighs grow cold like stones. (Sotah 11-b)
6. R. Jose, son of R. Hanina said: It teaches that he solicited them for immoral purposes but they refused to yield. (Sotah 11-b)
7. Rab and Samuel (differ in their interpretation). One said they are the priestly and levitical houses and the other said they are the royal houses. The priestly are Moses and Aaron, and the royal houses for David, a descendant from Miriam. (Sotah 11-b)
8. We may not write with ink upon these stones (of the Ephod)

229

nor cut into them with a knife, but we write with ink on them, and show the Shamir on the outside and these split on their own accord. (Sotah 48-b)

9. R. Helbe said: proselytes are as hard for Israel as a sore. (Yebamoth 47-b)

10. R. Kattina said: whenever Israel came up to the Festival, the curtains were removed for them and the Cherubim were shown to them, whose bodies were intertwisted with one another and they would be addressed thus: "Look, you are beloved before God as the love between man and woman." (Yoma 54-a)

11. Seven prophetesses. Who are they? Sarah, Miriam, Deborah, Hannah, Abigail, Huldah and Esther. (Megillah 14-a)

12. R. Johanan said, Three keys, the Holy One, blessed be He, has retained in His hands, and not entrusted them into the hand of any messenger; namely, the key of rain, the key of childbirth, and the key of the resurrection from the dead. (Taanith 2-a)

13. R. Abdimai, son of Hama, who was the son of Hasa, said this teaches us that the Holy One, blessed be He, overturned the mountain upon them like an inverted cask and said to them, if you accept the Torah, well and good, but if not there shall be your burial place. (Sabbath 88-a)

14. Which is considered a plague? If a town that has five hundred grown up men and had three dead within three consecutive days, it is considered a plague; if less it is not a plague. (Taanith 19-a)

15. The entire foreskin which covers the glands should be torn with the nail and shoved down on all sides. The penis should be sucked until the blood from distant places comes out. If circumcision was performed without sucking, it is considered as though the circumcision had not been done at all. (Shulhan Arukh on Circumcision #4)

16. There were two men whom Satan incited against each other. Every Friday evening they wrangled with one another. It hap-

pened that R. Meir came and restrained them three Friday evenings running, till he made peace between them. Then he heard Satan cry: woe is me; R. Meir has driven me away from my house. (Gitin, 52-a)

17. For R. Anani Ben Sason said: Why is the portion about the priestly garments placed next to the portion about the sacrifices? It is to tell you that just as sacrifices procure atonement, so do the priestly garments. (Arak., 16-a)

18. The Rabbis taught: Kimchith had seven sons and all ministered as High Priests. They said unto her, what hast thou done to merit such honour? She replied: Throughout the days of my life, the beams of my house have not seen the plaits of my hair. (Yoma, 47-a)

19. Raba said: It is the duty of a man to mellow himself (with wine) on Purim, until he cannot tell the difference between "cursed be Haman" and "Blessed be Mordecai." (Megillah, 7-b)

20. Rabbi Ada of Jappa said: The ten sons of Haman and the word "ten" should be said in one breath. What is the reason? Because their souls departed together. (Megillah, 16-b)

21. The twenty-fifth day of Tebeth is a day of Mount Grizim on which no mourning is permitted. It is the day on which the Kuteans demanded the house of our God from Alexander, the Macedonian, so as to destroy it, and he has given them the permission. Whereupon some people came and informed Simon the Just. What did the latter do? He put on his priestly garment, rolled himself in priestly garments, some of the noble men of Israel went with him, carrying fiery torches in their hands, etc. When he saw Simon the Just, he descended from his carriage and bowed down before him, etc. (Yoma, 69-a)

22. R. Johanan said in the name of Simeon ben Yohai: Every commandment which the Holy One, blessed be He, gave unto Israel, He gave to them publicly, except the Sabbath which He bestowed upon them in secret. (Betzh, 16-a)

231

23. When Moses ascended on high, he said to Israel, I will return at the end of forty days, at the beginning of the sixth hour. At the end of forty days Satan came and confounded the world, etc. Whereupon he showed them a vision of his bier, etc. (Sabbath, 89-a)

24. As for the likeness of their faces, the four had the face of a man, and the face of a lion, on the right side; and the four had the face of an ox on the left side. (Ez. I, 10)

25. R. Akiba said, jesting and levity lead a man on to lewdness. (Abboth III, 13)

26. R. Isaac said: when God said to him; go get thee down, Moses' face darkened so that he became as one blind on account of his many troubles and did not know which side to descend. The angels then sought to slay him, saying: Now is the time to slay him, but God knew the intention of the angels. What did He do? said R. Berekiah, etc. The Lord opened unto him a wicket under His throne of glory, and said to him: go get thee down, and it says, "and the Lord said unto me, arise get thee down quickly from hence." (Shemoth Rabba, 42)

27. R. Samuel b. Nahmani said in R. Jonathan's name: That he was suspected of (adultery with) a married woman, as it is written "they were jealous of Moses in the camp." R. Samuel ben Yitschak said, from this we infer that every man was jealous of his wife. (Sanhedrin, 110-a)

28. "And they looked after Moses." R. Hama says that there were those who said "look at the neck of the son of Amram" and their friends would answer "what do you expect from a man who was in charge of building a Tabernacle? Don't you think that he should be rich?" (Midrash Rabbah, 52)

29. "And he returned to the camp," etc. R. Abbahu said: The Holy One, blessed be He, said to Moses "Now they will say, the Rabbi is angry and also the pupil is angry, what will become of Israel? If you move your tent back to the camp, well

and good, but if not, Joshua the son of Nun, your disciple, will take your place." (Berakoth, 63-b)

30. R. Kahana said: R. Hama, the son of the daughter of Hassa related to me (that) Rabbah bar Nahmani died through persecution because information having been laid against him to the state. Said they (the informers), etc. (Baba Metzia, 86-a)

31. The king (Hadrian) said to Rabbi Joshuah ben Hananiah: I should like to "see your God." Whereupon Joshuah replied: You cannot see Him, etc. (Hullin, 59-b)

32. And the Tables were the work of God. (Ex. XXXII, 16) And he hewed two tables of stone like unto the first. (Ex. XXXIV, 4)

33. We have learned that, when Moses ascended on High, he found the Holy One, blessed be He, sitting and writing "longsuffering." Said he (Moses) to Him: Sovereign of the Universe, "Longsuffering to the righteous?" Then He replied "even to the Wicked," etc. (Sanhedrin 111-a)

34. For when R. Aha bar Ada came (from Palestine) he declared in the name of R. Isaac: They decreed against (heathen's) bred on account of their oil. But how is oil stricter than bred? Rather should the statement say that they made a decree against their bred and oil on account of their wine, on their wine, on account of their daughters, etc. (Abodah Zarah, 36-a)

35. Abba Hilkiah was a grandson of Honi the Circle Drawer, and whenever the world was in need of rain, etc. (Taanith, 23-a)

36. "And they heard the voice of the Lord God walking in the garden towards the cool of the day." The Shekinah was principally in the lowest (part of the world). When Adam sinned the Shekinah moved up to the first heavens, after Cain sinned the Shekinah moved up to the second heavens, after Enosh's generation's sin — to the third heavens, after the flood — to the fourth. When the generation that built the Tower of Babel came, the Shekinah moved to the fifth heavens. After the gen-

eration of the Sodomites — to the sixth and after the Egyptians in the days of Abraham — to the seventh. (Bereshith Rabbah, 19)

37. For if it is agreed with R. Jose the Galilean, behold he has said "faint hearted," i. e., he who is afraid because of the transgressions, he had committed, etc. (Sotah, 43-a)

38. Said R. Hiya son of Abba, "R. Simon b. Yohai when he saw his mother chatting a lot, he would tell her: Mother, today is Sabbath." (Jerushalmi, Sabbath, Chpt. XV, 3)

39. The daughters of R. Nahman used to stir a cauldron with their hands when it was boiling hot. R. 'Ilish was puzzled about it. It is written (he said): "one man among a thousand have I found," etc. (Git. 45-a)

40. Said R. Johanan son of R. Eliezer, son of R. Jose the Galilean, who says that even if there are nine hundred and ninety-nine angels declaring him guilty and but one angel declares merits, the Holy One, blessed be He, turns the scales to "merits," etc. If half and half? R. Jose b. Hanina says "forgiving iniquity." R. Abuhau said it is written "forgiving" what does the Holy One, blessed be He, do? He snatches one of his guilts away, and the merits will balance. (Jer., Kedushin Sect. I, 10)

41. For Samuel said: a change of diet is the beginning of bowel trouble. It is written in the book of Ben Sirah "all the days of the poor is evil, etc." (Kethuboth, 110-b)

42. He who withholds an employee's wages is as though he deprived him of his life, etc. (Baba Metzia, 112-a)

43. R. Eliezer b. Jacob says: if one misappropriated a "seah" of wheat and kneeded it and baked it and set aside a portion of it as "Hallah," how would he be able to pronounce the benediction? He would surely not be pronouncing a blessing but pronouncing a blasphemy, etc. (Baba Kama, 94-a)

44. Said Raba: there are two arguments against this opinion. First that a man cannot obtain atonement with something which he obtained as the result of a transgression, etc. (Temurah, 20-b)

45. His robbery is prohibited, for R. Huna said: Whence do we learn that the robbery of a Heathen is prohibited, because it says, etc. (Baba Kama, 113-b)

46. We have learned: Amram was a great man of his generation. (Sotah 12-a)

47. R. Safra would singe the head (of an animal); Rabba salted "shibuta"; R. Huna lit the lamp; R. Papa plaited the wicks; R. Hisda cut up the beet-roots. Rabah and R. Joseph chopped wood. R. Zera kindled the fire, etc. (Shabbath, 119-a)

48. "Speaking words" that thy speech on the Sabbath should not be like thy speech on weekdays. (Sabbath, 113-b)

49. A court of heathens is considered disqualified by the Mosaic Law. (Git., 9-b)

LIST OF AUTHORITIES AND AUTHORITATIVE SOURCES QUOTED IN THE "TZEENAH U-REENAH" ON EXODUS

ABAYE: Real name Nahmani, but nicknamed "Abaye" ("little father"), by his uncle, who adopted him. Abaye was a Babylonian Amora who lived in the 4th Century and was head of the Pumbeditha Academy.

ABBAHU: Palestinian Amora; B. 279; D. 320. One of the great authorities on the Bible.

ABIN: There were two outstanding rabbis by that name to whom the "Tzeenah U-Reenah" may be referred. One was a Babylonian Amora of the 4th Century; the other was an eminent Cabbalist of the 11th Century.

ABRAHAM RABBI: Rabbi Abraham Saba, author of the frequently quoted Tzror-Hamor, 15th Century, Germany.

AKIBA: The father of Rabbinic Judaism, one of the most revered personalities in Jewish history, who supported Bar Kochba's revolt. B. 50; died a martyr's death about 132.

AZARIAH: Azariah ben Ephraim Figo, who was a famous preacher and homiletical writer of the 17th Century in Venice.

BAHYA: Full name Bahya ben Asher ben Halawa; distinguished Biblical exegete, who lived in Spain in the 13th Century.

BA'AL HATTURIM: The name of a work written by Jacob ben Asher 1280 - 1340 A.D. The author was a Talmudist and Mystic who made use of the numerical value of words in his method of interpretation.

BAR NAHMANI: Babylonian Amora 270-300; pupil of Rabbi Huna of Sura and of Rabbi Judah ben Ezekiel of Pumbeditha.

ELIEZER BEN HYRKANUS: A prominent Tanna and the most brilliant disciple of Rabbi Johanan ben Zakkai; 1st Century A.D.

ELIEZER BEN JACOB: There were two by that name. One

was a Tanna of the 1st Century A. D., an authority on the Jerusalem Temple and is mentioned in the Mishnah and Haggadata. The second was a Tanna of the 2nd Century and was the founder of a school known in the Talmud after his name "Debé Eliezer ben Jacob."

HANANEEL: Rabbi Hananeel ben Jusiel, author of a commentary on the Pentateuch. Rabbi of Kairwan, Africa; Biblical and Talmudical commentator, born 990, died 1050 A. D.

HILKIA ABBA: Saint and miracle worker of the 1st Century B.C. Son-in-law of Honi Ham'aggel the "circle-drawer."

HAZZEKUNI: Name of a commentary on the Pentateuch by Hiskia ben Manoah who lived in France in the 13th Century.

HIRTZ: Rabbi Naphtali Hirtz ben Eliezer Treves; Cabbalist of the 16th Century; Frankfurt a. M.

HOSHEN MISHPAT: Name of the 4th part of the Shulhan Arukh by Joseph ben Ephraim Caro, dealing with civil and criminal law.

IBN SHU'AIB: Preacher and Cabbalist 14th Century.

ILISH: Babylonian scholar of the 4th Century.

IMRE NO'AM: This is the name of an allegorical and mystical commentary on the Pentateuch, published first in Constantinople in 1546. The author of the commentary was Jacob de Illescos, a Biblical commentator of the 14th Century. There are other works bearing the name "Imre No'am," but they are of a later date than the "Tzeenah U-Reenah."

ISSERLES: Full name Rabbi Moses Isserles, who lived in Poland between the years 1520 and 1572. He was a rabbi in Krakow and author of a well-known work called "Mapa," which consists of supplementary material to the Shulkhan Arukh.

JEHUDAH: Judah ben Asher, German Talmudist and Authority on Rabbinics, born in Germany 1270, died in Spain 1349.

JOSHUA BEN LEVI: Palestinian Amora of the first half of the third Century, head of the School of Lydda in Southern Palestine.

JOSE' RABBI: Jose Ben Halafta, Palestinian Tanna who flourished in the 2nd Century A.D.

MEIR: Palestinian Tanna, 2nd Century A.D. One of the foremost exponents of Jewish learning and a well-known miracle worker. In later tradition he is called Meir Ba'al Ha-ness.

MENORATH HA-MAOR: Name of an ethical work written by Isaac Aboab of Toledo, 14th Century.

NAHMAN: Son-in-law of Rabbah ben Abuha, who lived in Babylon, 3rd Century, and noted for his aphorisms contained in the Talmud.

PIRQUE DE RABBI ELIEZER: An Haggadic-Midrashic work on Genesis, part Exodus, and a few sentences of Numbers, ascribed to Rabbi Eliezer ben Hyrkanus. The work, however, was composed in Italy after 833 A. D.

RABBAH BAR BAR HANAH: Babylonian Amora who lived in the 3rd Century; known for his fantastic adventures.

RABBAH HUNA: Bar-bar-Huna, Babylonian Amora of the 4th Century, head of the Academy of Sura.

RABAN: ראב"ן Rabbi Eliezer ben Nathan of Mayence, Halakist and liturgical poet, flourished in the first half of the 12th Century.

RAMBAN: ראמב"ן Full name Rabbi Moses ben Nahman, also called Nachmanides. Born in 1195 in Georna, Spain; died 1270 in Palestine. He was a rabbi and a physician; an eminent scholar and writer in the field of Biblical exegesis and mysticism.

RASHI: רש"י Full name Rabbi Solomon ben Isaac. Most popular expounder of the Bible and the Talmud; born Troyes, France, 1040; died 1105. His commentary on the Bible is included in the text of almost every Jewish edition of the Pentateuch.

SAADYA: Gaon, born 892 in Egypt; died 942 in Sura, Babylon. Bible commentator, philosopher, and champion of Rabbinism against Karaism. Head of the Jewish Academy in Sura.

SEFER HAGAN: A commentary on the Pentateuch by Aaron ben Joseph, who lived in France in the 13th Century. The commentary is called גן because the numerical value of the two Hebrew letters amount to 53, corresponding to the fifty-three weekly portions of the Pentateuch.

SHIMON BEN HALAFTA: Tanna of VI generation. Disciple of Judah Hanassi.

SIMON THE JUST: There were two high priests by that name. One lived in the 4th Century B.C., and was honoured by Alexander the Great. The second lived in the 2nd Century B.C., and was famous for his piety and charity.

SIMON BEN LAKISH: Outstanding Palestinian Amora; 200-275 A. D.

TANCHUMA: Name of three different collections of Haggadah on the Pentateuch but not necessarily the work of Rabbi Tanchuma. They are so called because of certain homilies ascribed to Rabbah Tanchuma bar Abba who was a Palestinian Amora of the 5th Century.

TANNA DEBE ELIAHU: Name of a Midrashic work by an unknown author, compiled around the 10th Century. The compilation consists of two parts, one called Seder Eliahu Rabbah, the other called Seder Eliahu Zuta. There are several books under that name but of later dates.

TURNOS RUFUS: Spelled also Tineius Rufus; governor of Judea during the Bar Kochba insurrection; known for his acts of oppression.

TOLDOTH YITSCHAK: The name of a famous book by Isaac ben Jacob Caro of the early 16th Century. The book was first published in Constantinople but later also in Italy, Poland and elsewhere.

TZROR HAMOR: Name of a mystical commentary on the Pentateuch by Abraham Saba, 15th Century.

UKBA MAR: Exilarch of Bagdad, 10th Century.

YALKUT: Name of a compilation of various Midrashic material, arranged according to the Biblical verses to which they apply.

YITSCHAKI: Rabbi Solomon ben Isaac, also known as Rashi. (See under Rashi.)

ZE'ERA: Palestinian Amora, third generation. Occupies a prominent place in the Halakah as well as in the Haggadah.

LIST OF ABBREVIATIONS

A. V.	Authorized Version
R. V.	Revised Version
ADPB	Authorized Daily Prayer Book
Ap.	Appendix
Ch.	Chapter
Ibid.	Ibidem
Ket.	Ketuboth
Cp.	Compare
P.	Page
V.	Verse
Tz. U.	Tzeenah U-Reenah

REFERENCES AND NOTES

INTRODUCTION

1. Moses did not tell about the wonders which God performed on Mount Sinai, about the fire and vapours. (Cp. XVIII: 1)
   (און (משה) וואר ניט זאגן די וואונדר פון "שטים" און פייאר.
2. The goats came on their own volition. Cp. XXXVIII: 8. (sounds like Plural of "game") די גיימן קאמן
3. "The author for all pious women."
4. The History of Jewish Literature, Warsaw, 1928. (In Yiddish)
5. Cp. page 221.
6. Cp "translations" page 26.
7. Encyclopedia Judaica Volume 3, P. 472-473. art. on Askenazy, Jacob ben Isaac.
8. Rabbi Joshua be Levi Palestinian Amora (200 B.C.)
9. Cp. Baba Kama page 30.
10. Hullin page 60.
11. Cp. Page IX.
12. Cp. Page XI.
13. Cp. Page XII.
14. Cp. Page XIII.
15. Cp. Page IX.
16. Cp. A. A. Roback: The Story of Yiddish Literature Page 64.

CHAPTER I

1. Proverbs XXV: 12.
2. A boy assumes religious responsibility at the age of 13 on

his בר מצוה when he becomes a full member of the Synagogue.

3. Proverbs XIII: 24.
4. Verse 5 follows verse 7 in the text; but has been transposed to its Biblical order.
5. Cp. Commentary on Verse 1.
6. Chapter I, verse 5. Hebrew text. יצה ירך יעקב
7. Genesis XXXII: 25.
8. Cp. Appendix II, 1.
9. Joseph.
10. Cp. Genesis IX: 11.
11. See Genesis IX: 11.
12. Sanhedrin Fol. 106A.
13. Cp. Numbers XXXI: 8.
14. This passage follows verse 11 in the text, but was transposed for better coherence.
15. Cp. Appendix II, 2.
16. Cp. Appendix II, 3.
17. Cp. Appendix II, 4
18. Cp. Appendix II, 5
19. Cp. Appendix II, 6
20. Cp. Appendix II, 7

CHAPTER II

1. Cp. Appendix II: 47.
2. In the text verse 2 is a part of verse 3, but has been separated here and placed according to Biblical order.
3. About February.
4. About June.
5. Verse 4 comes after verse 5 in the text, but was transposed according to Biblical order.
6. Cp. IV: 10 Footnote Page 52.

CHAPTER III

1. Amram not mentioned by name in the Biblical text.
2. Jewish reverence for parents was so great that a son would not accept any honour which would exalt him above his father.
3. The reference to Joseph is found in Genesis, Chapter L: 24, but there is no such verbal reference with regard to Jacob.

CHAPTER IV

1. There is a Jewish legend which states that when Moses was still a child, Pharaoh played with him, and that on one occasion, while they played, little Moses seized the crown from Pharaoh's head. Cp. Louis Ginzberg, "The Legends of the Jews," Ed. 1910 p. 272, Volume II.
2. Cp. Appendix II, 15.

CHAPTER V

1. According to Jewish law a priest is not permitted to visit a cemetery, so that he may not defile himself. Cp. Leviticus XXI: 1-3
2. The "Tzeenah U-Reenah" amends the Biblical text, changing the words "Lest He fall upon us" into a warning against Pharaoh. This is very interesting, because pestilence was one of the ten plagues used against Pharaoh and there is no reason why it should have been brought against Moses and Aaron.

CHAPTER VI

1. Our text uses the abridged form יְיָ for יהוה
2. The Jewish New Year.
3. Passover.

CHAPTER VII

1. Leviticus 15: 19

CHAPTER VIII

1. Division of chapter follows the English Bible.
2. תקופה. For explanation see Appendix I, #2, page 228.
3. Repetition. See Chapter VII: 19.

CHAPTER IX

1. Verse 24 in our text comes in the middle of verse 33, but was transposed to its Biblical order.
2. For missing passage see verse 24, which was transposed in keeping with the Biblical order.
3. Proverbs XXIX: 23.

CHAPTER X

1. Proverbs XXVIII: 14.
2. The text refers to the common root of אדם man and earth אדמה
3. Exodus XXXII: 12.
4. Cp. verses 1-20.
5. According to the Biblical text, the darkness lasted only three days.

CHAPTR XI

1. Verse 7 was transposed from XII: 1 in keeping with the Biblical order.

245

CHAPTER XII

1. Our text refers to Mitzraim as the capital of Egypt, while the land of Egypt is called Eretz Mitzraim.
2. Text repeated in Verse 30.
3. Compare with Verse 34, where verse is repeated.
4. This explanation seems to contradict the one given in verse 8.
5. A repetition of Chapter XI: 7, with a different interpretation of the text.
6. Several passages have been transposed to Verses 5, 6, 7, 8.
7. The verse "Neither shall ye break a bone thereof," is recorded here in accordance with the Biblical order, although in our text it precedes Verse 39.

CHAPTER XIII

1. Cp. Genesis IX: 26.
2. Cp. Daniel III.
3. The text here is verbose and repeats itself too much. It had to be shortened for the sake of clarity.
4. Proverbs XXI: 31.
5. This is a play upon the word חמושים, and חמשים which in Hebrew may mean either "armed" or "fifty."
6. Potiphar.

CHAPTER XIV

1. Cp. Chapter VIII: verse 19.

CHAPTER XV

1. In the text verse 2 comes after verse 3, but was transposed to the Biblical order.

2. This interpretation of נערמו is based on the derivative rule frequently employed in Jewish exegesis, by which the meaning of a word is derived from another one with the same root, or merely possessing the same number of letters but in a different order. For instance, the meaning "wise" is superimposed upon the word by referring to its root ערום which means wise or sly. (Cp. Genesis III: 1)
3. Verse 12 was recast to follow the Biblical order.
4. Cp. Appendix II, 12.
5. For the missing passage, see Verse 22.
6. Lit "Song."
7. Megillah 14-a. Cp. Appendix II, 11.
8. Exodus XII: 36.
9. See commentary on Chapter XIV: verse 6.
10. This play upon the word is accomplished by transposing the letters. See note #2 above.

CHAPTER XVI

1. Psalm CXXVII: v. 2.
2. Psalm LXXVIII v. 25. The author plays upon the words (mighty) אבירים and (bodily members) אברים.
3. Verse 5 comes after verse 6 in our edition, but it was transposed to keep with the Biblical order.
4. Psalm XI: verse 5.
5. Cp. Exodus XVI: 5.
6. Two he-lambs cp. Numbers XXVIII: 9.
7. The Hebrew text uses the emphatic form by repeating twice the word מות יומת.
8. Cp. Shulhan Arukh, on הלכות חלה.

CHAPTER XVII

1. Cp. Numbers XX: 16.

2. Cp. Chapter XVII: 13.
3. Obadiah I: 21.

CHAPTER XVIII

1. Proverbs XV: 4.
2. "Throat" in the text.
3. Chapter XVIII: 16.
4. Chapter XVIII: 27.
5. Verse 16.
6. Missing in the Hebrew text.
7. Cp. The Hebrew text.
8. The text says that Hur died a long time ago in connection with the making of the Golden Calf. Obviously, there is some confusion, since the giving of the Ten Commandments and the making of the Golden Calf came later.
9. Verse transposed according to Biblical order.

CHAPTER XIX

1. A prayer said on the Sabbath beginning with the words, "Moses rejoiced." Singer S.A.D.P.B.; P. 138.
2. Verse transposed to the Biblical order.
3. Verse transposed to the Biblical order.
4. Isaiah XXVII: 13.
5. Paragraph reverted to its Biblical order. From Verse 23.

CHAPTER XX

1. Cp. comments on Verse 7.
2. In the text verse 4 comes after verse 5. This, however, was rearranged in accordance with the Biblical order.

3. I Samuel XIV: 24-46.
4. II Samuel XXI: 1-9.
5. *Ibid.* v. 12.
6. Cp. Shulhan Arukh, Chapter XX, on "Things Forbidden on the Sabbath."
7. See Appendix I.
8. A Sabbath evening prayer. See Singer's Prayer Book, pages 211, 211a.
9. The author resumes commentary on verses 12 to 17.
10. By "stranger" a non-Israelite is meant.
11. Exodus XXIV: 7.
12. Verse 24 comes in the "Tzeenah U-Reenah" at the end of Chapter XXV, but it was transposed here in accordance with the Biblical order.

CHAPTER XXI

1. Proverbs XXIV: 23, A. V.
2. Exodus XVIII: 23.
3. Gittin 9-b.
4. Our "Tzeenah U-Reenah" text says "If he be married to a Jewish woman."
5. Idolatry.
6. Genesis IX: 22-23.
7. Cp. Appendix II, 14.

CHAPTER XXII

1. Text transposed to its Biblical order.
2. Proverbs XXI: 14.
3. The rule can be best expressed in the words, "Charity begins at home."
4. Isaiah XLIX: 13.
5. The same passage is also recorded earlier.

CHAPTER XXIII

1. In our text Verse 3 comes after Verse 5, but was transposed to Biblical order.
2. In our text Verse 4 comes after Verse 5, but was transposed to Biblical order.
3. Cp. Exodus XXIII: 19; XXXIV: 26; Deuteronomy XIV: 21

CHAPTER XXIV

1. June-July
2. Yebama 47-b.
3. Cp. Leviticus X: 1-2.
4. According to Jewish tradition there are six hundred and thirteen precepts which a Jew has to observe.
5. Cp. Deuteronomy IX: 9, 18, 25.

CHAPTER XXV

1. Proverbs VIII: 10. A.V.
2. Here the text contains a dislocated verse from Genesis XXV: 25, which reads "And the first came forth red." Esau went out red from his mother's womb.
3. Psalm CXXXII: 17.
4. Leviticus XIX: 35-37.
5. Sota 48-b
6. Pesikta Rabbati
7. Our text says "shadow."
8. Ecclesiastes VII: 12.
9. Proverbs III: 18.
10. Verse 11.
11. Verse 24.

12. For instance, in connection with royalty the word לו is used in Deuteronomy XVII: 18.
13. Numbers XXV: 13.
14. Yoma 54-a.
15. By the rule of Notarikon, a form of Biblical exegisis, which stresses the numerical value of the letters.
16. Proverbs XX: 27.
17. Proverbs VI: 23.
18. Job XXXVII: 22.
19. Jewish mysticism has several names for Satan which begin with the initial letter ס as for instance סטרא אחרא, the evil side, as contrasted with the right (good) side.
20. Git. 52a
21. The prayer begins with the words "a shield to our forefathers."
22. ספר הגן
23. For missing passage, see Chapter XX: 24.

CHAPTER XXVII

1. The "Tzeenah U-Reenah" omits Chapter XXVI.
2. Proverbs XXVII: 9.
3. Psalm CIV: 31.
4. Missing passage transposed to Biblical order. See next paragraph.

CHAPTER XXVIII

1. Erakin 16-a.
2. Later editions say accidental killing.
3. Reference is here made to verse 4 of same chapter in the Biblical text, where only six articles are enumerated. The "Tzeenah U-Reenah" text, however, enumerates all eight articles.

4. A four-cornered ritual garment.
5. Cp. Genesis XXXV: 22 and XLIX: 4. Our text calls Bilhah, Reuben's stepmother, Jacob's concubine, and Rachel's handmaid.
6. The English Bible translates the Hebrew word יהלם by "Diamond." However, the Hebrew and English Lexicon by Brown, Driver and Briggs is doubtful of the exact meaning of the word. The "Tzeenah U-Reenah" translates יהלם by Mother of Pearl.
7. Yoma 47-a.

CHAPTER XXIX

1. Deuteronomy XXV: 17.
2. Read on the Sabbath preceding the month of Adar.
3. Read on the Sabbath preceding Purim.
4. Read on the Sabbath preceding the month of Nisan.
5. Read on the first Sabbath of Nisan.
6. Cp. Esther VII: 4.
7. Megillah 7-b.
8. Esther III: 6.
9. Esther III: 8.
10. סכות
11. שמיני עצרת
12. Esther IV: 16.
13. According to the Shulhan Arkuh, fasting on the Passover is prohibited. The idea of the author is to emphasize here the gravity of the situation which forced the children of Israel to fast on the Passover.
14. Megillah 16-b.
15. Esther IX: 6.
16. Esther IX :13.

CHAPTER XXX

1. Proverbs X: 27.
2. Hebrew
3. Zephaniah III: 9.
4. The text uses the term העלבליגג instead of gerahs. An häblung was equal to the half of a German pfennig and was the predecessor of the heller; Cp. "The Dictionary of Numismatic Names" by Albert F. Prey.
5. The author resumes his commentary on verse 12.
6. Proverbs XI: 4.
7. Cp. XXX: 12.
8. The word צדקה righteousness may also mean alms-giving.
9. Palm Branch.
10. Osier Branch.
11. Citron.
12. Myrtle.

CHAPTER XXXI

1. שבת הגדול the "great Sabbath," is the Sabbath preceding the Passover.
2. שבת שובה is the Sabbath falling between the Jewish New Year and the Day of Atonement.
3. Yom Tob 61-a.
4. Cp. Verse 17 of same Chapter in the Bible.
5. Shabbath 119 a
6. The word comes from a common root כלה, which may also mean bride.
7. The Hebrew Old Testament is divided into 24 books.
8. A. V.
9. Deuteronomy XXXI: 28.

CHAPTER XXXII

1. The text derives the number six from the word כי בשש. It is a play upon the double meaning of the word.
2. Sabbath 89-a
3. The missing passage has been transposed to verse 4 in accordance with the Biblical order.
4. The text probably takes the name to derive from the word מכה.
5. Joseph's nickname is supposed to have been "Ox." The notion seems to be based on a mistaken reading of עלי שור for עלה שור Cp. Genesis XLIX: 22.
6. Cp. Ez. I: 10
7. Missing passages transposed according to Biblical order. Cp. Verses 13, 15.
8. Jeremiah II: 4.
9. Psalm II: 4.
10. Psalm XXXVII: 13.
11. Samuel XXV: 29.
12. Verse 7 in our text comes after verse 15, but it is transposed to the Biblical order.
13. Verse 7 follows verse 15 in our text but has been transposed to the Biblical order.
14. Cp. The Shulhan Arukh on chapter entitled "Amidah."
15. Psalm VII: 6.
16. We have here a play upon the word אף.
17. Lit. Samaritans.

CHAPTER XXXIII

1. Verses 4, 7 and 8 somewhat confused and were transposed to Biblical order.
2. The writer plays upon the words חרות and חרות Cp. XXXII: 16.

3. Cp. the use of the term נרו בהלו in Job XXIX: 3.
4. Sanhedrin 110-a
5. Midrash Tanhuma, section Pekude XXX: 8. Cp. Appendix II, 28.
6. Talmud Berakoth 63-b
7. Samaritans
8. Cp. Footnote 2.
9. Cp. Verse 6.
10. השוכר את הפועלים, Baba Metzia page 86-a2.
11. Cp. Treatise Shabboth, Chapter II.
12. Hullin 59-b to 60-a
13. The word עכו״ם comes from עובד כוכבים ומזלות idolaters, who worship the stars and the constellations.
14. Isaiah XL: 5.
15. Exodus XXXIII: 19.

CHAPTER XXXIV

1. Ketuboth 10-a
2. Sanhedrin 111, a&b.
3. Numbers XIV: 17.
4. Jerushalmi, Kiddushin I: 10.
5. Abodah Zarah 36-b
6. Pesahim, Page 118A.
7. Parts of the Mishnah might have had their origin as far back as the Babylonian-Persian captivity; but the compilation of the Mishnah, as we know it, was made by Rabbi Judah Hanassi, who lived in the years 135-219 A.D.
8. Rabbi Judah Hanassi, often called just "Rabbi."
9. Cp. Commentary on XXXIII: 18.

CHAPTER XXXV

1. Psalm XC: 17. Also Cp. S.A.D. Prayer Book, Page 211.
2. Cp. Appendix II, 36.

3. Genesis III: 8.
4. The Habhdallah Service marks the end of the Sabbath. Cp. Shulhan Arukh, on the laws concerning the Habhdallah.
5. Kiddushin, 49B.
6. Kiddushin, Chapter IV.
7. Sotah 43, a & b
8. Shabbath 113
9. Jerushalmi, Sabbath, Chpt. XV, 3, Cp. Appendix II, 38.
10. Verse 20 follows after verse 22 in the text, but is transposed to its Biblical order.
11. Ecclesiastes VII: 28.
12. Exodus XXXII: 4.
13. Gittin 45-a
14. Samaritans
15. Verse in our text precedes verse 20, but has been transposed to the Biblical order.
16. The Toldoth Yitschak differs from Rabban in this respect.
17. The text says, "grosh," which is one hundredth of a Polish zloty.
18. Ta'anith 23a, b.
19. Cp. Ketuboth 67-a.
20. For missing passage, see end of verse 20.

CHAPTER XXXVIII

1. Proverbs XV: 16, 17.
2. Aboth IV: 1.
3. Proverbs XV: 15.
4. Baba Kama, Page 119A, and Baba Metzia 112a
5. Baba Kama 94a.
6. Temurah 20b
7. Isaiah LXI: 8
8. Psalm X: 3.
9. Baba Kama 113b
10. Exodus XXXVIII: 21.

CHAPTER XL

1. The court of the Tabernacle, according to Chapter XXVII: 9 and 12, was 100 cubits long and 50 cubits wide.
2. אהל מועד
3. Isaiah LII: 8.

APPENDIX

1. Cp. Louis Ginzberg: *The Legends of the Jews,* Vol. V, page 111.
2. Cp. Maimonides, *Kiddush Hahodesh,* Chpt. IX.

BIBLIOGRAPHY

ABRAHAMS, ISRAEL: Chapters on Jewish Literature, Philadelphia 1899.

ARTICLES: "Judeo German" Literature in Jewish Encyclopedia. Yiddish Literature in Encyclopedia Britannica 14th Ed. New International Encyclopedia.

GINZBERG, LOUIS The Legends of the Jew. (English translation) Philadelphia 1947.

GRUNBAUM, M. Jüdischdeutsche Chrestomatie, Leipzig 1882.

ERIK, M. Geschichte fun der Yiddischer Liteuratur, Warsaw 1928.

LEVNER, J. B. The Legends of Israel (Translated by Joel Snowman), London 1946.

MIESES: Die Yiddische Sprache 1924.

NIGER, S. Studien Zu der Geschichte fun der Yiddischer Literatur, Wilna 1912.

REJZIN, ZALMEN: Lexicon of the Yiddish Literature. Press and Philology. Warsaw 1926-1930.

ROBACK, A. A. The Story of Yiddish Literature. New York 1940.

STAERK UND LEITZMANN: Die Jüdischdeutschen Bibel Ubersetzugen, Frankfurt am Main 1923.

STEINSCHNEIDER, M. Jüdischdeutsche Literatur Serapeum 1848-1849; 1864, 1869.

WAXMAN, MEYER A History of Jewish Literature Vol. II, New York 1943.

WEINREICH, MAX Tableaux of Yiddish Literary History, Wilna 1930.

WEINER, LEO: History of Yiddish Literature 1898.